A Psychodynamic Approach to Brief Therapy

WITHDRAWN
FROM
STOCKPORT COLLEGE
LEARNING CENTRE

STOCKPORT COLLEGE

096032

Brief Therapies Series

Series Editor: Stephen Palmer
Associate Editor: Gladeana McMahon

Focusing on brief and time-limited therapies, this series of books is aimed at students, beginning and experienced counsellors, therapists and other members of the helping professions who need to know more about working with the specific skills, theories and practices involving in this demanding but vital area of their work.

A Psychodynamic Approach to Brief Therapy

Gertrud Mander

SAGE Publications
London • Thousand Oaks • New Delhi

© Gertrud Mander 2000

First published 2000

All rights reserved. No part of this publication may be
reproduced, stored in a retrieval system, transmitted or utilized
in any form or by any means, electronic, mechanical,
photocopying, recording or otherwise, without permission in
writing from the Publishers.

 SAGE Publications Ltd
6 Bonhill Street
London EC2A 4PU

SAGE Publications Inc
2455 Teller Road
Thousand Oaks, California 91320

SAGE Publications India Pvt Ltd
32, M-Block Market
Greater Kailash – I
New Delhi 110 048

British Library Cataloguing in Publication data

A catalogue record for this book is available
from the British Library

ISBN 0 7619 6005 8
ISBN 0 7619 6006 6 (pbk)

Library of Congress catalog record available

Typeset by Mayhew Typesetting, Rhayader, Powys
Printed in Great Britain by Biddles Ltd, Guildford, Surrey

STOCKPORT COLLEGE
LIBRARY

| 69219 LR1343 | 18·6·01 |
| SL 096032 | 616·8914 MAN |

Contents

Acknowledgements

I am indebted to Paul Keeble, former Head of Training, and to Ruth Archer, Head of Counselling at the Westminster Pastoral Foundation (WPF), for enabling me to do in-house training in brief therapy; and to John Tydeman for my induction and training in the Balint–Malan model of brief focal psychotherapy. I am very thankful to Ann Kutek, former Clinical Director of Counselling in Companies (CiC), Westminster Pastoral Foundation, for giving me years of stimulating supervisory and therapeutic work in solution-focused brief therapy for CiC. I also owe thanks to Mary Anne Coate, Head of Training at the WPF, and June Roberts, Course Organizer of the WPF post-Qualifying Certificate in Time-Limited Counselling, for sharing their ideas and experience of time-limited work with me, and Penny Spearman, former Deputy Head of WPF Counselling. But most of all I want to thank the many clients, patients and supervisees I have worked with and learnt from during my years of involvement in brief work for the WPF. The case vignettes are drawn from this work experience but all identifying details have been changed.

To see a World in a grain of sand,
And a Heaven in a Wild Flower,
Hold Infinity in the palm of your hand,
And Eternity in an hour.

William Blake

1

Introduction and Overview

The aims and structure of the book

The aim of this book is to describe how the psychodynamic approach is applied to and used in the practice of brief counselling and psychotherapy by an adaptation of the fundamental principles of the psychoanalytic theory practised by analysts and psychotherapists. It starts with a brief outline of the theory from Freud onwards to the present day, proceeds to a description of the basic concepts and techniques of psychodynamic clinical practice, and then describes the psychodynamic understanding of change in terms of the patient's mental functioning and interaction with others.

Chapter 3 will discuss the historical development of psychoanalytic treatment methods, from classical analysis to psychoanalytic psychotherapy and psychodynamic counselling, and describe the reasons why some of Freud's colleagues felt the need to experiment with shortened versions of the therapeutic methods developed and taught by him, which led to a whole series of brief therapy models based on psychodynamic theory. Different modalities of brief, short-term and time-limited work will be introduced one by one and the differences and agreements described in terms of duration, techniques, the contexts for which they were developed and the basic theoretical principles on which they are based. This will lead to an examination of the fundamental difference in aims between long-term and short-term counselling and psychotherapy, and the specific techniques employed by each approach, allowing for these differences in terms of needs and personality structures rather than expressing a definite preference for one or the other.

The intention here is not to take sides, but to weigh carefully the evidence for and against the various treatment choices, avoiding a dogmatic stance in favour of either, and taking realities into account such as what is suitable for the institutional in contrast to the private practice setting and how far necessities and choices dictate the length and intensity of work contracts. Another important consideration, the difficulty of deciding how much is enough and when to leave well alone, also needs to be discussed at this point, bearing in mind the inescapable uncertainty of evaluating treatment outcome when there is no way of knowing what the future after therapy will bring and whether the results and changes at the point of termination will be lasting.

Chapter 4 will deal with the basics of practice and structure in brief work and take the reader through the vertical and the horizontal aspects of brief casework. Starting with assessment, the main diagnostic and selection criteria for brief and time-limited psychodynamic work will be outlined, compared and contrasted with those obtaining in the open-ended and ongoing modality. Stress is laid on the importance of selecting and formulating a psychodynamic focus from the inchoate mass of clinical material offered by the patient during the assessment session and strictly maintaining this focus throughout the therapeutic contract, in contrast to long-term *laissez-faire* strategies. This is justified on the assumption first formulated by Otto Rank, that making a positive difference in one selected area of the patient's life and mental functioning will inevitably lead to other positive changes and movements in the overall picture, as a therapeutic process will have been set in motion that will take its beneficial course.

Equally highlighted is the emotional impact of an assessment interview in which the problem is presented, identified, hypothetically linked to dynamic events in the past, and probably understood by the patient for the first time. Its therapeutic effectiveness as a psychodynamic experience can determine the outcome of a piece of brief work, as it initiates the working through and removing of an impasse or of the stubborn conflict in the patient's inner world that has made him/her seek help in the first place.

Next, Chapter 5 moves to the therapist's specific task and role in brief and focal work, which is described in detail as relating, containing, process-monitoring, judicious interpreting, all of this in terms of selective attention and selective neglect, particularly in relation to the inevitable transferences and countertransferences which arise in the dynamic process of therapeutic dialogue. A discussion of such issues as ambivalence and disappointment, specifically arising in the middle period, will be followed (Chapter 6) by detailed instructions of how to prepare for, observe and structure the ending of the contract, how to handle its emotional impact in terms of separation anxieties, regressive demands for continuation, aggressive sabotaging or bland denying of loss and grief, which potentially apply to both participants.

Issues of 'after therapy – what?' comprise planned follow-ups and reviews, referring on or priming for further therapy work, and long-term or successive contracting, including the controversial ethical question of whether a short-term contract can be or should be converted into ongoing long-term work with the same therapist. As this divides the practitioners of short-term work almost as much as does the widely diverging interpretation of outcomes, improvements and therapeutic results in brief work, Chapter 7 raises important general points relating to therapeutic orientation, boundary issues and flexibility, and will be illustrated by relevant clinical vignettes.

Finally, the discussion of contexts and treatment settings, of politics and cost-effectiveness (Chapter 8), will be followed by a section on supervision and training, on ethics and issues of personalities, research and evaluation (Chapters 9 and 10).

Brief therapy: an overview

The psychodynamic approach has been gaining ground in the field of brief therapeutic interventions since 1955, when psychoanalysts Michael Balint and David Malan set up an innovative research workshop at the Tavistock Institute in London to develop and test a model of brief focal psychotherapy. They deplored the constant lengthening and inconclusiveness of therapeutic contracts, which put analysis out of reach for most people in need of help, and experimented with an adaptation and shortening of the standard clinical setting, which favoured perfectionism and comprehensiveness but was often also interminable. In 'Analysis terminable and interminable', Freud (1937) had tackled the issues of when and how to end magisterially, but when Sandor Ferenczi tried to introduce a more active stance into his consulting room in order to shorten the analytic procedure, Freud was not interested in this tampering with his open-ended analytic style and considered the analyst's deliberate self-involvement a dangerous mistake. He was, however, well aware of the problems of interminability, and had himself suggested a 'psychotherapy for the people' in which the 'pure gold of psychoanalysis' would have to be 'compounded with the alloy of suggestion' (Freud, 1919), which is just what Ferenczi had tried to do, when he was boldly breaking the frame, stepping out of the transference and becoming real with his patients, which, of course, infringed the analytic rule of abstinence!

No such sacrilegious digressions from the straight and narrow analytic path for the Balint–Malan team. To set a limit from the outset and to select a specific area to work on was the new approach they pioneered. Wisely they also avoided focusing on the patient's symptoms, choosing instead dynamic issues, preferably of oedipal origin, in their patients' clinical material. They developed what they called a method of 'selective attention and selective neglect' that served the purpose of containing and structuring deliberately what was brought by the patient for therapeutic exploration, on the assumption that the part would represent the whole in some way. The pressing task was seen as the systematic working with a carefully selected dynamic focus in order to resolve unconscious conflict interfering in the patient's psychic functioning and leading to symptom formation.

Balint and Malan achieved what they set out to do in many cases by interpreting to the patient the unconscious and the therapeutic processes in the transference, honouring the limited duration agreed upon, while planning to establish a series of follow-ups to determine whether therapeutic results noted at the end of the brief therapy contract proved durable and lasting.

This model was an ingenious device that allowed them to retain the most important analytic tools – transference and interpreting – while sacrificing such secondary concepts as therapeutic passivity, open-endedness and complete character transformation. It included a scientific method of evaluating the usefulness of their experiment. Malan's extensive research diagrams and tables and the assessment and therapy forms for scores of patients served as the solid evidential base for a presentation of conclusive results, which defined improvement as the 'experience of old problems in the relationship with the therapist – but with a new ending' – in other words as 'a corrective emotional experience', as first hypothesized by F. Alexander and T.M. French (1946).

To the researchers' surprise a wide range of complaints could be tackled with this method, and also quite far-reaching and lasting improvements were achieved. The importance of careful assessment criteria was noted, as was the need for high motivation and enthusiasm in both participants in the brief therapeutic enterprise. In the UK, Balint's and Malan's publications (Balint, 1972; Malan, 1963) of their visionary focal psychotherapy experiment heralded the beginning of a new psychoanalytic psychotherapy method, practised and taught at the Tavistock Institute, which promised greater availability of public psychotherapy services as the numbers that could be treated were much larger. Now, half a century later, brief psychodynamic counselling and psychotherapy is practised in many forms, durations and theoretical models, varying widely in fundamental concepts of time boundaries, choice of patient, frequency of sessions, evaluation and referral methods. But they all go back to the work done by these pioneers.

The debate still continues in the profession and in public as to the ultimate value of brief methods based on psychoanalytic principles and as to the motives of the counsellors and psychotherapists offering these. The language of long-term clinicians when discussing brief work is full of expressions such as 'compromise', 'expediency', 'short cuts' or 'short changing the client' (Halmos, 1965: 145–7.), while the defenders of brief work point to research studies which show that on average patients stay for 10 sessions in publicly funded psychotherapy settings (Garfield, 1978). There are many factors entering into this important ongoing debate, which will have to be carefully discussed and researched. However, the truth of the matter is that short-term, time-limited and brief work has come to stay, has become the treatment of choice for many agencies, employers and health services, and now provides the maximum numbers of patients with a minimum of service that is affordable and sustainable.

I do not intend to go at length into the pros and cons of the two approaches here as this has been done extensively elsewhere (recently by Feltham, 1997), and will always depend to some extent on the faith of the counsellors practising what they have been trained to do, on what they have received themselves and what they consider optimal for themselves and others. Also there is always the match of personalities, the temperaments and experience levels to consider. 'I am not a racehorse, I am a carthorse' was a comment I received when I was advocating the merits of brief work to a colleague. This remark highlighted an important factor that is rarely analysed and always fraught with subjective opinions. Not everybody works well fast and briefly. Certainly not the beginner, whose short-term work is often unplanned and results in patients voting with their feet. Versatility and flexibility certainly are requirements of the therapist who practises in both modes, as is an ability to let go, if necessary, the capacity to mourn, the willingness to bear uncertainty and not to expect perfect results.

In his paper on endings in therapy, Holmes (1997) compares brief work to the short story, in contrast to the novel, which can be used as an analogy of extended analysis. I have often found it useful to talk of the 'brief encounter' with the patient and of the 'chapter' in a narrative of life that is concluded when a brief contract comes to an end – which implies that there are (or can be) other chapters, other brief encounters, involving other therapists and narrators. As with the two literary genres so with the two therapeutic modalities, the goals are qualitatively different. In the first, there is a choice of modest focus: author and therapist home in on a critical moment in a life journey and attempt to deal with the crisis by giving it a meaning and helping to find a resolution. In the second, the intention is to do a full reconstruction job, to encompass a whole world and round off a vast panorama. When there is no structure, no direction and no goal, this could be endless, as the unfolding proliferation of detail makes it arbitrary and difficult to call a halt – unless there is a death, of subject or author. In fact, the novelist is usually quite selective, creating order out of chaos and constructing a plot that satisfies authorial and audience needs, while the therapist is restricted by expectations of outcome as much as by the realities of time, place and finance.

Both scenarios are to some extent set apart from the real world and hence depend on decisions and choices made by the participants on the basis of certain sets of criteria determining when to end and why. In therapy there are agreed general goals such as crisis management, symptom removal, problem-solving, support, ego functioning, enabling autonomy, improving relationship skills and the ability to work. Another main difficulty here with structuring, timing and ending is that the therapeutic relationship involves strong attachments, separation anxieties, resistances and transferences, and that the work always needs to be done with and against these adhesive and repellent forces, particularly when it uses the 'fundamental principle' of free association.

The quantitative difference between the 'brief encounter' (of brief work) and the long-term relationship (of analysis and intensive psychotherapy) is apparent, while the qualitative difference – in terms of impact, effect and meaning – is more intangible. The brief therapist's belief is to strike the iron while it is hot, i.e. to make use of the moment of optimal receptivity in patient and therapist. First impressions may be partial and deceptive, but they are powerful, like electric charges, and release energies and creative forces in the mind. The skill is to harness these potentially destructive forces for the good of the patient, before they can become squandered, eroded or overwhelming, calling forth ever new resistances and a strong degree of dependence which are difficult to resolve.

Setting a time limit is a prime method of containment, creating temporary safety, territorial delineation and a measure of certainty: in short, boundaries. But this, of course, has its down side too. There is no going back on it, and the end is there from the beginning, which is threatening and paralysing to some, while liberating to others. The Roman motto *carpe diem* was an exhortation to make use of the limited time of the human life span before the certainty of death. Not everybody is capable of this fruitful use of the moment, because of overwhelming anxieties or of defences against these anxieties like denial or withdrawal which are usually bound up with infantile experiences of separation and deprivation. The brief therapist (Mann, 1973) intends to make these anxieties conscious and hence focuses on issues of loss and mourning by building in an ending in advance. What s/he cannot do, however, is allow a repetition of the (death) experience, for purposes of a repeated working through, though the experience can and must be prepared for. The Balint–Malan model has therefore built in a monitoring device to establish whether the mourning work has been done and borne fruit (Freud, 1919): the follow-up, which enables the therapist to find out whether the therapy, like the 'lost object', has been internalized, has either started a process of self-reflection or is remembered as a good experience that can be repeated if necessary.

The literary analogy with short story and novel can be extended to include notions of journey or life stage and of the therapist's place in these as parent, apprentice master or temporary companion, chosen according to individual need and preference by the action of transference and countertransference. This allows for the symbolic function of therapy, for its 'as if' quality of parenting and guidance as well as for its practical function of management and containment. Dogmatic claims made by defenders of either method that only their approach is effective and hence 'infallible' have been unhelpful and confusing. These often carry undertones of fanaticism and religious faith, and are clearly scientifically unprovable. It is better to look at what works, when and why, and, instead of Either/Or, to allow for Both alongside each other. Balint and Malan mentioned the existence of a radical and of a conservative view in relation to brief work – the former promising likely results with most conditions, the latter reserving the method for specific cases of light symptomatology. Because of the results they achieved in their cases and on the basis of their carefully written-up research they arrived at a conclusion which surprised them very much – namely that the former won the day when the clinical work was carefully done.

Provided that there is careful initial selection and preparation, a holding of the boundaries and a maintenance of the working alliance, brief therapeutic encounters are usually positive, though they may not always be effective in the long run (which is the same for long-term work). Malan told his patients that, once they had entered the therapeutic process, they might well want more than the number of sessions offered and contracted at the beginning, and that this could be granted if it were mutually agreed, but not with the same regular therapist, as he did not believe one should alter a contract in midstream.

The change of plan from short-term to long-term work could therefore mean two things: on the one hand, a discovery by the patient that s/he wanted to continue a process experienced as an eye-opener, or as an attractive taster of meaning-making and understanding that could transform life in the ways s/he wished and found useful in order to lead a balanced existence; on the other hand, the request for more therapy could mean that the positive bonding had led to a dependence in the transference, and due to this an ending might be experienced as catastrophic or traumatic, repeating early childhood experiences of separation and trauma that had so far remained hidden and hence not been worked through.

There are two ways of dealing with this situation, and opinions differ sharply on which is the preferred scenario. Either the brief therapist turns into a long-term therapist by switching technique and renewing the contract. This is not what Balint or Malan would have recommended. They favoured a change of therapist at this point, because it was quite likely that the therapist's dependence on the patient, and his or her own unconscious separation anxieties, might have contributed to producing the situation.

The second choice is referral of the patient to another therapist, which would indicate that the brief contract was concluded as planned, while the patient's dependency needs were addressed, too. The message is: 'If you feel you need more than you had from me, it is up to you to get it. However, I will help you in the task by recommending a colleague.' Both scenarios require the therapist to explore his/her own feeling reactions towards the patient honestly in relation to ending, preferably in supervision, as they would be contained in the countertransference material. In his book *My Work with Borderline Patients* (1986), H.F. Searles points to the importance of the therapist's monitoring of separation anxieties, and defences against these. He is referring there to what happens in analysis with borderline patients, but this does not restrict his findings to that mode of clinical work. The brief therapist, in fact, has to be particularly aware of his/her in/ability to mourn, separation anxieties and attachment behaviour in order to honour the contract in focal work, and also so as not to stray from the focus which a slipping into dependency would amount to. The skill is to become attached quickly, to the point of intimacy, and then to detach equally quickly, in spite of the inevitable feelings of loss and mourning which arise at the end of work. The patient and the therapist are both together in the ending and in the grieving, and the achievement of this is one of the main therapeutic goals of this kind of work. Without avoidance and denial, they are asked and forced to go through a cathartic and emotionally corrective experience.

The difficulty and the consummate skill is how to make conscious these strong unconscious defences against anxieties of having to live (and relive) powerful and previously unbearable feelings of loss and letting go and allowing them to become cathartic, transformative and bearable.

It has been said that the therapist who is drawn to brief work is temperamentally inclined to develop intensive scenarios, to work in short, sharp bursts, to enjoy (reap) the satisfaction of quick results. I am convinced that there is a particular personality type – more extrovert than introvert – who is best suited to this demanding style in which 'the clock is ticking' all the time and opportunities rarely turn up more than once, where fast thinking and sharp reacting are at a premium and where quickfire choices have to be made all the time. There is little time for 'reverie' in the sessions, for sitting back and waiting, or for regret; and detours or backtracking have to be kept to a minimum. Anyone who has seen Habib Davanloo at work on video or in the flesh will agree with this thumbnail sketch of the optimal brief stylist and will have admired the virtuoso performance of the quick mind. One is reminded of the surgeon who is total concentration for the time it takes to wield the scalpel and perform an operation, for the lancing of a boil: thrust, twist, removal of the knife. Feelings are brusquely addressed but not dwelt on, the encounter is brief, intense and charismatic, it will linger vividly in the mind. There is love, but no mercy or reprieve.

Not everyone has the ruthlessness and determination this requires. It is known that the impact of personality alone can be a therapeutic agent, and that therapists like Laing, Jung and Carl Rogers used their charismatic personalities to affect patients profoundly. Their ability to establish instant intimacy, to read the patient like an open book and to create rapport has made them famous. Because of this, the one-session-therapy or the two-plus-one approach clearly have to be taken seriously. In these moments, the patient's capacity to 'heal him/herself' can become activated as if by the turn of a switch: a well-conducted initial interview, a well-timed mutative interpretation, an intuitive and felicitous linking of dissociated material will lead to a flashing insight, which is like the 'moment of truth' in a novel or drama when the protagonist becomes aware of some blinding knowledge which marks the turning point, the peripeteia, of a plot or a life.

Davanloo was a master at this make-use-of-the-moment technique: in his case it was a deliberate go for the jugular, the pinpointing of bottled-up aggression in the patient's relating with self and others. Similarly, the medical physician Balint gathers the patient's symptoms into a correct diagnosis which determines the course of treatment. Hobson's successful cases of two-plus-one therapy (Barkham and Hobson, 1989) hinged on the intuitive linking of two apparently disparate statements in the patient's material which pinpointed the origin of the present dilemma (fear of thunder) and cast it in terms of past trauma. This is analogous to the stone thrown into a pond which causes ripples and concentric rings to spread far and wide to the banks of the pond. If the mind is compared to a pond, the ripple effects of a therapeutic intervention, however brief, should be inevitable and obvious. Of course, these can also become destructive, if a patient is fragile and close to a breakdown.

These days in supervision one meets increasing numbers of patients who report a good first experience of brief counselling, and who have returned for more work because this first attempt has become a stepping stone, enabling them to open themselves up to another, to cross the threshold of another consulting room and ask for more of the stuff that helped them survive a critical stage in their life. These patients characterize a situation which could be called 'successive contracting', i.e. an engagement in therapy at recurring points in their personal life when the memory of a good therapeutic experience in the past – whether of a single session, a course of brief work, an extensive bout of psychotherapy, or a creative group experience – has prompted a wish for a top-up or for the resumption of unfinished work, and has led their attention to previously unknown problems triggered off by new life developments.

Erik Erikson (1950: 239) was the first theoretician to point to the need for recurrent therapy when a new stage in the life cycle is reached and needs negotiation, is setting off a temporary crisis and triggering the twofold reaction of onward or regressive movement. This important hypothesis can be linked to what Freud (1937) said in 'Analysis terminable and interminable', when he cautioned that new pathological material needing further analysis was likely to emerge in the ongoing course of an analysand's life, as it was impossible to foresee what was going to happen to the patient and also impossible to practise preventive analysis.

All this takes us back to what was said earlier about the danger of talking in terms of Either/Or, instead of And/And. For some people one therapeutic experience may last a life-time, for others, a series of therapeutic encounters, a form of intermittent therapy, may enable them to go through and manage life without major breakdowns. A literary analogy of the latter is Christian, the hero of Bunyan's *Pilgrim's Progress*, who sometimes strays from the straight path, is joined by various companions for part of the way, sheds his burden when he passes the cross, and finally arrives at his point of destination, the City of Light: maturity, death and transfiguration. When we conceive with Erikson of life as an ongoing journey fraught with difficulties and crises, with Jung as a journey of individuation which leads in circuitous ways through many stages to its inevitable end, and of the patient as the pilgrim in search of a holy grail (be it Freud's psychic equilibrium, Erikson's 'ego integrity', Rogers' 'self-actualization' or Christianity's 'redemption'), then counselling and psychotherapy are options of helpful companionship for shorter or longer periods of time.

The important point of the comparison with Bunyan is that the traveller is on a life-long journey of discovery, a precarious journey of becoming himself in the world. He moves on and forward in an ongoing process, in the external world and in his internal world, impelled by hope without knowing what he will find and where and how he will eventually find himself. In the course of this he constantly seeks, enters into and leaves behind relationships with others, as his nature is object-seeking and object-relating, loving and hating, at times of the very same object.

Therapy becomes part of this journey and is a journey in itself, when the traveller has seriously lost his way and stopped in his track. Here, however, the pilgrimage image begins to fall down, as the spatial and temporal dimensions of the therapeutic journey are infinitely complicated by unconscious processes in the psyche, obeying laws of their own, appearing and disappearing in unpredictable ways. The harnessing and identifying of these is the task of the psychodynamic therapist, who endeavours to help the patient reorientate and refind him/herself. Does this simply involve a psychological repair job to refit the engine, a return, so to speak, to the status quo, of which we are sometimes accused by detractors? Dr Rivers in Pat Barker's novel *Regeneration* (1991) knows that his patients, who have recovered from shell shock with his help, have to return to the trenches, where they will again be exposed to experiences like the one which traumatized them. The counsellor of an employee suffering from work-related stress symptoms knows that he is likely to return to the situation which caused the stress in the first place, after he completes his course of counselling. How can he be 'immunized' sufficiently not to succumb to the stress again? In other words, what will be psychically different the second time round when he re-encounters similar stress?

These are big questions which I will address later in Chapter 2, which deals with psychic change and therapeutic results. Here they are flagged up merely to mark a territory that is hotly disputed and fought over by brief and long-term therapists who are constantly asking themselves these questions and are constantly being asked to produce evidence of lasting change in their patients due to their therapeutic interventions. One of the biggest questions (asked by Eysenck and other therapy sceptics in the fifties) is whether change would happen anyhow, spontaneously so to speak, as the psyche is in constant dynamic movement and (apparently) self-regulating. This is practically unanswerable as there is no experimental research that could tackle the problem conclusively with the help of control groups and repeated trials – not even the regular follow-ups conducted by Balint and Malan, which came closest to proving that their focal work had removed the troubling symptoms for fairly long times. Less specific desired results like ego-strengthening, improved capacity for mourning and bearing strong feelings remain in the realm of inspired guesswork.

2

The Psychodynamic Model and Its Development

Theoretical base

Nowadays many counsellors and psychotherapists call themselves 'psychodynamic', which can mean different things to different people in terms of clinical practice and theoretical orientation, though the base-line seems to be an acceptance of the existence of unconscious dynamic forces operating in the mind and of the necessity of working with these constantly in the therapeutic enterprise. A good definition of the psychoanalytic tradition from which psychodynamic counselling derives is as follows:

> At its core is a belief in the role of the unconscious in the development of intrapsychic conflict and disturbance. Through the careful unfolding of the therapeutic relationship, within a defined setting, it is understood that resolution of conflict and disturbance may be achieved: This is chiefly made possible via the agency of the transference–countertransference dynamic, the operation of which focuses the relevant issues between and within the two members of the counselling relationship. It is understood that during this relationship the client and counsellor will face anxiety, defence and resistance and that much of the relationship will attend to the painstaking mediation of these difficulties. (MacLoughlin, 1995: p. xi)

Quite often there is an implication, when referring to trainings or to practitioners, that the psychodynamic approach is a lesser breed than the psychoanalytic one, perhaps somewhat watered down, or, as I have heard it described, more broadly based, eclectic, flexible and enriched by ingredients from the social dimension in addition to 'strict and tendentious psychoanalysis', as Freud (1919) put it. In terms of the process, 'psychodynamic' is descriptive of a connection between the inner and the outer world in relation to the therapeutic interaction in each individual case, while 'psychoanalytic' can be seen as referring both to technical aspects of clinical practice and to a rigorous stance of analysing and interpreting clinical material in the transference, which excludes other, more 'real', active or direct forms of intervention. This distinction is important as it implies a fundamental difference, as between purity and admixture, and a juggling of different styles and approaches as befits the occasion, while at bottom retaining fundamental articles of belief, of which the 'pure gold of psychoanalysis' is the most essential.

In principle, the psychodynamic approach in counselling and psychotherapy is based on a body of theory that was developed over the past hundred years by several generations of psychoanalysts, beginning with Freud's studies on hysteria, his theorizing about the psycho-neuroses and his construction of a hypothetical model of the human mind, which had topographical and structural features and assumed conscious as well as preconscious and unconscious ways of mental functioning. Studying clinical material from patients and analysing his own dreams, Freud came to hypothesize that the mental apparatus consisted of the three different parts of superego, ego and id which control the mental and instinctual processes in varying degrees, operating together, or in conflict with each other, in the course of human development, depending on the satisfaction and gratification of the human being's sexual instincts which are activated by his or her oral, anal and genital needs. Provided the child's development from initial dependence to gradual autonomy proceeds well, is managed adequately by parental caregivers, and not disturbed by traumatic interferences from within or without, Freud assumed a steady progress from infancy through adolescence to adulthood, leading naturally from the dependant nursing dyad with the mother via the interdependent oedipal triad from which the child should emerge strengthened to form mutually satisfying relationships with parents, siblings and peers, and eventually arrive at mature adulthood and at the ability 'to love and work'.

In other words, the human infant, according to Freud, develops from primary narcissism as babe-in-arms to an active social existence of interdependence and interaction with others with whom s/he identifies, from whom s/he learns language and other survival skills, and whom s/he also needs to fight in order to establish a mental equilibrium and an identity of his/her own.

This hypothetical map of human development is in fact a system of mental functioning reconstructed from observations Freud made with patients suffering from psycho-neurotic and psycho-pathological symptoms which had apparently been caused by traumatic life events, severe deprivation or unmanageable instinctual conflicts, and had resulted in arrested emotional development, insecure bonding and immature attachment patterns. Followers of Freud like Klein, Winnicott and Bion (to name only the most important) developed this basic model of sexual and instinctual development further and included the area of human object relating. By postulating a primary human need for secure attachment, basic trust and active interaction with significant others, it was found that individual patterns of relating are laid down and developed in the early phases of feeding and holding, of being weaned and of learning to explore the environment in the presence of mother, or of the primary caregiver. Because of the powerful feelings of love and hate, and the ensuing persecutory and depressive anxieties which are experienced in this primary relationship, where instinctual needs for gratification and security are overwhelming, the management of this phase becomes crucial for the healthy functioning of the individual in later life. If it has not been satisfactory, strong defensive mechanisms are activated to counteract fears of annihilation and abandonment, and these defences are necessary for survival, but they may stunt or inhibit the growth of the individual's mental and affective life and have severe consequences for the future development of his/her capacity to relate, cope and become an adult.

In his self-analysis Freud had discovered a complex system of unconscious defensive mechanisms that are triggered off automatically in the event of unmanageable anxieties and fears relating to weaning and castration that are experienced as threats to the adequate functioning of the individual ego. He focused explicitly on the infant's sexual or 'libidinal' experiences of pleasure and unpleasure, for which he claimed a regulatory system based on the energy model of discharge and cathexis. The object relations school headed by Klein, Winnicott and Bion took his original discoveries of unconscious processes further and made a distinction between primitive defences (of splitting, projection and denial) and more mature defences like repression, intellectualization, reaction formation, reversal and identification with the aggressor. All these defence mechanisms were seen as necessary and normal to enable the individual to survive external and internal pressures dangerous to his/her survival, but when used excessively or beyond their appropriate developmental stages they would become crippling to healthy ego functioning and were liable to lead to neurotic or psychotic anxieties that would obstruct an individual's affective and thinking operations and hence affect his/her perception of inner and outer reality. The mother's function in containing and mediating her infant's instinctual anxieties and in responding appropriately to his/her developmental needs was considered vital, as any interruption in the continuity and quality of her task would have severe pathologizing effects on the child's growing ego and self and halt the necessary process of identity formation.

Freud's focus had been on the oedipal development, which firmly establishes the genital phase after mastery of the oral and anal phases. The object relations school, by contrast, emphasized the pregenital mother and her role in the child's progress from symbiosis to separation and individuation (Mahler), initiating social processes of interaction, interdependence and identification with parental imagos that are internalized and become internal objects. By coining the concept of the 'transformational object', Christopher Bollas (1986) further developed Winnicott's (1971) notion of 'the use of an object', and this linked up with the new thinking on narcissism in which many concepts of the object relations school received a radical redefinition.

More recently, theorists of self-psychology described the formation of narcissistic disturbances in the emergent self structure when the infant's early need for self objects is not satisfied, or when s/he does not receive empathic attunement from the mother which is necessary to experience him/herself as real and alive. Thus both Winnicott and Kohut recognized the infant's primary need for mirroring by the mother, which is the experience of being seen, held and encouraged to respond from his/her own self. This notion connects with Bion's concept of the mother as container of the infant's anxieties, which are projected into her and transformed by her reverie into manageable mental content, a transformation of what he calls beta elements into alpha elements, of unbearable anxiety into knowledge and thinking, which will eventually lead to a capacity for self-containment and anxiety management, to separateness and a strong sense of self.

This brief overview of mainstream psychoanalytic thinking must also include John Bowlby's attachment theory, which postulates a necessary primary experience of secure attachment and the establishment of a secure base from which will develop healthy patterns of attachment, strong ego functions, and a growing capacity to explore and relate to external reality. When there is no secure base, the attachment behaviour may be insecure, clinging, ambivalent, hostile, avoidant, disorganized, and all these categories are characterized by high levels of separation anxiety leading to difficulties in relationships with others during the life cycle.

The psychodynamic counsellor and psychotherapist will be familiar with most of these psychoanalytic formulations of human development, hypothesize on the basis of psychoanalytic models of mental functioning and the psychodynamics of primary human needs, and will base his or her therapeutic work on some or all of these constructs when assessing and hypothesizing about clinical material and answering requests for therapeutic assistance. S/he will conceive of the task in terms of the clients' developmental needs, their problems in object relating or their attachment patterns, and be prepared to be used as a significant other, with whom unfinished or inhibited developmental tasks can be undertaken, repaired and taken further. S/he will be mindful of offering the containment the clients may require, the sensitive mirroring and attunement they might not have had from the mother. S/he will initiate a dynamic therapeutic process of reflection and meaning-making, of making conscious what seem to be unconscious conflicts in the clients' inner world, obstructing the smooth functioning of their psychic processes and impairing their relations with others and with the external world.

Malan (1979) described the basic principles of dynamic psychotherapy in terms of the interpretation of two 'triangles of insight', called 'the triangle of conflict' and 'the triangle of person'. The first of these names Defence, Anxiety and Hidden Feeling, which together create the unconscious conflict that makes the patient seek help and that is identified by the therapist in the assessment interview.

> This triangle is related to the second triangle by the fact that the hidden feeling is directed towards one or more categories of the triangle of person, namely Other, Transference, and Parent, represented by O, T and P, respectively. The fact that there are three categories of person in the second triangle means that there are three possible links – the O/P link, where feelings directed towards Other are derived from feelings directed towards Parent; the O/T link, where some kind of similar feelings are directed towards Other and Therapist; and the T/P link, where Transference feelings are derived from feelings about Parents.

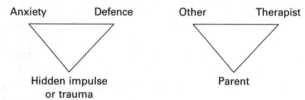

Anxiety   Defence   Other   Therapist

Hidden impulse   Parent
or trauma

Figure 1   Malan's two triangles

> Each triangle stands on its apex, which represents the fact that the aim of most dynamic psychotherapy is to reach, beneath the defence and the anxiety, to the hidden feeling, and then to trace this feeling back from the present to its origins in the past, usually in the relation with parents. The triangle of person thus can also usually be represented by a triangle of time: Other corresponding to current, or recent past; Transference to here-and-now; and Parent to distant past. (1979: 80)

In these triangles Malan found a 'device that can be used to represent almost every intervention that a therapist makes, and that demonstrated that much of a therapist's skill consists of knowing which parts of which triangle to include in his interpretation at any given moment' (1979: 80). I have quoted him at length as he is such a master at describing complicated dynamic processes lucidly and at indicating the logical sequence of events when an intervention is made on the basis of a patient's clinical material. In effect, he compresses the psychodynamic method into a diagram that is the perfect working tool as long as it is not used mechanically nor becomes a cerebral exercise. The triangles prove that, in reality, the psychodynamic counsellor and psychotherapist always works on more than one level spatially and temporarily, connecting inner and outer reality, past and present memory, feeling and experience, and making verbal links between all these factors in order to facilitate insight and under- standing in the patient.

Add to this Erikson's theory of the life-cycle, which takes human development from the cradle to the grave and far beyond the so-called 'formative' early years, then the work can be seen in the wider context of a person's personal narrative, both at the actual stage of his/her life, and the stage to which s/he has regressed in the event of a crisis around making a transition. Erikson conceived of the eight ages of man as each revolving around the performance of specific tasks, e.g. basic trust in infancy, identity in puberty, intimacy and generativity in adulthood, whose non-performance would result in its opposite, e.g. basic mistrust, role confusion, isolation, stagnation, etc. The function of regression is to return to and attempt to repair an unfinished developmental task which allows the individual several attempts at achieving maturation and going over the same ground with the increased resources and the different perspectives of a later stage.

When Freud (1914) described the therapeutic task with the patient as one of 'remembering, repeating and working through' and the goal as enabling the patient to 'love and work', he anticipated the Erik- sonian model of successive stages, crises and tasks in a therapeutic methodology with the fundamental aim of facilitating the mastery of developmental life tasks, of assisting in the resolution of instinctual conflict, in the management of neurotic anxiety and the containment of aggression by lending ego strength and insight. He himself was doubtful whether patients beyond midlife could be helped to change their malfunctioning defence mechanisms, and considered many con- ditions untreatable by psychoanalysis (like narcissistic damage or psychotic states), while his successors, Jung, Klein, Bion and other post-Freudians, have since conceptualized and tackled these success- fully.

Jung also introduced the useful concept of 'individuation' (1921, and *passim* in his *Collected Works*) as a dynamic process of becoming and of self-realization, which accelerates in midlife and leads to the integration and unification of the self, to a 'separate indivisible unity or whole' of the person. To assist in the development of this individu- ation process can be seen as a primary therapeutic aim, particularly when, as is often the case, it is preceded by a midlife crisis (Jacques, 1965) in which the patient becomes depressed at the realization of diminished life expectation and potency and experiences a sense of failure, loss of purpose or intimations of mortality. In the therapeutic relationship the patient can work through the depressive crisis threatening his/her potency, his/her sense of identity and purposiveness, and enter a stage of mature acceptance of reality, of resignation to the time-limited life expectation, and of 'ego integrity', which Erikson defines as the task of Old Age, which follows mature generativity.

Another clinical concept introduced by Jung was that of the 'shadow', which he simply defined as 'the thing a person has no wish to be' (Jung, 1945: CW16, §470), the negative, darker side of the personality, the disavowed, primitive aspects of human nature:

> Everyone carries a shadow, and the less it is embodied in the individual's conscious life, the blacker and denser it is. If an inferiority is conscious, one always has a chance to correct it, but if it is repressed and isolated from consciousness, it never gets corrected and is liable to burst forth suddenly in a moment of unawareness. At all counts, it forms an unconscious snag, thwarting our most well-meant intentions. (Jung, CW11, §131, quoted in Samuels et al., 1986)

For Jung, the aim of psychotherapy was to develop an awareness of those images and situations most likely to produce shadow projections in one's individual life. To admit and to analyse the shadow is to break its compulsive hold, and it is an integral part of individuation to withdraw one's shadow projections upon others. This can be linked up with Malan's triangle of conflict, with the psychoanalytic notion of projection as defence, and in particular with Melanie Klein's use of the concepts of splitting and projective identification (which Jung called 'participation mystique'), both of which she identified as early defences, prevalent in what she called the paranoid-schizoid position of infant development, when the object is split into good and bad, and the anxiety is paranoid, i.e. a fear of persecution and attack (Klein, 1952).

In the early months of life, according to Klein, the infant splits the image of the mother so as to possess the good and control the bad aspects of her, and projects unwanted parts of him/herself into her, which results in her being experienced as if she were the projected content, i.e. a shadow projection. Jung postulated the need for the withdrawal of projections in order to heal the splits, while Klein contrasted the early paranoid-schizoid position with the later depressive position in which good and bad aspects come together in the infant's mind, first in guilt and ambivalence and then in efforts to make reparation and to synthesize the opposites. Since it is impossible to eradicate the shadow, it is impossible to stay in the depressive position, as there is a constant movement back and forth from one to the other position, depending on the state and kind of anxiety experienced – persecutory or depressive – and the experiences and conflicts that have to be managed. At best, the shadow 'can be come to terms with', or anxieties can be managed by using more mature defences than splitting, projection and evacuation (Bion, 1963) and by facing reality, one's own dark and bad parts, rather than blaming others or retreating into phantasy.

Freud has to be given credit for calling attention to the split between the light and the dark sides of the human psyche and to the human tendency to deny and to defend against the primitive, aggressive and evil aspects of human nature. His belief that there are two instinctual forces, a life and a death force, both of which seek expression in conscious and in unconscious, in direct and in sub-limated ways, led him (and his followers, in particular Klein and Jung) to the therapeutic methods of analysing and making conscious the projective and introjective processes which cause psycho-neurotic suffering and psychic imbalances, incapacitating mental and affective functioning and preventing individuation, psychic equilibrium, growth and well-being, in short, what Rogerians call 'congruence' and wholeness.

When Bion (1967) coined the concept of 'not knowing', he was echoing an idea the poet John Keats had communicated to his brothers in December 1817 when he described 'negative capability': 'when a man is capable of being in uncertainties, mysteries, doubts, without any irritable reaching after fact & reason'. The ability to stay with uncertainty enables the poet to access his creativity and his imagination. For the therapist and the patient this negative capability becomes a 'capacity for tolerating frustration . . . which enables the psyche to develop thought as a means by which the frustration that is tolerated is itself made tolerable' (Bion, 1967: 112). The capacity to tolerate frustration is another way of describing the capacity to face anxiety without denying or defending against it, which is, ultimately, the capacity to face the truth, however difficult and apparently unbearable. And, according to Freud, it is the capacity to face truth, not cure, that is the true goal of psychoanalysis. Hence his famous dictum in *Studies on Hysteria*: 'much will be gained if we succeed in transforming . . . hysterical misery into common unhappiness' (Freud, 1893–5: 305).

Basic clinical concepts

The psychodynamic model is anchored in a number of basic clinical concepts formulated by psychoanalysis which form the essential toolkit of the practitioner of this approach and the structure of his/her clinical practice. To start with, the *analytic setting* and the *analytic frame* mean laying down the fundamental principle of commitment and containment which enables the therapeutic work to be done. Winnicott defined the setting as the 'sum of all the details of management more or less accepted by all analysts which becomes more important than interpretation with regressed patients'. Bleger expanded Winnicott's term by the suggestion that it should be

> applied to the totality of the phenomena that are included in the thera-
> peutic relationship . . . both the phenomena that make up the process
> (which are what is studied, analysed, and interpreted), and the non-
> process, i.e. the frame – that is – those constant elements within which the
> process takes place – that only becomes evident when it breaks down, and
> that . . . can become the depository of the most primitive part of
> personality, the psychotic part. (quoted in Momigliano, 1992: 34)

This constant structure of the analytic frame has the same function for the patient which the maternal holding environment has for the child's developing ego. Flegenheimer compared it poetically to 'the darkness in a cinema, the silence in a concert hall' (quoted in Momigliano, 1992: 35).

The analytic insistence on the setting or frame which offers firm boundaries, security, constancy and continuity, relates to

> the radical otherness of this human encounter, to the privileged sense of
> time and space that is experienced on entering and leaving the therapeutic
> container. It is time with a difference, related to the timelessness of the
> unconscious, to existential, subjective time, when past, present, and future
> come together, can form links and meanings and produce intense experi-
> ences for the two participants in an encounter qualitatively different from
> other relationships and in a dialogue that is not like ordinary conversa-
> tion. In this safe space people go into trancelike states, go temporarily
> mad, have visions and delusions They also learn to speak a new language
> and they remember, imagine, and communicate in ways they never knew
> they were capable of. This is the peculiar magic of this particular hour,
> potentially curative or destructive depending on the handling of the
> opportunity and the timing of responses. (Mander, 1995: 9)

André Green wrote about the necessity

> to maintain the isolation of the analytic situation . . . the closeness of
> contact which is restricted to the sphere of the psyche and, at the same
> time, the certainty that the mad thoughts will not go beyond the four walls
> of the consulting room. It ensures that the language used as a vehicle for
> these thoughts will remain metaphorical, that the session will come to an
> end, and it will be followed by another session. (1975: 22)

The frame is sacrosanct, implying sanctuary and sanctity. It can be translated into Winnicott's clinical image of holding and providing, like the mother, a facilitating environment, an intermediary, inter-actional space. Bion's concept of container/contained is a further elaboration of the frame which implies the maternal activity of reverie in relation to the infant's unconscious communications by way of projective identification.

The therapist is responsible for holding the frame when a negative therapeutic reaction makes the patient fearful or unwilling to enter it, makes it difficult to be in it together for long stretches of time and sometimes even impossible to use it constructively. The beginnings and endings of sessions are the critical points to watch, as are cancelled sessions, breaks and demands to change appointments, all of which acquire a symbolic meaning in relation to the analytic work done and to the patient's inevitable resistances to getting on with it.

The multifaceted therapeutic relationship embodies the *working alliance* which, according to Greenson, constitutes the

> relatively nonneurotic, rational relationship between patient and analyst which makes it possible for the patient to work purposefully in the ana-lytic situation. It is the rapport that is necessary before an interpretation should be given. The alliance is formed between the patient's 'reasonable' or 'observing' ego and the analyst's analyzing ego, and indicates a partial and temporary identification that the patient makes with the analyst's attitude and method of work while they are concentrating together on the problems, conflicts, and the neurotic suffering that have brought him/her into therapy. (1967: 46)

The patient's ability to oscillate between the working alliance and the neurotic transference reactions is a prerequisite for doing the psycho-analytic work. This ability is parallel to the split in the patient's ego between a reasonable, observing, analyzing ego, and an experiencing, subjective, irrational ego. The ability to form a working alliance presupposes the existence of a relatively stable part of the individual. It can be regarded as

> being based on the patient's conscious or unconscious wish to cooperate and his readiness to accept the therapist's aid in overcoming internal difficulties. This is not the same as attending treatment simply on the basis of getting pleasure or some other form of gratification. In the working alliance there is an acceptance of the need to deal with internal problems and to do analytic work in the face of internal or (particularly with children) external (e.g. family) resistance. (1967: 47)

In short-term work the establishment of a working alliance is as crucial as in long-term work, and depends on the patient's moti-vation to make use of the limited time on hand. This will be apparent at the assessment, and it needs to be constantly fostered as there is no time to lose in digressions and regression. Equally, signs of *resistance* have to be noted carefully as these will counteract the willingness to work. Freud's definition of resistance and his admonition to interpret it constantly is one of the cornerstones of the psychodynamic approach, though the levels of resistance (depending on the individual and the intensity of the therapy) and the techniques to tackle it vary considerably. Resistance has been defined positively and negatively: as an assertive stance against being influenced and overwhelmed; as an expression of anxiety about change; as a need to control and sabotage the analytic work; as a regulation of self-esteem. It is the largely unconscious defensive attitude adopted by the patient towards the therapist which indicates transferential and real fears of the unknown factors in the therapeutic process and acts as a brake to the changes initiated by the analytic work. The experience is that by making resistance conscious appropriately, patients will feel understood and supported to face anxieties and habitual blockages they are not aware of, and the skilful therapist can gather much useful information from monitoring the patient's resistance. In analysis, interpreting the resistance constitutes as large a part of the work as does interpreting the transference, while psychotherapy and counselling will work with both more sparingly, though constantly and vigilantly holding them in mind.

All these concepts describe closely linked dynamic aspects of the therapeutic relationship. *Transference*, Freud's perhaps most startling and most creative discovery, is embedded in them all as the powerful unconscious force active when two people come together for the purpose of attending to the emotional problems of one of them, and it constitutes, in the words of Waelder,

> an attempt of the patient to revive and re-enact, in the analytic situation and in relation to the analyst, situations and fantasies of his childhood. Hence transference is a regressive process. It develops in consequence of the conditions of the analytic experience, viz., of the analytic situation and the analytic technique. (quoted from Sandler et al., 1973: 44)

This classical formulation is somewhat restrictive, and many additions and expansions have been made to it, also to include transferences occurring outside the analytic situation (i.e. between doctors and patients, teachers and pupils, priests and congregrants, or between friends and enemies), but 'the classical analytic situation does appear to provide conditions which foster the development of transferences and which enable the phenomena to be examined in relatively uncontaminated forms' (Sandler et al., 1973: 46).

The largest area of disagreement is between Kleinians, Freudians and Jungians, with the former insisting on including all aspects of the patient's relationship to his/her analyst in the transference. When Betty Joseph used the phrase of the 'total situation', she was referring to this idea that 'everything in the patient's psychic organisation based on his early and habitual ways of functioning, his phantasies, impulses, defences and conflicts will be lived out in some way in the transference' (1989: 157), and hence that all the patient's associations are essentially referring 'to some thought or feeling about the analyst', as being a repetition of past (usually very early) relationships and hence available to transference interpretations. This is echoed in Patrick Casement's remark 'somebody is angry with someone' (Casement, 1985: 38) apropos of patients' unconscious communications in the transference, which sums up the 'total situation' beautifully – whatever material the patient may bring and whomever s/he is talking about, it is certain to carry a transferential meaning. Not every therapist would take matters to this length, though Casement's cases are skilfully and convincingly scanned for their transferential cues.

Whatever the detail in definition, transference is omnipresent in all relationships. It has probably been most succinctly defined as a 'specific illusion which develops in regard to the other person, one which, unbeknown to the subject, represents, in some of its features, a repetition of a relationship towards an important figure in the person's past' (Sandler et al., 1973: 47). Moreover, transference elements enter to varying degrees into all relationships, and these (i.e. choice of spouse, friend or employer) are often determined by some characteristic of the other person that (consciously or unconsciously) represents some attribute of an important figure in the past.

For the psychodynamic practitioner, transference is a given, a guiding principle, a central 'fact' with which he or she has to reckon from the moment a contact has been made that will (or will not) lead to a therapeutic engagement with the patient. The question for him/her is not whether transference exists, but rather when and how to work with it. This depends on the personality, as much as on the therapeutic contract, but there is no doubt that short-term work in particular requires a careful and deliberate decision about how much, if at all, to interpret or to foster the identified transference, and this is influenced by factors such as lack of time, the necessity to attend to many other pressing tasks and the once-weekly frequency of meetings. The crucial difference here is how much needs to be held in mind and how little can be used to effect without opening floodgates that cannot be closed to material that cannot be channelled.

The best method in this case is to work with one's *counter-transference* responses, which convey essential information about the patient's unconscious projections, when variations in the feelings and attitudes towards the patient can lead to increased insight into processes occurring in the patient. Paula Heimann called the countertransference 'an instrument of research into the patient's unconscious', and she maintained:

> Our basic assumption is that the analyst's unconscious understands that of the patient. This rapport on the deep level comes to the surface in the form of feelings which the analyst notices in response to his patient in his 'counter-transference'. This is the most dynamic way in which his patient's voice reaches him. In his comparison of feelings roused in himself with his patient's associations and behaviour, the analyst possesses a most valuable means of checking whether he has understood or failed to understand his patient. . . . Often the emotions roused in him are much nearer to the heart of the matter than his reasoning, or, to put it in other words, his unconscious perception of the patient's unconscious is more acute and in advance of his conscious conception of the situation. The analyst has to be able to sustain the feelings which are stirred up in him as opposed to discharging them (as does the patient) in order to subordinate them to the analytic task in which he functions as the patient's mirror reflection. (1989: 75)

In contrast to the Kleinian notion of the 'total situation' and its constant active interpretation, which can be experienced as intrusive and therapist-centred by the patient, this understanding of the therapist's emotional responses relates to the basic passive functions of listening and attentiveness which serve the containment and facilitation of the patient's material.

The brief therapist will train his/her attention to pick up counter-transference cues sensitively rather than busily interpreting the transference, which may lead to regression in the client and away from the agreed focus. As long as s/he keeps constant tabs on the complexities of the emotional field, involving projections, transference and countertransference, the work can progress 'briefly' and analytically.

When Freud described the analytic work with the patient as a task of 'remembering, repeating and working through', he stressed the detailed and repeated therapeutic process of analysing the patient's clinical material, which consists of a free-associative flow of memories, and the description of daily events, emotions and phantasies. He also emphasized the fact that the patient's unchecked reminiscing according to the fundamental rule can produce long-forgotten memories which are experienced as 'unthought known' once interpreted and analysed in the therapy. He further emphasized that the patient also acts out, i.e. compulsively repeats, habitual behaviour which goes back to his/her infancy, and that this is another, unconscious, way of remembering something unthought known. Inhibitions and defences, pathological character traits, painful conflicts, traumatic experiences, incomprehensible symptoms and other 'clinical facts', by being interpreted in the transference, are then transformed into memories which had remained repressed and repeated in the form of constantly renewed resistance.

Once named and interpreted, there is a flash of intellectual insight, the well-known 'moment of truth', but this is rarely enough in itself when it happens once, as resistance is a repetitive and a persistent habit which needs to be worked through often and repeatedly before there can be lasting change.

> *'Working through'* is taken to be a sort of psychical work which allows the subject to accept certain repressed elements and to free himself from the grip of mechanisms of repetition. It is expedited by interpretations from the analyst which consist chiefly in showing how the meanings in question may be recognised in different contexts. (Laplanche and Pontalis, 1985: 488)

In other words, emotional discharge or abreaction is not enough, while working through allows the subject to pass from merely intellectual acceptance to a conviction based on lived experience of the repressed instincts which are 'feeding the resistance'.

> Working through is a third term after remembering and repeating in which the other two are combined. It is undoubtedly a repetition, but one modified by interpretation and hence liable to enable the subject to free himself from irrational repetition mechanisms. It is a form of work accomplished by the patient, an acquisition of insight in a more lasting way. (Laplanche and Pontalis, 1985: 488)

In brief work, there is little time for this slow and patient activity of working through, which gathers wild flowers by the wayside. The lack of this repeated activity of going over the same ground in order to relive an experience and to consolidate its meaning is its most striking limitation. Only through conducting follow-ups can it be established whether there has been an ongoing therapeutic effect of work done briefly, in the sense of an ongoing working through after completion of a contract and termination of the relationship because the desired process of self-analysis has been set in train and is taking its course.

The psychodynamic understanding of psychic change

The basic goal of psychodynamic therapy could be described as a concerted effort to make the unconscious conscious and to create meaning where there is anxiety, confusion or futility. In other words – Christopher Bollas' words, to be correct – it is an effort to analyse the 'unthought known' (Bollas, 1986) and, by doing this, to produce a psychic change that is experienced as a liberation, from depression, manic defence, compulsive or obsessional behaviour, all of which amounts to an experience of the ego as 'not being the master in its own house', in the classic definition by Arthur Schopenhauer, which long predates Freud's discovery of the unconscious and its defences. Another way of defining the ultimate goal of psychodynamic psychotherapy and counselling could be to say, in a paraphrase of Freud's words 'from neurotic misery to ordinary human unhappiness', that the client is enabled psychically to establish the rule of the reality principle instead of the pleasure principle, which means s/he moves from the predominant use of phantasy, illusion or hallucination as a means of psychic survival to the use of thinking, staying with and bearing feeling and affect, however painful, frustrating or anxiety-provoking. The therapist as the 'transformational object' is taking on the parental task, failed for the patient's infant, of a gradual facilitation of thinking the unthinkable, saying the unsayable, bearing the unbearable. The 'potential space', the intermediary area between the two participants in the therapeutic endeavour, is, as with mother and baby in the earliest phase of life, the arena and the frame where difficult psychic experience is shared, mediated and transformed, and where psychic change can happen.

Change is, of course, something most people fear as much as hope for, and much defensive behaviour, including resistance to the therapist, indicates this fear of change and the uncertainty it brings with it. 'When Bion mentioned change', Momigliano reminds us, 'he usually qualified it as "catastrophic", to indicate the feelings of risk and uncertainty which the thought function is exposed to because of its very growth process, the new idea may represent the psychotic catastrophe of breaking the container' (1992: 71). There are some therapeutic modes of intervention which unfortunately do not take this need for 'safe containing' sufficiently to heart, and initiate change without safeguarding adequately against the consequences a sudden breaching of emotional barriers may have. Active methods like rebirthing, marathon encounter groups or active imagination which lead into previously uncharted territory without sufficient equipment or time for debriefing may abandon clients in an uncontained or distressed state that can result in breakdown or severe depression. In brief therapy with short time contracts it is essential to watch the rate of change for danger signs in order to wrap up the process safely at the end, to stop emotional matters from hurtling out of control, and, if necessary, to arrange for a quick referral-on in which the tempo of change can be braked and the uncontained material gathered in and worked through.

Anna Freud distinguished between insight-producing therapy and 'developmental help', a distinction which came out of her experience of child analysis, but is equally applicable to work of short or long duration with adults. The 'rehabilitative' function of therapy is based on the use of language, involving the patient's self-representations and mental representations of the object world, and it proceeds as constantly shifting narrative work on the 'unexamined life', aiming 'gradually to remove the obstacles which have impeded the normal lines of emotional and cognitive development' (Fonagy and Target, 1986: 32). The distinction is important in that it describes different stages in a process of self-exploration and psychic change, of identifying a problem, an emotion, a deficit, a recurrent behaviour pattern, and of linking this to something relevant in the past – a significant relationship, a life event, a memory, perhaps a dream.

There is insight when the link is meaningful in terms of something hidden that was avoided because facing it might have involved pain and suffering, the abandonment of a cherished phantasy, the acknowledgement of an unpalatable truth. Such individual insight is a necessary part of a whole series of further insights which accumulate, build up into knowledge and gradually initiate a clearing away of the invisible emotional obstacles that have impeded the natural progress of development. Bion speaks of the therapeutic task of transforming beta elements (bad experience) into alpha elements (good experience) with the help of knowledge, which is his idiosyncratic short-hand for the analytic processing of life experience into a personal narrative and life story that makes sense, can be owned in the present and inspire hope for the future. It is this process of 'learning from experience' (the title of one of Bion's books) that is the basis for 'becoming', i.e. trusting the transformative developmental and maturational processes which are normally active in the life cycle of individuals.

The difference between Anna Freud's two analytic modes is one of depth, intensity and duration. The former can be brief, it promotes self-sufficiency and initiates a sustained process of self-exploration and self-analysis that continues outside the therapeutic relationship and after the therapy has ended. The latter has to do with holding, nurturing and working together over long periods of time until a substantial internal restructuring of defences, repair of internal objects and changes in self-representations and mental functioning have occurred which amount to a task of reparenting, a strengthening of ego functions and the achievement of a psychic equilibrium that underpins emotional experience throughout its inevitable ups and downs. Wordsworth called it 'recollection in tranquillity'. Neither work is ever complete, and psychic change is rarely permanent, though when it occurs it can be the opportunity to make external changes – which will set in train other events and happenings in the external or internal world, and at best establish a dynamic process of self-reflection and self-examination which makes the patient feel that s/he is in charge of his/her life and able to take risks, analyse and confront fears and rely less on defensive strategies like blaming, withdrawing or aggressive acting out. In Melanie Klein's words, the process shifts from the primitive functioning at the paranoid-schizoid position, in which the experience of persecutory anxieties leads to their denial and splitting off, to the depressive position, where anxieties are faced, where guilt feelings and concern for others lead to attempts at reparation, and where the individual assumes responsibility for his/her own actions.

When patients seek help, they usually come with the expectation of solving problems, of finding answers to difficult dilemmas or simply 'sorting themselves out', all of which sounds as if the process could be painfree and swift, a mental exercise, a set of prescriptions, a magic cure. Notions of quick discharge and abreaction are usually in evidence too, as if something could be taken away once and for all, and then there might be 'peace of mind' for ever. They soon realize, however, that the reliving of painful experience and emotion, the revisiting of buried traumata, the return of forgotten and repressed distress, is inevitable and a necessary part of the therapeutic endeavour, as the previous avoidance of these is the very cause of the troubling problem, and they learn to accept that they will have to go through fire in order to come into life. The unconscious fear of loss of control, because of a strong regressive pull to the source of pain ('the point of maximum pain', Hinshelwood, 1991), is a pervasive symptom in anxious novices to the process, but this changes markedly with the experience of sustained therapeutic attention, of being patiently listened to, reliably supported, constantly mirrored, trusted and understood. It is replaced by subtle and constantly shifting therapeutic interactions which amount to a process of metabolic transformation, of metamorphosis, transfiguration and gradual psychic change.

When this process has become established, we may speak of 'having turned a corner', and we probably notice subtle changes of mood, of body and verbal language, or differences in the quality of relating. Some would call this shift the 'corrective emotional experience' of therapy, but this phrase (Alexander and French, 1946) has become controversial as it can mean different things to different people, ranging from misplaced offers of concrete mothering to allowing an experience of relating that is qualitatively different from anything the client has ever known. This does not mean directly making up for something missed, like good parenting or appropriate weaning, but, rather, the painful discovery of this deficit in the past, and the stoic acceptance of this immutable reality, which can lead to acts of creative reparation, like choosing an activity that allows a constructive channelling of personal experience and learning. In other words, an old problem can find a solution for the first time. This is the simple principle underlying solution-focused brief therapy, where a problem area is identified by the two participants for which a solution can be found in a relatively short time which fully involves the client's cooperation, imagination and his/her good memories of previous problem-solving experience. It constitutes an act of decision, trial-and-error, risk, and, if successful, will lead to insight (I can do it) and hope (I can do it again). The psychic change involved may be small, and yet manifold, rewarding and liberating enough to make a significant difference. Its 'rehabilitative' function can be measured in terms of what consequences will follow.

3

The Historical Development of Brief
Psychotherapy Models

The most important Brief Psychotherapy Models

We have already mentioned the brief focal psychotherapy model developed by Michael Balint and David Malan at the Tavistock Clinic in the 1950s (Balint, 1972; Malan 1963). This was by no means the first attempt to shorten the increasingly lengthier processes of psychoanalysis, practised by Freud's followers in their private consulting rooms in their endeavour to implement his teachings; but it was the first truly systematic and research-based attempt at developing a time-limited and deliberately focused model of analytic practice, after Sandor Ferenczi's experiments with a shortened version of analysis that involved manipulation and physical gratification of the patient, much to Freud's disapproval. It was, in some respects, also the purest in terms of using basic analytic clinical concepts. However, like all other brief models, it did away with the 'fundamental rule' of free association and with it the analyst's passivity, which meant a departure from Freud's 'evenly hovering attention', and from Bion's exhortation to use reverie 'without memory and desire', and it radically reinterpreted the 'holistic' analytic method which considered every important aspect of the personality as closely related to, or implied by, every other aspect. It did this by concentrating on what French (1958, 1970) had called the 'focal conflict' and the 'nuclear conflict', in his attempt to develop a systematic and teachable method of approaching psychoanalytic clinical data, in order to obtain guidelines for the clinician's interpretative activities. The focal conflict was defined as follows:

> a disturbing motive (an impulse or a wish) is in conflict with a reactive motive (a superego or ego response) creating the necessity for finding a solution (an adaptive or defensive compromise). Focal conflicts are derivatives of deeper and earlier nuclear conflicts . . . which presumably originate during crucial developmental periods in early life. These remain mostly dormant, repressed or solved, with one of them becoming activated (or having remained active) and continuously appearing to underlie behaviour in the form of focal conflicts . . . which can be identified as variations of the same theme. (quoted from Balint, 1972: 11)

In other words, when a patient comes for treatment, s/he usually presents with symptoms which are semi- or preconscious manifestations of this unresolved focal conflict and point the way to what needs to be analysed (in the transference) to free the patient from the nuclear conflict that has been an ongoing developmental obstruction in her/his psyche. All subsequent forms of dynamic brief therapy, even the solution-focused models which have proclaimed that 'making a difference' is all that needs doing, have used French's formulation of the 'focal conflict' as a basis for the brief therapeutic activity when they advocate resolving the presenting problem and producing necessary change. This is not the same as behavioural symptom removal, as the focus has a psychodynamic dimension reaching into the past and connecting past feelings and attitudes with the present (as demonstrated in Malan's triangles of conflict and person).

The focus: Balint and Malan

The secret and the magic of brief psychotherapy lie in the therapist's ability to assess the patient and to choose the correct *focus*, the core focus (or complex) which causes the patient's distress. This was conceptualized and systematically implemented by Balint and Malan, the latter of whom defined the 'limited aim' of focal brief therapy as 'briefly working through a given aspect of psychopathology' with the therapist keeping in mind an aim or 'focus' which should ideally be formulated in terms of an essential interpretation on which therapy is to be based (Malan, 1963: 209). Malan pursued this focus single-mindedly, using selective neglect and starting with an initial successful interaction between patient and therapist that is succinctly described thus: 'a) the patient offers material, which b) enables the therapist to formulate a focus, which c) the therapist offers to the patient, which d) the patient in turn accepts and works with' (1963: 210).

The corrective emotional experience: Alexander

Another important aim of the brief therapy mode was defined by Alexander (Alexander and French, 1946) as the '*corrective emotional experience*', which results

> from the difference between the original parental response and the response of the analyst during analysis which provides the patient with an opportunity to correct his distortions. The emotional experience in the transference lends conviction to and is the necessary underpinning of insight. Having thus reached some stability this insight elicits new, more up-to-date and reality-orientated solutions to old conflicts. (quoted in Balint, 1972: 9)

Alexander considered this experience as the key therapeutic factor in the standard analytic procedure, as formulated by Freud, and its first formulation occurred to him when he was pondering Ferenczi's abortive attempt at shortening analytic treatment and at correcting the over-intellectualized procedure of psychoanalysis by reviving the abreaction theory of cure (discarded by Freud after his attempts to use hypnosis with hysterics, which is described in *Studies on Hysteria* [1893–5]). Alexander, like Ferenczi, resorted to a variety of activities in the hope of improving the standard procedure, which he described as follows: 'The standard procedure can be improved by rendering the corrective influence of the transference situation more effective by giving increased attention to the interpersonal climate of the treatment situation'. He hoped to achieve this by (a) changes in the frequency of interviews, (b) temporary interruptions of the treatment (to deal with excessive dependency problems) and (c) replacement of the analyst's spontaneous countertransference attitudes by assuming a deliberately planned stance, the opposite of the parental attitudes, to enhance the corrective emotional experience. He was fiercely attacked, not only for his manipulative recommendations on the therapeutic process, but because he seemed to believe that he was offering an improved form of psychoanalysis, when it was in reality an alternative.

The trouble with the application of the concept of the 'corrective emotional experience' was and is twofold. On the one hand, it was falsely taken to mean 'gratifying the patient's emotional and narcissistic needs – for parenting, nurturing, being loved'. On the other hand, it was misunderstood as a 'concrete form of gratification and replacement' instead of the enabling of insight, i.e. as an advocacy of therapy as making up for a lack or deficit, to the extent of physical hugging, holding, rebirthing and other, potentially abusive forms of boundary-breaking. Both these notions involve a rather concrete caring for the patient, instead of the symbolic containment in the analytic space and frame which operates as the facilitating environment and offers an experience of safety in which the past parental failure and developmental deficit can be faced, and the patient's deficient relating to others can be changed through reworking his/her early developmental stages in the transference.

The basic therapeutic principle is to re-expose the patient under more favourable situations to emotional situations which s/he could not handle in the past and which s/he will now experience with a new ending, such as acceptance, understanding, forgiveness. In Winnicott's paradoxical way of thinking, the therapist can never make up to the patients for what they have suffered in the past, but what he can offer is to repeat the failure to love them enough and then share with them and help them work through the feelings about this failure. He believed that the therapist has to fail, but this time round the patient would be able to bear the failure, and the therapeutic relationship would survive the re-enactment of original failure and enable the patient to relive and work through it:

> Corrective provision is never enough. What is it that may be enough for some of our patients to get well? In the end the patient uses the analyst's failures, often quite small ones, perhaps manoeuvred by the patient . . . and we have to put up with being in a limited context misunderstood. The operative factor is that the patient now hates the analyst for the failure that originally came as an environmental factor, outside the infant's area of omnipotent control but that is *now* staged in the transference. So in the end we succeed by failing – failing the patient's way. This is a long distance from the simple theory of cure by corrective experience. (Winnicott, 1965: 258)

This is part of the crucial developmental move from infantile dependence to autonomy, to mastery and to the acquisition of a capacity to bear anxiety and uncertainty (Keats and Bion).

As insight, coupled with a lived experience of the habitual and compulsive problem finding a new and different solution, the 'corrective emotional experience' is the goal of all therapeutic experience that aims to involve the patient's understanding. When talking about the first examples of brief therapy, frequent mention has been made of Freud's treatment of Bruno Walter (e.g. Coren, 1996: 23), in which, after a brief consultation, he recommended to Walter a holiday from opera and a trip to Sicily to cure his paralysed arm, 'instead of questioning me about sexual aberrations in infancy', as Walter had feared. On Walter's return, Freud recommended he use his arm again, and after a short time Walter had overcome his neurosis. This 'neglect and counter-stimulation' technique was more akin to Milton Erickson's 'uncommon therapy' techniques than to Alexander's experiential insight method. It does, however, emphasize an important element of all effective brief (or long-term) therapy – the *element of surprise*, which has been minted by most charismatic consultants from Winnicott (in his doodling at clinical consultations) to Davanloo (in his assessments), and such latter-day or present-day practitioners of one-(or two-plus-one)session therapy as Laing, Lacan and Hobson, who seem to be able to fit the key in the lock in a magic, open-sesame sort of way that causes a 'moment of truth', and becomes the revelation of a conflict resolution which constitutes a therapeutic cure comparable to Bruno Walter's experience. What seems to be at work is the impact of the doctor's, therapist's or healer's personality, which has been used in placebo cures from time immemorial and which depends on the patient's faith in his authority and method.

It would be foolish to neglect this curative aspect, particularly in brief work; and with reputable therapists whose fame may depend on the development of a new method or the pronouncement of a new theory that promises better results, it is surely always present. This is the element of 'suggestion' that Freud (1919) talks about when he recommends a psychotherapy for the people 'alloyed with the copper of suggestion'. All well-known brief therapy models have been developed by such personalities and bear the imprint of their individual and idiosyncratic character and style, their temperament and beliefs. The caveat to other therapists that should, but doesn't always, follow is: 'See whether you can do it, and whether it suits you too.' All too often, unfortunately, the method is advertised as a panacea and a dogma, instead of another, newer version among many others, probably equally valid ones.

Freud, the founder of psychoanalysis, has also been called the original brief therapist, particularly in relation to his earliest recorded cases, when he was still experimenting with and developing the practice of psychoanalysis. When Davanloo stated that 'we have forgotten how to do brief therapy', he was clearly referring to the pioneers of psychoanalysis (of whom Jung, Adler, Rank and Ferenczi are only the best known), whose cases rarely lasted longer than a few months. In a way, like so many reformers and pioneers, he was demanding a return to the beginnings and the giving up of acquired bad habits that no longer made sense to him (and did not suit his personality). But it is the Either/Or instead of the And/And which makes no sense as it leads to strife, impoverishment and dogmatism.

The concept of time: Mann

This brings me to the third and probably most important principle of brief therapy, the *concept of time* and timelessness, which constitutes the most radical departure from the open-ended process of analysis and imposes structure, goal and finiteness on the apparently random progress of therapeutic discourse that relies on unconscious associative material. Instead of reaching an end when the work done satisfies both participants' expectations (or when one of them decides it is enough), a time limit is set at the beginning and is honoured no matter how the work proceeds. Moreover, this is done with the intention of furthering the therapeutic aims and in the firm belief that limiting time is one of the principal curative factors and that practical considerations of economy, cost-effectiveness and workload are certainly important, but not the primary motive for shortening the work.

The most articulate theoretician of this aspect of brief therapy is James Mann (1973), whose 12-session model exemplifies a philosophy of developmental needs concentrated into beginnings and endings, with issues of attachment, separation and loss the central focus of the clinical work. His clinical experience had convinced him that in conventional psychotherapy therapist and patient come to need each other, and that this dependence, coupled with an illusion of time-lessness, undermines the therapeutic effectiveness of open-ended work and should be minimized. Time is intimately connected with mortality and other unpleasant limitations of the human condition, so it is unconsciously avoided by both therapist and patient. Mann became convinced that 'Time should be quite deliberately employed to achieve certain ends that will be of use to the patient' and also maintained

> that the problem of time with its meaning of separation, loss, and death is as vital in the emotional life of the therapist as it is in that of the patient, [thus] only by setting a fixed time limit [could] the ambiguity about ending treatment be eliminated. In short: A fixed time limit forces both therapist and patient to confront the issue of termination with a minimum of evasion. (1973: 36)

In order to harness the useful potential of this insight, Mann advocated

> twelve treatment sessions as the minimal time required for a series of dynamic events to develop, flourish, and be available for discussion, examination, and resolution. The recurring life crisis of separation–individuation is the substantive base upon which the treatment rests which emphasised the fact of repeated separation crises on the manner in which later similar crises are managed. (1973: 15)

Total mastery of this basic anxiety, he maintained, is, of course, beyond mortal reach, and all human beings remain susceptible to this anxiety throughout life. In this kind of time-limited psychotherapy, however, mastery of separation anxiety becomes the model for the mastery of other neurotic anxieties, albeit in a somewhat derived manner. The logic is simple and convincing, and leads to a statement of basic universal conflicts, in the manner of Erik Erikson (1950):

1) Independence versus dependence
2) Activity versus passivity
3) Adequate self-esteem versus diminished or loss of self-esteem
4) Unresolved or delayed grief. (Mann, 1973: 25)

In Mann's evaluation session the patient's central issue is identified, usually painful feelings that the patient has had about himself or herself over a long period of time. While this sets the tone for treatment, the definiteness of the termination date provides the shape. The patient is asked to agree with the treatment plan.

The first treatment phase is used to allow the patient to return to an earlier phase of development where the sense of timelessness was prevalent. The patient re-experiences the 'golden glow' of childhood omnipotence, setting the stage for the first conflict with the therapist, who brings the patient back to the central issue and hence confronts him/her with reality. The therapist must not be seduced into working on side-issues in order to stay with the reality of the treatment situation.

In the second phase, the re-emergence of reality, the patient's resistance appears, together with disappointment and ambivalence towards the therapist. The treatment proceeds on two levels: the manifest level with patient and therapist working psychotherapeutically to understand and clarify the central issue as it relates to the past, the present and the therapist; and the latent level, which represents the patient's struggle with the limitations of time in the therapy, and, in connection with this, with the limitations of reality.

In the third phase, termination, the two levels of treatment come together. Some aspect of the central issue is related to the actual ending of treatment, and the separation experience is consistently interpreted in the transference, which becomes essential for the therapeutic results of the work. 'Active and appropriate management of the termination will allow the patient to internalise the therapist as a replacement for the earlier ambivalent object, thereby making separation a genuine maturational event' (Mann, 1973: 28). Without acknowledgement to Alexander, Mann was clearly describing a 'corrective emotional experience' as the positive result of his brief therapy method, which has since become widely and effectively used. When it did not work, however, because of acting out of separation anxiety on the part of the patient or because some traumatic event (e.g. a death) may have occurred during the course of the therapy, Mann extended the length of treatment, seeing the patient for a few additional sessions some time after termination, or arranging for additional therapy after a period without, to establish whether the patient was able to consolidate the gains of therapy after treatment had ended. In either case eventual termination with the brief therapist became possible. But the hard and fast rule had become flexible, possibly with serious implications relating to boundary-breaking (Langs, 1994).

This model is the easiest method of brief therapy to teach, and to practise. Its effectiveness depends on the therapist's belief in the method, his/her ability to hold the focus and honour the contract, and the firm attitude that no further treatment will be needed. The three phases of treatment develop quite naturally because of the time limit, and the level at which the therapy is conducted is similar to the beginnings of long forms of therapy. It also requires the acquisition of some new skills, in particular the formulation of the central issue, and the ability to work with the ending from the beginning, which is best taught and learnt through individual supervision. Its main difficulties are encountered in the countertransference, in the shape of 'guilt, thwarted narcissistic gratification with respect to the dependence of patients, and anger, grief and the problem of tolerating separation and loss which relate to the therapist's reparative needs'. These have to be carefully monitored in supervision and acknowledged by the therapist. Not everybody can tolerate them in the long run.

Assessment and evaluation: Malan, Davanloo and Molnos
The setting of a fixed time limit for brief therapy as initiated by Mann was accepted in principle by Malan, Davanloo and Molnos, to name but three of the innovative brief therapists whose writings have influenced the most recent brief therapy boom in the UK. But none of them are as strict and single-minded as Mann in their planning and implementation of time limits. Their individual methods have been shaped by differences in personality and context: the Tavistock Clinic in London for Malan and Molnos; the American clinical consultancy position for Davanloo, who was a one-man band difficult to imitate. All three therapists laid great emphasis on *assessment and evaluation*, most particularly Davanloo, whose public demonstrations of videoed casework demonstrate that most of the work after the lengthy assessment session, which was seen as 'trial therapy', was repeating and re-enacting in a relentless and confrontative pursuit of defences and resistances what had been uncovered and confronted in the very first encounter. The therapy itself hence became a continued working through of issues uncovered at assessment, connected with the original conflict and the buried anger with primary carers that was creating relationship difficulties.

Davanloo maintained that the original conflict is generated not in a one-to-one relationship, but within multiple relationships in the primary environment involving mostly the mother, but also the father, siblings and other significant people. The child starts by being in conflict with at least two people. As a result, powerful impulses arise of hatred, jealousy, envy, of feeling excluded and wanting to exclude. Those feelings reappear in later relationships and create the difficulties the patient cannot resolve by him/herself. In this sense, the three single letters T, O and P on the vertices of Malan's triangle of person represent an oversimplification: only T (Therapist) stands for one single person; P (Past) usually involves more than one person; and O (Other) is likely to be equally complex. During the working-through sessions the therapist and patient go over this pattern of relating in a dynamic technique of repeated back and forth movements that enables the patient to feel an equal participant and shaper of his/her therapy, while being firmly held by the therapist. The conflict is thus activated within the therapeutic relationship, is no longer internal and can be tackled and resolved.

Balint's and Malan's brief focal psychotherapy, an 'example of applied psychoanalysis', as indicated in the subtitle of Balint's book (1972), was the product of an experimental workshop at the Tavistock Clinic in the fifties and sixties. It was long by today's treatment standards, usually 25 to 30 sessions, or 6 months (including breaks and missed sessions). Balint and Malan pioneered several of the essential features of most brief work, stressing the priority of thorough assessment, the importance of patient motivation (for change), of recent onset of the problem, of some degree of psychological-mindedness in the patient and of willingness to be cured, the ability to accept treatment or 'cure' in terms of the presenting problem and to feel reasonably satisfied with this. They also introduced the notion of the therapist's 'selective attention, selective interpretation, selective neglect', and recommended the use of 'trial interpretation' to test the patient's suitability for insight-oriented work with the help of the two triangles.

They both considered that their focal therapy was on a continuum with psychoanalysis as it was restricted to interpretative interventions, and they insisted that the aim of treatment was the clarification of the two triangles which Malan, adapting and expanding Menninger's (1958) triangle of insight, had called the triangle of person and the triangle of conflict. By repeatedly interpreting the patient's defence, anxiety and hidden feelings with the help of the triangle of conflict, and by further interpreting the transference (to the therapist), other relationships, and relationships with parents with the help of the triangle of person, the patient acquires insight into his/her basic conflicts and their no longer constructive defensive strategies, and hopefully is able to let go of or modify the latter.

The importance of creating an atmosphere conducive to success, which is dependent on the therapist's confidence and authority, is another significant point stressed by Balint and Malan, as was their careful choice of a psychodynamic focus, which Balint suggested should be found in 'ten-minute psychotherapy', by a flash of understanding, a moment of truth, the meeting of two minds. This experience, he insisted, needs to be felt and recognized by both partners, and then translated into a precise formulation, without which no focal plan can be devised that would enable the therapist to use selective attention or selective neglect. The focus must be quite specific to each patient, not general like 'homosexuality' or 'oedipal conflict', and it needs to be sharply delineated and unambiguous, perhaps best expressed in the form of an interpretation that could be given meaningfully to the patient towards the end of the treatment.

An alternative to this 'flash' method was formulated by Malan in the idea of a

> crystallization of a focus, i.e. not a flash but a gradual emergence in the give and take between patient and therapist which would deal with doubts and other emerging foci along the way. The chosen focus limits and predicts the therapeutic results; equally, there is probably a close correlation between motivation and outcome. (1963: 208)

> The ideal focus is one where the current symptomatology and its precipitating stresses can be related to the original conflict in childhood. This does not have to be, although it frequently is oedipal in nature. (Flegenheimer, 1982: 106)

Sometimes the conflict is interpreted in the transference first, in the belief that the transference–parent links are the most important factors in successful therapy. Dreams and fantasies are not analysed as fully as they would be in long-term treatment. The therapist needs to be neither unduly confronting, nor need s/he shrink from deep interpretations, as long as these are kept to a minimum.

The main qualitative differences between brief and long-term psychotherapy are in the limitation of the patient's regression, in the careful avoidance of dependence, and in the virtual elimination of the working-through phase of treatment. Most of the factors operating in long-term psychotherapy are present in the brief therapy situation: the patient–therapist relationship, the opportunity for abreaction, the opportunity for insight, and the use of dreams, fantasies, associations and the manifestations of the transference. The striking difference in technique is a rapid back-and-forth movement between patient and therapist, with both participating actively in an equal interaction which is the norm of human communication and does not have to be learnt, as does the long-term therapy method of communication, by free association and interpretation. This serves to keep the therapy focused and retards regression in the patient. In addition, the therapist brings to the situation a sense of confidence and optimism, symbolized by the time limitation, which indicates to the patient that the therapist hopes that a great deal can be accomplished in a short period of time, and that it is up to the patient to do most of the work. The therapist frequently makes comments which highlight the patient's responsibilities and is quick to intervene when the patient tries to sit back and let the therapist do the work. All these factors tend to heighten the tension and the emotional content of the patient–therapist interaction.

Dangers for the therapist in using this method are that s/he may drift into old patterns and analyse anything that comes along without staying within the focus. This will inevitably lead to long-term therapy and sabotage the treatment plan. Another danger lies in becoming overly ambitious and doing 'wild' analysis, making deep interpretations for the sake of it and losing the momentum of the clearly focused process.

A further distinctive feature of the Balint–Malan model is the use of repeated follow-ups after termination of contract to establish whether the achieved therapeutic changes have been lasting and whether the patient has benefited from the therapy. Follow-ups can be up to four years after termination, sometimes by letter. Malan's research is based on these follow-ups, which showed a success rate of 44 per cent, and proved that the patients continued the process of self-reflection and working through that was started by the thereapy, often over many years, and seemed to have internalized the therapist in a creative way.

Other tasks recommended by the Tavistock team are a step-by-step supervisory screening of individual sessions, with the help of forms notating expectations, atmosphere, interventions given, thought of, and not given, focal aim and afterthoughts, all of which allow a systematic evaluation of the structure of sessions, of the treatment as a whole, and of the outcome in relation to predictions. An essential requirement for practitioners of this method is a fluent ability to interpret, to consistently hold the frame, and to process clinical material in the light of assessment hypotheses and predictions. Inexperienced therapists will need intensive supervision, preferably in a group; they will also need to learn and develop good assessment skills, the ability to establish instant rapport and to make quick decisions without regret about when to intervene, and to know what to interpret and how to leave well alone, particularly in relation to transference and resistance interpretations. Finally, the therapist should not be tempted to think that s/he is giving the patient a second-best, but s/he has to believe in the method chosen and carry it through firmly to the best of his/her ability.

Malan (1963: 8–9) listed 12 reasons why psychotherapies had tended to get longer and longer. It might be as well to give these here:

1. Resistance,
2. Over-determination,
3. Necessity for working through,
4. Roots of neurosis in early childhood,
5. Transference,

6. Dependence,
7. Negative transference connected with termination,
8. The transference neurosis,
9. A tendency towards passivity and the willingness to follow where the patient leads,
10. The 'sense of timelessness' conveyed to the patient,
11. Therapeutic perfectionism,
12. The increasing preoccupation with ever deeper and earlier experiences.

Many of these items constitute fundamental psychoanalytic concepts and principles first formulated by Freud and handed down to his disciples. Malan was well aware of this, but he was not afraid to claim that 'a rationally based technique of brief psychotherapy must be based on a conscious opposition to one or more of these factors, particularly those in the therapist. This list provides a good frame of reference within which the different kinds of technique may be considered' (1963: 9).

Malan's most gifted pupil, the Hungarian Angela Molnos, followed up his brief work a generation later with a spirited defence of the time-limited method, which rests on the blunt statement that 'psychotherapy should be as short as possible and as long as the patient really needs it' (1995: 23). Molnos consolidated some of Malan's teaching and took it further by stating her belief 'that to the extent that analytic psychotherapies offer a space within which the timelessness of childhood – which coincides with the timelessness of the unconscious – can be reexperienced, they also awaken powerful resistances against its disruptions' (1995: 18). She believed that the shortening of therapy had to be at the beginning before the patient has had time to rally his/her forces and mount strong resistance against the therapist. She also emphasized the importance of the therapist's 'good intentions', doing therapy briefly and hopefully. To this end she was eager to stress the subjective factors influencing why one would prefer brief rather than long-term psychotherapy.

> For instance, one's personality might be more suited to it or there might be unconscious reasons on the part of the therapist, such as magical fantasies of curing someone instantly, omnipotence, rivalry with slow colleagues etc. None of these and other wrong reasons are specific to brief psychotherapy. Obviously any therapist who is keen on brief work because of such hidden, self-orientated destructive motives is either in need of psychotherapeutic help or should not be a therapist at all. . . . Whatever we do we should heed the warning against overtreating the patient. (Foulkes, 1975: 73, cited in Molnos, 1995: 22–3)

In her book about the essentials of brief dynamic psychotherapy Molnos outlines a model which elegantly expands the two triangles of Malan into four and describes the usual sequence as follows:

The patient comes with his problem. No matter how he presents it, while we explore it, we soon find out that the core of the problem is some disturbance in his relationships with others. As we take his history we look for patterns, and we discover similar patterns in his past. Finally, sooner or later we see the same pattern appearing in the here-and-now. Knowingly or not, when we take the patient's history we are looking for patterns, and by doing so we are using the four triangles: the conflict now, out there; the problem in the past, there and then, and, finally, the problem here-and-now. (1995: 36, see diagram)

This sounds deceptively simple, but is, of course, quite complicated when applied to individual situations brought into therapy by distressed patients which need to be stripped to their core conflict. On the other hand, when Molnos describes her way of working in brief psychotherapy, she manages to condense her original approach to 'healing destructive anger' very plausibly into a sequence of therapeutic moves by which she breaks through the 'wall' of defences systematically right at the beginning of therapy 'when both the need for the therapist's help and the determination to change are strong and the patient's unconscious has not yet learnt to out-manoeuvre the therapist's particular approach' (1995: 76). In her approach the 'strong but fair ' challenge which she borrowed from Davanloo 'is combined with a completely secure psychic holding'. Molnos goes on to challenge the resistances until the moment when the patient is suddenly in touch with the anger against the much-needed therapist and expresses this, which 'has a magic, liberating quality. It is a moment of separation within a good relationship', something the patient may never have expressed before, or felt before, in a good relationship. Molnos maintains that 'immediately after the healing anger positive feelings appear, the current and past conflicts are linked with the one in the here and now', and by doing this repeatedly and for the remainder of the therapy, she achieves her therapeutic aim, i.e. 'the expression of negative feelings towards the person on whom [the patient] most depends is an eminently healing experience' (1995: 75). In a way, by doing this she has once again demonstrated Freud's classic sequence of 'remembering, repeating and working through', albeit in a very shortened version of his technique, particularly the important working-through part of it.

Gaining freedom from repressed anger and acquiring the ability to express anger (and other repressed feelings) is certainly one of the prime goals of all psychotherapy. Molnos's convincingly described brief method seems to work for her, but it clearly requires the patient to possess the psychic strength (the ego strength) to bear the unavoidable pain that is to come. She claims that, in contrast to the more conventional therapist (but in line with the Kleinians), her immediate aim is not to lower the initial anxiety but to use it to help the patient break through the defensive wall and get to the core of the problem as fast as s/he can bear it. Molnos has learnt from her second master, Davanloo, that in the first session, or 'trial therapy', the therapist tests whether the patient has sufficient ego strength to go beyond his/her habitual defences and to experience his/her true feelings to the full in the here-and-now. In all cases, moreover, the therapist will make sure that there is a good rapport at the end of the first session.

What it boils down to in the end is the patient's ego strength as much as the therapist's determination to challenge the defences. How many patients, one wonders, can really stand up to such a dynamic technique of relentless confrontation and battering? And how many therapists *can* trust their gut feelings and go into the offensive armed with such a strong belief in the healing power of anger? Neither Molnos nor Davanloo has provided as much research evidence as Malan to vouch for the efficacy of their recommended approach in other, less capable or fearless hands. In the enthusiasm created by the laboratory conditions in which they worked, it seems likely that they fell for the magic of the moment when the confrontation worked and when the relentless struggle against the barrier of defences came to a sudden end in the warm feelings of rapport experienced as a real mutative event of healing in the actual relationship. They firmly believed that the aims formulated by Freud, namely 'overcoming the patient's resistance' and 'making the unconscious conscious', are consistently achievable in their brief therapy of confrontation and psychic holding, 'in which the therapist's intermediate aim at any one point in the therapy is to follow and apply the basic analytic principles, thus facilitating corrective emotional experiences, together with the correct cognitive recognition of internal and external reality as well as bringing about behavioural changes in his daily life' (Molnos, 1995: 87).

As a blueprint for successful brief psychotherapy, Angela Molnos's methodology and philosophy of healing anger is admirable, but there must be a snag in it otherwise it would have caught on more widely. As with Alexander and French, this may have to do with the confused area between the transference and the real relationship, and the surprising result may be a transference cure rather than consolidated psychic change. Also the method requires a measure of brutality in the therapist that few of us can muster – the best comparison I can think of is surgery, an art that requires precision, strong nerves, supreme expertise and the kind of confident personality that is rare.

In this context it might be useful to mention Roy Schafer, who cautioned against the 'mental magic' of brief therapy, as its results are inherently unstable, even though continuing contact with the doctor, if only in fantasy, can sometimes fortify and sustain the magical gains over considerable time. . . . It follows that the patient would want to buck up in order to be loved by the doctor [transference cure]. The patient will do it for the conditional love of the doctor. And . . . the way to please is by developing a less disturbing and less obvious substitute neurosis – perhaps a phobic avoidance of tabooed depression and the adoption of a manic posture. . . . By its very nature a brief therapy cannot fully reveal all the unconsciously significant factors at work in it. One cannot even make that claim for full-scale analysis, however informative they are in comparison to brief therapy. . . . The therapist tries to deny how difficult it is to bring about change based on true and insightful modification of defenses and how magically conceived and unstable many of the apparent benefits of brief therapy are likely to be. The unyielding patient is a threat to an overeager therapist's defenses. As a result the therapist may make excessive claims for the penetration and the results of brief therapy.

In this respect, I would mention that even Dr. Mann's careful analytic account of his method includes what I would consider an excessive claim; in one place he says that his method helps 'bypass the patient's customary defences. . . .' It is questionable whether customary defenses can ever be bypassed, for they are too important to the patient and too pervasively applied by him or her. Rather than thinking of end runs around defenses, I would suggest instead thinking that under certain transferential conditions, the patient may re-align important defenses in a compromise move that allows some limited exploratory work to be done and some limited change to occur for reasons that combine irrational repetition and rational change. To some extent this seems to be true in every treatment approach but it is especially true in brief therapy. (1982: 150)

These sceptical comments are well worth pondering in relation to the method recommended by Angela Molnos and practised by her mentor David Davanloo, whom the later David Malan had come to admire, too. But they apply to short-term therapy modes as a whole, and also to some long-term work when issues of collusion and seduction are ignored.

Cognitive analytic therapy: Ryle
I have outlined three explictly psychodynamic brief therapy models whose practitioners influenced and were influenced by each other in their endeavour to remain true to the basics of the analytic approach while shortening its treatment duration. Next I want to describe Dr Anthony Ryle's cognitive analytic therapy (CAT) model. This was developed at London's St Thomas' Hospital in an effort to use the scarce resources of the psychiatric outpatient clinic more effectively by shortening the prevailing psychotherapeutic procedures, and it explicitly states that it is integrated and eclectic in order to achieve its aims briefly and thoroughly.

Any psychotherapist who runs a district service can calculate that for each 50 hours of therapy per week that can be offered, the choice lies between treating 25 patients weekly for two years, 50 patients for one year, 100 patients for six months or 150 for four months. Responsibility for populations implies that we can only afford to offer those who reach us a minimum sufficient intervention. Despite this there are still many services where contracted brief therapy is seldom or never offered and many psychotherapists with no experience of, and no trust in, work within time limits. Given the emphasis placed upon long-term personal analysis and on treating long-term patients in the training of dynamic therapists, this is not surprising. Moreover, psychoanalysts with a commitment to brief therapy have seldom been granted very much respect by the psycho-analytic establishment. However, the general preference for supposedly more intensive or longer term work has more tradition than evidence to support it and I believe that psychotherapists owe it to their potential patients, currently denied treatment, to consider the value of time-limited work. (Ryle, 1992: 401)

CAT combines psychoanalytic theory, cognitive psychology and the cognitive therapeutic approach into a time-limited model that allows therapist and patient to work jointly at the reformulation of the patient's 'relationship procedures and self-procedures', to help him or her change neurotic patterns which are self-reinforcing and self-repeating. Object relations are translated into relationship procedures, and a repertoire of reciprocal relationship procedures deriving from their earliest relationships are identified for each patient. Based on the history and on the early interaction in the room, the therapist helps the patient construct 'a renarration of his own story in order to recognise the ways in which this history has left the person with certain "procedures" or ways of going about their life which don't work and which for various reasons they have been unable to revise' (Ryle, 1995: 568).

The aim of CAT is thus very modest: it is to stop people from going on doing the things that maintain their damage.

In the therapy there are 3 R's: *Reformulation* is the first, the reshaping of the history and description of the present. Therapy is occupied with the patient being helped to learn to *recognise* the recurrences of these unrevised patterns so that they can become open to *revision*. This is done partly in daily life through homework and self-monitoring, and centrally in the therapy relationship, into which of course the patient will tend to bring their range of problems. (Ryle, 1995: 569)

In CAT the use of cognitive techniques like homework has a dual purpose: on the one hand, it serves to shorten the therapy time by instructing the patient to use the time between sessions construc-tively; on the other hand, it is intended to involve the patients actively as equals in the therapeutic work and to strengthen their usually deficient self-reflection by setting them the task of identifying their habitual relationship patterns and finding ways of changing these. In the basic model of the procedure their maintenance depends on the anticipation of the consequences – and getting them confirmed or not. In a relationship procedure the main consequences are the reciprocation by the other, the reciprocal role played by the other, and the recurrent patterns of reciprocal role procedures are seen as being formed in relations with caretakers. The originally parental and child roles can be reversed, and in playing one role one is involved in trying to get somebody else to play the reciprocation of it. The phenomenon of projective identification, the understanding of transference and in fact the maintenance of day-to-day relationships can all be understood in terms of patterns of reciprocal role procedures and their elicitation or attempted elicitation from others. This early experience, Ryle maintains, is also the basis of our relationship with ourselves, with our self-procedures, so there is a parallel in how we relate to others and how we relate to ourselves.

> For CAT, pathology has two basic features: the neurotic patient has a narrow or particularly distorted repertoire, and there are failures of integration. Once this failure has occurred, the fragmentary partial self-states acquire a certain autonomy, which recur and need to be identified by the therapist in terms of their defences and relationship patterns. Instead of interpretation which is seen as a power imbalance, the CAT therapist uses description and the main tool of CAT is the jointly formed description of how the self is managed and how relationships with others are conducted. This recruits the patient for the task of thinking about him/ herself and provides equipment for that task. (Ryle, 1995: 571)

The central interest, Ryle emphasizes in a generalization about CAT, is in the interpersonal shaping of the intrapersonal.

CAT could be defined as the bold reformulation of psychoanalysis and object relations theory by a therapist who uses the therapeutic alliance as the location of a cognitive collaboration geared to shifting outmoded repertoires based on self-perpetuating infantile expectations and role routines and thus freeing and enabling the patient to integrate.

> In CAT we do a large airlift of supplies into the garrison and find that they very often open the gate. The reformulation actually leads to the recovery of memory, to greater access to dreams and feelings. CAT gives the experience of an all too brief, but manageably disappointing relationship within which the patient can mourn for and think about their task, and in most cases go forward much less restricted by the procedures which they acquired in the past. CAT strengthens the patient's mind. (1995: 574)

Once again, there are strong echoes of Freud's 'Remembering, Repeating and Working Through', though the latter is mostly left to the patient to get on with independently, once the 16 (or in some cases 24) sessions with the therapist have finished. There is also little emphasis on the transference in terms of encouraging, fostering and interpreting its manifestations to produce re-enactments of the original scenario, as this would lead to a power imbalance, to fostering regression or dependence, all of which undermine the time limit.

The emphasis on the equality of sustained thinking and reflection has led to it being said of CAT that it is 'an exhortation to being reasonable'. This applies, of course, to all cognitive and problem-solving therapeutic work, and presupposes good ego strength and manageable anxiety levels. Another criticism of CAT has been that 'it presupposes a stable therapeutic alliance and that its capacity to deal with negative therapeutic reaction has not been proved' (Scott, 1993: 94). Ryle has refuted both allegations by emphasizing the rigorous use of joint reformulations, but this, of course, always depends on the patient's willingness to cooperate and to trust the therapist's benevolent understanding, and his/her constant availability for thinking.

I have also heard that cognitive analytic therapists find the amount of paperwork and preparation that goes into the average CAT case (which includes rigorous supervision) somewhat exacting, but this is a charge that can be levied against much brief work as supervision, careful note-taking, verbatim reports or process recording are essential to achieve brisk results. In CAT there is in addition the reading material, which consists of the psychotherapy file that is given to the patients to read (Ryle, 1990). This describes the patterns of unrevisable, maladaptive 'procedures' described as Snags, Dilemmas and Traps, which, according to Ryle, characterize neurosis, affecting both self-management and problems of relationships. The therapist, moreover, presents a summary of his/her understanding of the history and its meaning, and checks this out with the patient, to be modified if necessary, and a final version is then written down, which subsequently will be supplemented by a sequential diagram. All this work is aimed to help the patients learn to recognize automatic procedures in time to consider alternatives. It is quite an arduous, but necessary part of CAT, which requires both participants to be literate, conscientious and willing to follow the instructions developed by Ryle to sharpen and shorten the observational and descriptive tasks inherent in the method.

Ryle's extensive research findings confirm the efficacy of CAT for many conditions, including borderline states. In his critique of Betty

Joseph's paper 'Addiction to Near Death' (1982), which compares her analytic method and his CAT techniques, coming out in favour of the latter as less prone to collusion with and persecution of the patient, he makes the claim that borderline patients would be better served by his gentler descriptive and collaborative approach than by the relentlessly interpretative stance practised by the Kleinian analyst. He reports that an ongoing research study of borderline cases treated by cognitive analytic therapists seems to prove that over half such patients show significant benefit after 12–24 weekly sessions:

> As around 10% of NHS psychotherapy outpatients suffer from equivalent disorders, with many of them being more literally close to death than Joseph's case, the practical implications of the theoretical differences considered here are of considerable importance; one year in analysis uses enough professional time to treat ten patients in this category with Cognitive-Analytic Therapy. I believe that this figure, combined with the relative absence of serious debate between the world of psychoanalysis and other positions, justifies the polemical tone of this paper. (Ryle, 1993: 92)

In terms of cost-effectiveness and democratic distribution of scarce resources, this argument is certainly convincing. It does not address the hot issue of 'patient's treatment of choice versus medical necessity', which is understandable from the perspective of an over-worked consultant in an under-resourced NHS hospital. He does, however, make another valuable point in favour of CAT when he calls it a 'very safe first intervention', a statement that applies to much brief psychotherapy when it is well done: as an introduction into the method and the way of thinking. CAT can initiate the patient into the therapeutic process, into a habit of self-reflecting, internal map-making, and identifying of procedures and patterns which are self-defeating, without promising to 'cure' the patient once and for all. As it offers repeated contracts in persistent cases, if necessary, and does not pretend to be designed for use in private practice, it is tailored to the specific needs of a state-subsidized context where patients are offered affordable therapy under the motto 'when less is more or at least enough' (Ryle et al., 1992: 401). This means, it is making a virtue of necessity, and, more modest than psychoanalysis, 'achieves a clearing of the road blocks', rather than fundamental and far-reaching characterological changes.

Solution-focused brief therapy
Ryle's integrated time-limited model, which has travelled a long way from the relatively purist focal psychotherapy mode designed by Balint and Malan, has since paved the way for several minimally psychodynamic approaches which are designed for use in GP practices,

student counselling services and employment assistance programmes, and are even shorter and more eclectic than his method, in the service of cost-effectiveness. Five or six sessions have become the norm in these settings, and the definition of brief has changed drastically. A mixture of techniques, some borrowed from cognitive and systemic therapy, others adapted from behavioural techniques, usually including tasks and homework, are current in these hybrid brief therapies, which are offered free to patients, students and employees in primary care, training and work contexts.

Developed and tried out in the US in the context of stress management, alcohol and drug counselling, these briefest of treatments are designed to assist persons suffering from incapacitating symptoms of 'stress' to focus on its likely causes and to enable them to make some changes which will alleviate their condition, help them regain their psychic equilibrium and restore them to adequate functioning in their workplace and personal lives. There is more talk of goals than of focus here and the expectations are modest, though the psychodynamic counsellor will aim beyond symptom removal towards 'making a significant difference' in the patient's life by his/her brief intervention, supporting a limited and realistic process of change, and enabling patients to make connections between their inner and their outer worlds. The change can be seen in terms of understanding or problem-solving, and is usually based on an awareness that current patterns of functioning and relating may be influenced by past events which are still alive in the present.

I have been working and supervising over a number of years for Counselling in Companies (CiC), a consultancy and counselling service set up by WPF Counselling, which offers solution-focused brief therapy (SFBT) for managers and employees of a number of major British companies, local authorities and charitable organizations. Contracts are for five sessions, including an extensive assessment interview, and the counsellors are psychodynamic in the sense that they help their patients link the troubling problems they come with to unresolved issues in their past, and work actively towards making changes in the way they relate to themselves and others. The time constraints require the use of a set of techniques which speed up the process of reflection and change in the patient, such as focusing on practical solutions of identified problems rather than spending time on analysing these, affirming and consolidating positive achievement and tackling issues which can be managed realistically in five sessions.

Patients do not only present problems about work, usually relationship difficulties and domestic issues emerge quickly, as work pressures always affect personal life and vice versa. The counsellor determines why the patient has come, what s/he expects, what resources s/he has and how these can be mobilized. He/she finds a focus, explores, with the help of the 'miracle question' ('when you wake up in the morning, what would have happened if there had been a miracle?'), whether there is a solution fantasy and whether there are examples in the patient's life that show an ability to find solutions to problems. This positive and constructive approach is based on the work of de Shazer (1985), who coined the slogan 'the solution is the problem' and echoed Ryle when he emphasized that 'people stick to unsuccessful ways of solving difficulties in order not to make matters worse'. The counsellor's push for change is usually resisted; however, when the client is made to realize that s/he is already doing what s/he is searching for or that all s/he needs to do is doing something different – in the words of Geoffrey Bateson (1960), 'making the difference that makes the difference' – then the space of five sessions is long enough to achieve the change in behaviour which can turn around his or her life. This approach is pledged to a strict time limit and has a planned ending which indicates that the counsellor believes that something can be done and that the goal that has been set for the therapy is realistic and manageable. The containing function of the time limit and of the counsellor's confidence in the possibility of change come together in the client's ability to chose a new solution to an old problem, and what may have felt like an intractable chronic situation can be seen as 'the persistence of a repetitively poorly handled difficulty – which no one so far has been able to solve' (O'Hanlon, 1989).

This modest approach to making changes in a client's life works surprisingly well when there is good rapport and high motivation in both participants, but it can, of course, have its limitations and, if necessary, clients are referred on for long-term therapy with another therapist (for which they are no longer funded by their employer). This, then, can become the solution to an old problem of not managing their lives, and the client's intial decision of seeking help is validated. In some respects de Shazer joins hands with Alexander, though the corrective experience is seen in terms of behaviour change rather than emotional development, because once the client has had the experience of finding a solution to a problem s/he has found persistently intractable, there is the likelihood that other intractable problems will also be soluble. And so on, and so on. There is no knowing how far the ripple effect that has been set off in one part of the system will affect the other parts and produce ongoing changes.

The CiC counsellors who practise SFBT use their psychodynamic armamentarium conscientiously to monitor the transference/countertransference situation that accompanies the solution-focused therapeutic dialogue in order to grasp the underlying conflict that has caused the problem, while not necessarily verbalizing it. In spite of de Shazer's statement that 'it is not necessary to have detailed descriptions of the complaint, it is not even necessary to construct a rigorous explanation of how the trouble is maintained' (de Shazer et al., 1986), the attentive SFBT counsellor will continue to take note of and identify the dynamics of the brief encounter in order to contain spillage and remain aware of incipient derailment, while using de Shazer's formula interventions and strategies to push for the client's change. This two-pronged approach resembles Ryle's model in that the cognitive and the analytic methods are combined into an inter-active style that enables clients to become aware of their hidden potential for taking charge of their own lives and their capacity to make choices and help themselves.

One- and two-plus-one-session therapy
Elsewhere I have stressed the hypothesis that all brief therapy models reflect the personalities of their originators, and many of them were indeed developed simultaneously with or independently of the others in the course of their originators' practice and within their particular working contexts. My short presentation of the various models was part chronological and part typological, and I have found myself constructing a spectrum reaching from almost purely psychoanalytic to more and more eclectic psychodynamic approaches, as well as from longer to briefer and briefest contracts, and I have now reached the end of the spectrum where therapists practise 'two-plus-one-' or one-session therapies, which are more or less like an extended assess-ment, a dynamic consultation or, in the words of Davanloo and Barkham and Hobson (1989), a 'trial therapy' with the function of an opening game, serving purposes of assessment, selection, establish-ment of rapport, induction, testing of motivation, etc., rather than deep-reaching changes or ongoing support.

   In this mode the patient is seen, assessed and instantly engaged in a therapeutic dialogue which pinpoints the area of turbulence, focuses on his/her affective functioning, establishes basic developmental levels and typical defences, while aiming to start off a process of relating in the here-and-now in which the therapist can be experienced as under-standing, as facilitating communication, and, hopefully, as making meaningful links between disjointed bits of the patient's narrative. The secret of therapeutic effectiveness in this briefest of modes lies in a combination of quick and clear thinking, of intuitive hypothesizing and instant rapport that allows for a shift in the context of relating and engages the patient in an emotional experience that constitutes a clinically relevant change – some new understanding, some behaviour modification, a measure of affective relief.

Through the identification and understanding of a key issue, the patient may have been enabled to 'experience him/or herself as making changes in their lives, breaking through an impasse so that s/he can resume the normal process of growth and development' (Bloom, 1981). When doing very brief, one-session therapy, Bloom asks himself: 'What have these clients failed to understand about their lives that could make a difference in how they are conducting themselves now and how they might manage their lives in the future?' (1981: 167–216), and consequently directs his therapeutic effort at an area in the client's functioning that seems amenable to immediate change.

Also in the eighties, the psychiatrist and Jungian analyst R.F. Hobson developed a method he called 'conversational therapy', which drastically modified the orthodox psychiatric consultation from a clinically detached diagnostic interview to a therapeutic dialogue based on mutuality and relationship and on the therapist's 'hope to be corrected, and thus able to facilitate a shared language of feelings' in which the patient can discover his or her 'missing capacity'. Two-plus-one exploratory therapy consists of two successive sessions in which the therapist attempts to 'determine the narrative point of origin' of and unravel the patient's problem, followed by a planned follow-up three months later which together create a therapeutic space of 15 weeks, serving as a holding environment in which 'what goes on between sessions may be more important in determining outcome than what happens in the sessions' (Frank, 1982). The 'conversational style' depends largely on 'how the therapist talks', using 'We' rather than 'I' statements, startling metaphors and patient negotiation, all of which enables the 'mutative respecting of feelings' which makes a significant difference in the patient's perception of relationship and brings about the 'corrective emotional experience' of which Alexander and French (1946) were the first to speak. Hobson's emphasis on feelings (see his book *Forms of Feeling: The Heart of Psychotherapy*, 1985) gives the 'conversational style' its particular charge and intensity, as he instantly moves as close to the patient as he can safely get, and with this opening game establishes the rapport necessary to make the patient feel safe and held. He relies on the physician's traditional paternal authority, which sets up a powerful positive transference situation of trust, hope and expectation of relief, and generously includes the patient in his therapeutic musings, which produce meaning, cooperation, faith and gratitude.

Winnicott's paediatric consultations with babies and mothers can be seen as similar one- or two-session or trial therapies, which pinpoint the couple's basic troubles and rely on the healing power of the doctor's apostolic function, as defined by Balint (1955: 207). This function allows him to set aside the ordinary preliminaries of conversation, to still the patient's anxieties and to have an instant therapeutic effect quite disproportionate to the time he spends with each patient (on average nowadays 15 minutes). His task is the alleviation or removal of symptoms, and his style is usually directive, prescriptive and conveying of expertise. The example of Dr Hobson conducting a two-plus-one therapy fits this style and aim, despite the emphasis on feelings and their exploration. During this brief encounter the patient is involved in a clinical consultation where the doctor's guesses, hypotheses, promptings and the active drawing out of information combine seductively to produce an outcome of behaviour change and symptom relief, a therapeutic experience, but rarely a genuine psychic change.

In the clinical example the knowledge and the insight gained by the therapist are not transmitted to the patient, who never assumes the exploratory mode herself, but is the recipient of the doctor's findings, which she then confirms, even the acknowledgement that he is the first person to understand her. Is this the use of 'suggestion' Freud talked about when he mentioned 'the pure gold of psychoanalysis being alloyed with copper'? As in any diagnostic interview or assessment session, the therapist is making the links and checking out whether the patient has understood these. He may be right, and this is a relief for the patient, but he has not taught the patient how to make links herself, which would be the desired therapeutic goal. However, this usually requires some time and practice, particularly with the unsophisticated patient, like Dora in Hobson's case, for whom the thinking is done and who believes that the oh so understanding doctor must be right, to the extent that she goes and tells her husband, who promises to be more understanding (i.e. like the doctor) in future.

Barkham's and Hobson's two-plus-one model is explicitly described as a 'comprehensive' model, with a general theoretical base, not intrinsically restricted to a psychodynamic orientation. What they call negotiation, however, looks more like persuasion than interpretation, as when the GP gives a diagnosis and prescribes medication, both of which demonstrate that he knows best. The positive outcome at follow-up 'proves' no more than that the doctor's 'apostolic function' has effectively 'worked', and as the patient in question was enabled to make behavioural changes it did make a significant difference to her life, as would the placebo that enables a patient to shed a phobia or lose a symptom.

It may have become obvious that I question the legitimate inclusion of this brief therapeutic encounter into the psychodynamic family of brief psychotherapy, unless it remains labelled evaluation, assessment or preliminary exploration, and is seen as a prelude to therapy: therapeutic in itself, perhaps, but not therapy in itself. To be sure, a psychodynamic process is started in that the patient develops a transference to the therapist, but this is not used explicitly nor interpreted experimentally in order to induct the patient into analytic procedures of psychological insight, self-reflection or new meaning-making in his/her life story. There is no working through and the incipient transference relationship is used to be directive and didactic, authoritatively and paternalistically. The talk of 'sharing and respecting feelings' defines the humanistic basis of the effective helping relationship, but there is no acknowledgement of unconscious conflict or communication, and the realities of resistance and defence, which are the bedrock of psychodynamic understanding and practice, are bypassed.

As the last of the brief therapy models presented in this historical overview, one-session and two-plus-one session therapies should be linked up with the medical, psychiatric and psychological consultation, on the one hand, which establishes a diagnostic hypothesis, the symptomatology and the pathology of a patient from which treatment choices, and decisions relating to suitability, an indication or counter-indication for medication, a prognosis and other therapeutic actions are made. On the other hand, these modes remain intensive brief encounters full of potential and promise, first impressions, fantasies and speculation, but for the lasting imprint and the memory to be mutative, something out of the ordinary needs to have happened which may be the 'healing touch' of the charismatic personality, the spot-on prediction of the intuitive diagnostician, the casting of a spell and the open sesame of the shaman, and, last not least, the typical conversion experience which is a moment of grace. The shadow of charlatanism, false prophet and abuser, however, falls on all this and I remain sceptical of the lasting value of such activities (Guggenbühl-Craig, 1971).

The different aims of long-term and short-term work

A discussion of some of the fundamentally different aims of long-term and short-term psychodynamic work might as well be started by mentioning the areas of broad agreement. First: the basic therapeutic intention of enabling the patients 'to love and work', as Freud had put it simply, i.e. to gain (or regain) a sense of normal (healthy) psychic functioning, to free them from the disabling psychological or psycho-somatic symptoms with which they enter therapy by helping them make conscious the unconscious conflicts and complexes by which these may have been caused.

Freud further talked about 'transforming . . . hysterical misery into common unhappiness', by which he meant replacing unhelpful defensive strategies and immature structures of mental functioning by more serviceable ways of facing the realities of life. In order to facilitate this transformative process, the psychodynamic psychotherapists offer patients a therapeutic relationship in which they can feel safe and held through the difficult work of exploring and understanding what lies behind their pain and their problems of functioning (coping), at times also using this relationship with their patients to enable a deeper understanding of their problems in relating with others and with themselves, by facilitating and interpreting an enactment or re-enactment of these in the transference.

So much is clear and agreed by the general consensus. The specific ways of reaching these aims, however, and the extent of 'characterological' rather than symptomatic or behavioural change envisaged in the treatment, differ vastly for the long-term and the brief therapy modes, and apart from the theoretical differences, the chosen frequency of sessions and the varying duration of therapeutic contracts, there are quite substantial differences of opinion and of practice about how much and what kind of changes can be and need to be brought about in order to make a significant difference in a patient's disturbed and unsatisfactory functioning, significant enough to have a lasting effect and possibly to set in train an ongoing process of transmitted changes in other areas of his/her life.

The long-term psychotherapist allows the patient ample time to cover all the areas and the details of his/her actual and remembered life which emerge by association in the ongoing dialogue. S/he believes that a repeated retracing of the same ground will, spiral-fashion, uncover ever-new material relevant to the working through of identified unconscious conflicts and hidden feelings which are causing the suffering in the first place. By its open-endedness the therapy can lead into the complex ramifications of the patient's reminiscences and allow discoveries of hitherto unknown and unthought territories and depths, while the therapeutic relationship undergoes changes due to the transferences and resistances the patient develops towards the therapist in the course of a twofold movement towards dependence and regression, on the one hand, and autonomy and mastery, on the other, all of which will become the subject of the therapist's interpretations and the patient's increasing understanding of him/herself. This intricate therapeutic process will go through negative and positive phases, hopefully ending in a resolution and mutually agreed termination of the work when the patient's ego functioning and object relating have improved to a mutually satisfactory level, when his/her system of defences has been substantially restructured and a process of self-reflection and self-analysis has become established that will continue beyond the ending of therapy or analysis.

All this should amount to sustainable characterological changes and increased emotional maturation and could be called the reaching of the depressive position (in Kleinian terms), the attainment of the capacity for concern (in Winnicott's terminology), the acceptance of the reality principle (as envisaged by Freud) and the ability to bear uncertainty and not knowing (Bion). This kind of comprehensive therapeutic journey is lengthy and arduous, with its inevitable relapses and occasional retracings of one's steps, prone to considerable twisting and turning on the way, and leading into blind alleys, none of which can be predicted nor prevented. This has always been considered the necessary 'grist to the mill' in a process of 'learning from experience'(Bion), where the method is one of trial and error, of finding and discovering, rather than of a planned and straightforward strategy of action.

Long-term psychotherapy is not always successful. Many terminations are dictated by practical rather than purely therapeutic reasons, and the outcome is often surprisingly different from the initial expectations, which are invariably proved too limited or general. Some therapies get stuck in a stalemate, a 'malignant regression' or a negative therapeutic reaction that cannot be resolved (Balint, 1968). A constant process of erosion goes hand in hand with the persistent forward movement of change, which can result in periods of snail's-pace working alongside periods of brisk improvement and depends as much on the therapist's functioning as on the patient's willingness and motivation. This unevenness and unpredictability has been seized on by the sceptical critics of the analytic method and has to be taken into account and cautioned against on entering into the process. But I believe as a method for implementing the motto of the Delphic oracle, 'know thyself', it cannot be bettered, and as the examined life and the search for the truth is one of the legitimate life goals of *Homo sapiens*, Freud, for all his failings, has to be thanked for inventing it. To be alone in the presence of another (Winnicott, 1958) is an experience that should be available for every baby from the beginning of their life, to start them off in the process of acquiring 'basic trust' (Erikson) and a 'secure base' (Bowlby). But where this has been deficient, it can still be provided at a later stage in therapy, when hopefully it will help to correct the deficit and allow the patient to have another, more successful go at his or her life journey.

In my opinion, brief psychotherapy has a much less ambitious and comprehensive goal, something which, unfortunately, is not always admitted, as there is fierce competition between the two camps for first prize in effectivity, and there are false prophets in both camps who claim that only one or the other can be 'right'. I see the task of brief therapy *as different* and *sui generis*, or, to stay with the metaphor, it is merely one lap in a therapeutic journey, which is the process of individuation and amounts to a thorough rewriting of the patient's personal narrative. Brief therapy attends to a chapter, and its main tool and strength is the focusing on a significant clinical event, while long-term work ranges far and wide in its exploration, reflection and working through. The art and mastery of brief therapy lies in its limitation, and the image that comes to mind is that of a magnifying glass which picks out a small but central area in a large canvas and concentrates on the detail of this to the exclusion of everything else.

'Making a difference' has become a slogan, and a paraphrase of 'making a change' that emphasizes that this change has to be significant, meaningful and beneficial. There are changes and changes, and not all change is desirable nor lasting nor leading to desired or expected developments in a patient's emotional and practical life. The prerequisite of a psychodynamic therapeutic result is that something has been made conscious and put into words that was previously felt or sensed rather than understood, and it will therefore leave a distinctive mark in the complex tapestry of someone's life. To put it generally, a truth has been revealed, accepted and internalized that now provides a full understanding of a recurrent problem, dilemma, or blockage which had caused the patient distress and suffering.

An example is the case of a middle-aged woman who came for five-session solution-focused brief therapy with a motorway phobia that had started many years after her adored brother was killed in an accident, and had begun seriously to affect her life. Her husband had become impatient and uncommunicative as a result of her inability to drive – even with him in the driver's seat; at her work in a bank she had become unable to shut the door of her office and to assert herself with colleagues, and a recent cancer scare had so unsettled her that she decided to use her firm's offer of five free counselling sessions. With the help of her counsellor she put two and two together very quickly – in the third session she admitted that she had always been very envious of her brother, as she still was of her stepsister, whose 'irregular' family status she had only recently discovered. This envy had been murderous at times – and she had felt much guilt when her brother died, idealizing him in retrospect out of all proportion. The admission of envy to the counsellor, who helped her accept her envy as the natural consequence of maternal favouritism, had an electrifying result, as if her eyes had been opened to something she had always known but resisted because of her guilt. She became less phobic, less anxious and more assertive at work, and in the fifth session she described herself as 'completely changed', able to function in a new way in her relationship with her husband, her colleagues and with herself.

There is no doubt that counselling had made a significant difference and that something had been understood for the first time. But the counsellor had a sense of this step forward being almost too good to be true, or, to put it another way, that the client's effusive 'conversion' was only the beginning of a process of change that she would now have to manage by herself. He recommended she consider further counselling in future to consolidate the work she had done with him, and cautioned her that she might not be able to sustain the euphoria for long, as 'one swallow does not make a summer'. In long-term work there would have been the chance to help her absorb the realization that she had hidden her conflicted feelings about her brother for too long and to understand that her phobias and anxieties had been symptoms of her unresolved guilt and mourning. With therapeutic help she would have learnt to reflect on herself psychologically and gradually to tackle some of the somatic problems she also suffered from. As it was, however, she felt that she had got what she had come for, that the breakthrough was the true turning of a corner, and she was confident that she would be able to sustain the changes. In the counsellor's mind there remained a doubt that she might now idealize the counselling as she had idealized the brother and deal with its ending by denial and by asserting her independence. However, what had happened had happened and it was undoubtedly an experience of genuine change for her.

As this is usually shared by both participants, they can end on a positive note of achievement, though this will be intermingled with the sadness of parting after a moment of great intimacy. This powerful and complex emotional charge fuels the brief work to the point of producing truly astonishing results of sudden understanding, of confessing, remembering and taking action after paralysing indecision. But how can it be made to last and to have a significant influence on the client's future functioning and behaviour? The optimistic prognosis of the solution-focused counsellor is: 'Once you have been able to solve a problem, you will be able to solve other problems, too.' The more pessimistic expectation of the therapist who knows the persistence of repetition compulsion and acting out is that: 'Once is no guarantee for always,' and that only repeated action becomes evidence of true learning. This is borne out by observation and studies of children's learning behaviour – much trial and error and repeated going over the same ground eventually add up to the confident acquisition of a new skill. The same applies to insight, which alone is not enough and needs repeated confirmation with feeling and experience.

It follows that brief therapists need to be optimists in order to convince their patients as they are convinced themselves that change will not remain isolated but will usually engender more change and set something in motion that is irreversible. The client in the above example had become fired by that optimism and had set a number of things in motion which had made her hopeful that she would be able to make other changes. The transmission of hope and optimism is a vital ingredient of the effectiveness of brief therapy; in psychodynamic terms, it is a function of the positive transference which is powerfully active at the beginning of much therapy when it is in its honeymoon period. Instead of transference one could call it 'the initial impact', the 'shock of the new', the experience of the unexpected which alerts all systems and facilitates receptivity and vulnerability. It works in nine out of ten cases, the exception being patients who shut down defensively in fear of being overwhelmed by unbearable and uncontainable anxiety, anger or destructiveness.

Much brief work happens with people who are in an acute emotional crisis, which makes them cry out for instant help and open to any suggestion to improve their truly parlous state. They are suggestible in that they hand themselves over to the helper, who transmits confidence that they can be helped, and they are grateful for small mercies like the temporary relief of depressive or persecutory anxiety which comes with handing over the responsibility. Feeling contained by another who actively and constructively thinks for them reawakens good previous experiences of being held and thought about, and gradually mobilizes available inner resources of hope, trust and initiative with which their temporary helplessness can be conquered and transformed into mastery. In order for this to happen there needs to be a felt experience of regaining their ego strength as well as an understanding of what triggered off the crisis in the first place, e.g. an unconscious linking of present and past events and conflict that produced the anxiety of losing control. As with the patient described above, who, once she connected her murderous feelings for her brother (and stepsister) with her fear of herself (or her husband) getting killed on the motorway, was able to manage her anxiety and make significant behavioural changes.

Specific short-term and brief techniques

It is significant that the difference between long-term and short-term psychodynamic psychotherapy is mostly in the field of technique, while within the two camps themselves there are many variations of style from the orthodox/purist to the highly eclectic/flexible. There is probably more diversity among the short-termers than among the long-termers, who generally agree on the fundamentals of their craft: the 'fundamental rule' of free association, the use of interpretation, and, in particular, of the transference, of resistance, of dreams and unconscious phantasy. The patient is encouraged to use the couch and to do most of the talking, and what is brought to the sessions is left entirely to him/her. The long-term therapist imagines that his/her contribution to the therapeutic discourse consists mostly of interpreting the patient's free association clinical material and of keeping other forms of intervening like questions, explanations, suggestions or digressions to a minimum. There is no time limit and the boundaries of the analytic setting are strictly observed and interpreted.

Christopher Bollas in a recent talk, 'What is the Goal of Psychoanalysis?' (1999) maintained that while originally this goal was clearly the implementation of the 'fundamental rule', in reality the passive process of free association has become much less central over the decades as its exclusive implementation led to interminable, repetitive and inconclusive treatments and it has gradually become enriched with the more serviceable and practical goals of restructuring defences, enabling insight, strengthening the patient's ego, holding the frame and containing anxieties, which require a whole range of subsidiary, even non-verbal, techniques. However, the analyst's abstinence from active intervention, or, as Bion put it, his/her endeavour to be 'without memory and desire', has remained at the heart of the analytic process, preventing, in principle, any preconceived or planned treatment strategies on the part of the therapist which counteract the basic aims of facilitating the patient's self-analytic function and instinct management.

Brief therapists have no time to wait for the slow unfolding of themes, the gentle peeling off of psychic layers, the associative approximation to hidden psychic material which constitute the classical analytic process, and most of their techniques aim at shortening and concentrating the therapeutic process and at conducting a therapeutic dialogue in which both participants have an active part. For them, abstinence becomes concision, concentration, cutting corners, sticking to a focus, trimming excess fat and formulating strategies which get them to a goal in the shortest possible time. Outcome is as important as process. The clock is always ticking, which means no time must be wasted on the delicious detours and twisting rambles so familiar to the long-term practitioner, the wordy and carefully formulated interpretations, the pregnant silences and the patient waiting for responses which characterize much analytic discourse. They are not afraid of active questioning and aim at drawing out information from the patient which they consider relevant to their focal aim of treating an identified area of psychic disturbance. They intervene as frequently as they consider necessary and introduce material of their own whenever that seems apt to move the dialogue further.

Theirs is a craft of quick decisions, of no second chances, of striking the iron while it is hot and of ruthlessly pursuing an avenue once it has been chosen. There is no time for regrets at missed opportunities. Like their more passive and leisurely colleagues, brief therapists always work on several levels at once, processing and responding to the patient's communications while simultaneously monitoring the transference and countertransference constellation and the diagnostic hypothesis. However, in contrast to the passive analytic colleagues practising evenly hovering attention, they endeavour to stay on focus at all times, to exercise selective attention and selective neglect and to steer the therapeutic process briskly along a route that involves no hesitation or resting place. There is a clear purpose to every intervention, which will be linked to the chosen focus and to the known and anticipated ending of the therapy, and all of this serves to push the process as fast and as far as possible in the chosen direction. At the same time, there will be a constant close observation of the patient's ego functioning, as any sign of a regression to dependence needs to be recognized and if possible to be nipped in the bud, as will sidetracking manoeuvres on the part of the patient like being offered dreams, memories or new problems not directly relating to the focus.

This rigorous cognitive activity prevents the development of reverie recommended by Bion to the analyst. It requires an alert and active mind, an incisive and disciplined singlemindedness which may deliberately provoke the patient's hostility and resistance, while aiming constantly to draw his/her attention back to the focus, to the task and to the passage of time, in the individual session as well as in the therapy as a whole.

Other active strategies are the *setting of tasks* and of *homework* to facilitate a continuation of the patient's working through in between sessions. In contrast to the long-term mode, sessions are often spaced out in brief therapy at the patient's request to allow adequate time for the fermentation and sinking in of insights produced together in the sessions and to facilitate and initiate the patient's independent therapeutic activity, which will be necessary once the therapy has ended. The *spacing out of sessions* can be done in blocks or at a decreasing rate towards the end and is a creative (as well as a somewhat risky) strategy which both stretches the therapeutic container and dilutes the inexorable force of the time limitation. It can shrewdly prepare for the impending ending by providing a rehearsal of the coming separation and allowing a pause before the powerful finale of the last session, which has to be a review of what has been done and not done, provides an opportunity to look forward and backward, and a space in which to gather strength for the farewell and the separation. In the case mentioned in the previous section, Easter intervened between the first four sessions and the last session, and this pause before the end provided a breathing space, a time for review and for getting on with things by herself, which enabled the client to come for the last session well prepared to say goodbye, to look forward to savouring and getting used to her 'new self' and to express her gratitude mingled with regret that she could not carry on with her therapist.

The use of homework in brief therapy is a function of the lack of time for working through and of the therapist's deliberate encouragement of the patient to do his/her own processing and thinking about what is being explored and discovered in the sessions in order to arrive at a better self-understanding and improved self-worth by systematically practising the focusing and analysing undertaken in the therapeutic dialogue. As the name suggests, the homework set by the therapist (or later self-developed by the patient) has a deliberately educative function and consists of 'data-gathering, problem-solving and behaviour-changing tasks carried out by the patient in between sessions' (Macaskill, 1985: 134). In cases where the sessions are taped, the patient can be encouraged to play the tapes and to recall creatively what was being said in the sessions, in order to increase his/her understanding of the psychotherapy process. The strategy of homework was developed in the context of structural family therapy and is by no means universal in the brief therapy sector. It has been seen by some as an intrusion by the therapist into the patient's private space and constitutes a rather didactic approach to psychological problems which favours 'doing' over 'being' and relies on a cognitive, reality-based method as against a dynamic and intuitive way of investigation.

As always, much depends on the way it is done. The therapist who suggests the patient think constructively about a particular problem for 10 minutes every day, talk to his boss openly about a work issue he has resentfully avoided to mention for fear of being made redundant, or take his son to a football match in order to get to know him better can introduce these tasks gently as suggestions in the course of discussing the problem itself in the session. Or s/he can arbitrarily select a task at the end of a session in order to 'give the patient something to do in between sessions'. The former may become a natural and thoughtful carrying-on of the therapy in the absence of the therapist (Macaskill compares homework to a 'transitional object' in Winnicott's sense), while the latter may feel like a deliberate ruse to keep the patient engaged and is more likely to provoke his resistance than strengthen his motivation.

In fact, the way the patient responds to the assignment of homework can become a major therapeutic tool. 'Failure to report homework or beginning sessions with topics other than those directly related to the previous homework assignment, i.e. loss of focus, may alert the therapist to problems and resistances in therapy and call for prompt action,' writes Macaskill (1985: 134–141), and he maintains that homework-setting provides the therapist with a method of enhancing the patient's motivation and with an excellent indicator of 'resistance to change', of dependency conflicts, self-esteem issues and ego-weakness problems which can then become issues to be worked at. In other words, the assignment of homework is a valuable method of testing and eliciting patients' resistances, of learning about their defences and, hopefully, of teaching them more collaborative ways of being and relating.

Macaskill quotes Wolberg (1980), who recommended homework assignments as a tool to ensure the extended working through of problems after therapy has finished: 'The use of regular post-therapy self-constructed homework assignments is a means of optimising this potential. . . . Acquiring the ability to self-monitor and self-analyse problems during therapy via homework assignments gives them the confidence with which to face further problems once therapy is terminated.' The assumption is that a 'reduction of termination difficulties is most likely when the therapist has been careful to ensure that, as therapy progresses, the patient has been coached to become increasingly independent in constructing and monitoring his homework tasks' (Macaskill, 1985: 137). In other words, the therapist as a setter of homework tasks can become internalized as a good object, like the parent who teaches a child to master the environment and thereby encourages independence and growing up to adulthood.

In Cognitive Analytic Therapy Anthony Ryle sets his patients extensive tasks of self-scrutiny and teaches them the systematic monitoring of their behaviour patterns (called snags and traps) in order to strengthen the therapeutic alliance and to ensure a collaborative way of working together in which the patient experiences him/herself as potent and as able to understand, to tackle and to change his/her faulty ways of self-functioning, of relating and responding to others. As a short-cut method of condensing the lengthy analytic process based on free association, interpretation and resolution of the transference neurosis, this equates to Macaskill's suggestion that patients keep a daily diary, and to Wolberg's recommendation that they eventually self-construct their homework assignments in order to be properly equipped for the extended post-therapy working through which ensures the effectiveness of their brief therapy stint. The idea is that regular homework becomes a habit of self-maintenance like exercises or the daily brushing of teeth and enables patients to remain self-aware and actively working on their interpsychic conflicts and behavioural changes.

However, the main difference between the deliberate setting of tasks and the careful analytic working through of resistances lies in the strong element of paternalistic didacticism informing the former and in the primacy of a cognitive over an intuitive, insight-based approach which takes into account the unconscious dimensions of much human behaviour and mental functioning. Homework, one might say, enlists the supervisory functions of the superego, while the psychodynamic dialogue aims at strengthening the ego and at supporting it in its task of mastering the id. Learning, understanding and working through can happen on various levels simultaneously and interconnectedly, and not all of these are accessible cognitively.

Patients who refuse to do their homework, keep their diary or implement any of the other tasks recommended by the therapist indicate by this resistance that they are not ready or able to cope with the demands for systematic cognitive processing which are made on them by the therapist and by their superego. Macaskill would say that these patients are probably not suitable for brief therapy, which requires active participation, high motivation and the willingness to let go of or internalize the therapist. The carrying out of homework assignments is an indicator of ego strength and of the ability to work alone and carry through a task 'in the absence of the therapist'. It can also be a resistance to being told what to do, and a transference manifestation of issues around authority. In this case, one of the very reasons for recommending assignments, i.e. an avoidance of regression to dependence and the development of transference neurosis, might come into play and will need addressing.

Interestingly, one task set by Macaskill and recommended by Wolberg is the reading of selected chapters of self-help books. This amounts to an endorsement of individualistic methods of self-improvement while undervaluing the relationship aspect of therapy. It is as if the patient is told from the beginning to 'do it yourself, instruct yourself, and get on with it by yourself'. The therapist in the teaching role might eclipse the therapist in the relating role, emphasizing cognitive processing above experiential and emotional dimensions, and reality situations over intra-psychic states. Issues of rejection and isolation can be activated.

Confrontation is one of the active techniques common to all forms of short-term and brief therapy. It provides salutary shocks to the patients' system which are needed to keep up the urgency and to fuel the impetus of the therapy while testing ego strength, motivation and the ongoing ability to endure a rigorous therapeutic inquiry of their psychic and defensive systems. To infuse this stance with supportive firmness is a skill that requires total commitment and identification with the method and a high degree of self-confidence that comes from the experience that 'confronting works' (Molnos) when it is coupled with genuine concern for the client's wellbeing and not a game of one-up-manship or retaliation. It raises the anxiety levels to breaking point when hidden feelings burst through and become potentially liberating, creating intimacy and honesty and a good therapeutic experience.

Another technique borrowed from non-analytic therapies is the constant reviewing and feedback given of the joint work in progress in relation to the approaching ending and to the patient's expectations for change. This re-enforces the patient's active involvement, validates his/her ongoing participation in the interaction and keeps up the brisk pace of processing and reflecting. Furthermore, some other techniques used by cognitive and family therapists to influence the patient's thinking, like reframing, playing devil's advocate, using positive reinforcement and paradox, have become part of the brief therapist's kitbag alongside the basic psychodynamic armamentarium of linking past and present, identifying recurrent patterns of behaviour and relating, using the countertransference and transference (sparingly and judiciously) and listening to underlying meanings and conflicts. Along the broad spectrum of models outlined above, the basic psychodynamic analytic technique becomes more and more enriched (or diluted, depending on degrees of orthodoxy) by the active and reassuring techniques prescribed and tested in the behavioural and cognitive field; inevitably, I think, as contracts shorten and the pressure to deliver grows. The question is whether these actively promote a decrease in full self-understanding and an avoidance of the shadow aspects in a patient's life in the sense that so many self-help books recommend when they stress the value of positive thinking.

The most important technique, however, which the brief therapist of whatever hue has to develop and refine is the skill of assessment and evaluation, both at the beginning of therapy, when patients first present and are screened for their suitability to engage in and benefit from the therapy or counselling work on offer, and ongoing all through the therapy, in order to check and adjust the diagnostic hypothesis, as well as at the end of every contract and after termination. This all-important skill and the various techniques developed to conduct assessment and evaluate patients and their progress accurately will be the subject of the next chapter and is mentioned here merely to complete the list of essential and in many respects quite different skills required to do the brief psychodynamic therapy models developed over the last few decades. Taken from various medical and non-medical therapeutic disciplines, they all aim at making a difference, briefly, in patients' lives and to the presenting problems they show up with.

4

Assessment and Diagnosis in Brief and Focal Work

The assessment of patients for psychodynamic psychotherapy and counselling grew out of the diagnostic interview practised by the psychiatrist on first encountering the patient, in which a case study is prepared on basis of data obtained from the patient. This interview follows the classical scientific method of systematically collecting, arranging and recording data gathered from patients' medical and social history, and attempts to interpret the symptoms of their present illness dynamically in relation to biography, to the physical and psychological examination, and to environmental factors in order to arrive at a diagnostic hypothesis which will serve descriptive, analytic and evaluative purposes and 'becomes the working hypothesis for the planning of treatment and for a decision regarding prognostic probabilities' (Menninger, 1958: 235).

Menninger provided an imaginative definition of the 'psychiatric diagnosis' obtained 'as the result of a relationship established with the patient and those about him, a relationship which is a kind of transaction' (1958: 233–6). The diagnosis embraces the latitudinal and the longitudinal, the 'historical and cross-sectional studies' of the patient, which

> reveal as much of the life picture as is relevant to the correction of the troubled areas and deflection from the desired goals. A psychiatric diagnosis is always continuous and changing and diagnostic conclusions are arrived at by a process of accretion. . . . Prognosis is perhaps the most difficult part of diagnosis. Mental illness is of infinite variety and the particular course of any particular instance of disorganisation must be estimated by a determination of the forces contributing to it. (1958: 236)

Here, in a nutshell, is a description of the complex activity the medical profession calls the diagnosis of an illness. The psychotherapeutic profession, meanwhile, prefers to speak of assessment or initial interview, borrowing the medical examination and evaluation procedures in their broad outlines, while adapting and refining this carefully data-based process of assessment into an individualized encounter with the patient. During this encounter, the case study becomes embedded into a process of 'trial therapy' (Davanloo) that serves to determine the patient's suitability for the particular style of psychotherapy, conducted in a relationship with the therapist that demands the patient's active participation and interaction. The therapist's working hypothesis, arrived at with the help of this process, will serve as the basis for the treatment undertaken with the patient and is continually monitored, adjusted and corrected as new clinical data emerge in the course of ongoing therapy and persistent reflection on these.

Theoreticians of diagnostic assessment for psychoanalysis and psychotherapy like David Malan (1963, 1979), Nina Coltart (1988) and R.D. Hinshelwood (1991) are agreed on the difficulty, subtlety and complexity of the assessment task and on the basics of this introductory procedure to analytic treatment which serves to gatekeep and screen potential candidates. They insist on a careful gathering of biographical and clinical data, an observation of the anxiety levels, the demonstration of affect (or lack of affect), the defensive strategies used towards the assessor and, in particular, the patient's motivation, that difficult to grasp attitude which Coltart called 'the will to be analysed'.

Freud had said that for patients to be suitable for analysis he reckoned they needed to possess 'intelligence, and ethical reliability' and that there was no point embarking on the treatment of 'low-minded and repellent characters who are not capable of arousing human sympathy' (1893–5: 3–5). He added, 'the patient should be ill enough to seek help, but not too ill to make use of it'. He also made an important distinction between the necessary will to be analysed and the wish for recovery, which can be an appeal to the therapist to 'do something' and 'make things better for the patient' as if by magic. The former 'is a function of the autonomous ego and will lead to the necessary treatment alliance'. Coltart further defined this attitude as 'psychological-mindedness' and listed a number of ingredients which can be assessed by 'holding a number of queries in one's mind while doing an assessment interview':

1) Is there the capacity in the patient to take a distance from his own emotional experience?
2) Can the patient begin to reflect on himself . . . as a result of being listened to in this particularly attentive way?
3) Are various memories brought forward with different qualities and charges of affect? And are the affects, so far as one can tell, more or less appropriate?
4) Is there a capacity to perceive relationships between sections of history . . . and the patient's prevailing sense of discomfort?
5) Is there some capacity to recognise and tolerate internal reality with its wishes and conflicts and to distinguish it from external reality?

Furthermore: Does the patient show a lively interest and concern about his internal reality? . . . Is there a capacity for the use of the imagination? . . . Are there signs of a capacity to recognise the existence of an unconscious mental life? and Does the patient show signs of success or achievement in some, even if limited area of his life and some degree of proper self-esteem in relation to this? Here I would emphasise the areas of study or work and one or more important relationships. (1988: 129)

Limentani described this attitude as the 'analysand's capacity to move freely within his own psyche', to which he added 'his capacity to move freely within the interview situation' (1972, quoted in Coltart, 1988: 133). Summing up the assessor's complex, subtle and extremely skilful task, Coltart advised: 'you need to establish a certain rapport and keep it going and within that framework think about and learn to deploy all the skills you have to find out about this stranger's inner world. This may involve some questioning, some interpretation, some link-making comments, sympathy expressed only in your whole attitude of extremely attentive listening, and some concise summarising of your own views towards the end of the interview' (1988: 134).

Coltart's view that the interview may be 'one of the most momentous occasions in a patient's life' (1988: 128) is echoed by Hinshelwood when he emphasizes the effect of interpretation, which 'is to draw attention to those aspects of the patient of which he is unaware and of which, on the whole, he wishes to remain unaware' (1991: 174). 'It facilitates the patient leaving you without too much regret', according to Coltart (1988: 131), and Hinshelwood supplements this blunt statement by writing that 'the interpretation that grasps the uglier unconscious aspects of the patient as well as the positive ones presented to you will, like Strachey's mutative interpretation, tend to correct the primitive aspects of the patient's relationships and help him towards a more balanced frame of mind towards you' (1991: 174). Hinshelwood recommends a 'psychodynamic formulation' of the patient's 'point of maximum pain' in the assessment, which is arrived at by focusing on the three areas of object relations (the current life situation, the early infantile relations and the transference relationship) which are enshrined in Malan's triangle of person.

Even though he does not specifically mention assessment for brief psychodynamic therapy, Hinshelwood defines succinctly what the brief therapists Malan and Balint were the first to explore systematically, in the footsteps of Alexander and French, as central in brief therapy – the identification of the patient's focal or nuclear conflict, which, like the point of maximum pain, is the 'particular pain involved in the object relationship that makes sense of the way in which other object relationships are used *to avoid the pain*' (1991: 172). The skill of the assessor is to find and to put his or her finger on this point, and then to formulate interpretatively this psychodynamic focus in the course of conducting the initial interview with a patient, who can then be further tested as to his/her suitability for psychodynamic therapy of short- or long-term duration.

Between them, Malan and Balint did much of the systematic thinking on how to conduct, structure and evaluate this session, not only but also in preparation for brief work with the patient. Balint recommended an elastic interview technique, preparing an appropriate atmosphere, reassuring or anxiety-raising, as there is the need for different responses to different patients. He also spoke of assessment as a modelling of future therapy as it can be seen as a therapeutic situation in which psychoanalytic tools are used for diagnostic purposes.

Malan is eloquent about the fine detail of the task: how to elicit material, how to formulate a working hypothesis, how to establish rapport and a safe space for the patient, and, ultimately, how to give him/her 'a good therapeutic experience', in order to increase his/her motivation and 'wish to be analysed'. He recommends that the assessor should ask for a dream, a fantasy, a memory, when the patient was last angry, and, further to the important question 'why does the patient come now?', s/he should establish the precipitating factors which repeat situations from the past and constitute what he calls the patient's 'life problem'. Eventually, as in the medical model, the assessor will be making a diagnosis, formulating an explanatory hypothesis linking signs and symptoms together as manifestations of known pathological processes. It is advisable, he said, to obtain sufficient information and to formulate a minimum of hypotheses and of processes in order to be able to prescribe an appropriate therapeutic intervention.

Criteria for the selection of patients/clients for brief psychodynamic work

Malan (1979) advises the assessor to establish the patient's presenting problem and his/her underlying disturbance. This means that there will be a dynamic understanding of the *symptom*, its meaning and function. Also the therapist will evaluate the forces in the patient for or against improvement, and all through it is important not only what the patient says, but how s/he says it, when in the interview and in which sequence. Hence there is less description than in the medical model, but more exploration of psychopathology, more observation of dynamics and of relating. The interview should have a shape: a beginning, a middle and an end. It is not a psychiatric or a social history and not a psychotherapy session. It requires thinking on one's feet in relation to prognosis and appropriate intervention, thinking indeed on four different levels, namely

- psychiatrically;
- psychodynamically;
- psychotherapeutically;
- practically.

There is a checklist of what needs to be done:

- take care of the interview;
- take care of the patient;
- look out for ego strength and the severity of the problem:
    - establish whether the patient has had significant relationships in his/her life;
    - establish the patient's environment and support system (both internal and external);
    - draw inferences and formulate hypotheses;
    - deepen the rapport by making interpretations.

Throughout the interview it is important to

- remain aware of the possible effects of assessment: increased hope, increased disturbance, increased attachment.

Malan's Law of Increased Disturbance (1979: 220–21) implies that psychotherapy will make a patient as disturbed as s/he has ever been in the past, which means that previous breakdowns will need to be noted and the question asked: what have you been like at your worst?

Another important question the therapist will have to ask him/ herself is: can the patient work in interpretative therapy? In order to answer this, s/he needs to use some 'trial interpretations' and watch their side-effects on the patient, which could be relief or increased disturbance, the emergence of strong hopes and of strong attachment to the interviewer, increased motivation or motivation-decreasing anxiety.

Over the years analysts and psychotherapists have thought long and hard about exclusion and inclusion criteria for psychoanalytic therapy and they have, of course, disagreed and differed in their choice. Here are some of the lists they came up with.

Hildebrand (unpublished, quoted in Malan, 1979: 225) at the Tavistock Clinic listed as excluding factors:

- serious suicide attempts;
- alcoholism or drug addiction;

- long-term hospitalization and ECT;
- a homosexual wanting to be heterosexual;
- chronic phobic or obsessional symptoms;
- gross destructive or self-destructive acts.

Glover drew up a list in order of (decreasing) treatability:

- hysteria, conversion symptoms;
- compulsive neurosis;
- neurotic disturbance;
- character disturbance;
- perversions;
- addictions;
- impulsiveness;
- psychosis.

It is understandable that there are wide variants about treatability, and there is in fact a broad spectrum of opinion from the conservative view put forward by Hildebrand and Glover to the more radical views held by recent clinicians who are treating borderline patients (Searles, Kernberg), severely disordered narcissistic personality (Kohut) and patients with so-called 'endogenous depression', with paranoid or delusional fantasies which used to be considered untreatable.

In order to establish criteria for who can usefully be treated in brief focal therapy, Malan arrived at two hypotheses:

1 *Hypothesis A*: prognosis is best in mild illnesses of relatively recent onset.
2 *Hypothesis B*: prognosis is best when the patient shows willingness and ability to work in interpretative therapy.

In both cases it is important that the patient arrives for assessment at the 'propitious moment' in his/her life when s/he is willing and ready to make use of therapy.

Malan's selection criteria are:

Hypothesis A:
- patient shows up with oedipal problems;
- has satisfactory personal relationships;
- the illness is of recent onset.

Hypothesis B:
- patient shows high motivation;
- patient demonstrates good contact and response to trial interpretation.

From what has been said so far it must appear that the assessment for psychodynamic therapy, whether of long or short duration, concentrates on certain vital ingredients in the patient without which s/he is not treatable either way, with psychological-mindedness, high motivation and the ability to form and sustain a relationship high up among the list. This would indicate that chronicity, whether of depression, obsessiveness, acting out or self-destructive behaviour, but also an inability to self-reflect and to form relationships, would point to exclusion, as would all paranoid conditions (except in the temporary form of phobias after traumatization) and rigid defences whose dismantling could lead to breakdown.

However, the patient classification work done by Malan and his colleagues should not be considered as written in stone. Rather, it should be seen as a system of guidelines and rules of thumb which the assessor should hold in mind when examining individual patients who present for psychotherapy. In the end, most practitioners would agree that they allow themselves to be guided as much by their intuition and by the patient's manifest needs as by hard-and-fast diagnostic rules in the textbook when they make choices about whom to work with in psychotherapy. Individual rapport counts for as much as experience of what has worked in the past, and there are some clinicians who consider they can work with almost anyone as long as there is good enough initial contact and willingness on the part of the patient to risk the involvement in a helping relationship where his or her problems will be actively addressed.

Some assessment extends beyond the initial session when the assessor is not sure whether s/he has got a clear picture of the patient's inner world constellations and needs more time to establish anxiety levels, patterns of object relating or the full extent of emotional disturbance. In the second session the patient may show up much more disturbed, much less motivated or may even declare to be cured, all of which would indicate that the 'propitious moment' has gone and that it would be unwise to accept the patient for long- or short-term counselling/therapy. It has to be admitted that the momentous impact of a first session can also be anti-therapeutic, not necessarily because of the therapist's faulty assessment or faulty technique, but because the patient – for whatever reason – chooses not to go ahead. To respect this decision means accepting that the patient, no matter how much s/he might 'need' therapeutic help, is following an inner voice which says no to this now. Perhaps next time with a different therapist in a different context and constellation the moment will turn out to be more propitious. Moreover, the therapist's initial hunch that the picture was blurred can retrospectively be seen as an important indicator of the patient's blurred motivation.

This said to set the matter of early drop-out and apparent untreatability into a realistic context, I want to proceed to the description of what happens when a therapeutic alliance comes about in the initial interview and the two participants begin to engage in a meaningful interaction that will lead to the making of a joint contract. The therapist will be satisfied that s/he has enough information to recommend the patient for therapy, whether taking him/her on personally or referring him/her to a colleague for ongoing work. Either way, a choice will have to be made, on the basis of availability, desirability and practicability, as to which kind and which length of contract is considered appropriate; this will depend on the therapeutic goals and practical resources, which also have to be negotiated.

It will depend, moreover, on the context in which the patient presents for treatment. The settings in which Menninger, Malan, Coltart and Hinshelwood arrived at their definitions and descriptions of diagnosis and assessment, and for which they fashioned their recommendations, were either clinics or private practice. Thirty years on from Menninger and Malan, the scenario has changed, and there are many new settings, particularly in the world of counselling, where clients and patients are seen for therapy of various durations and intensities. Balint's and Malan's notion of brief work was 6 months or 25 sessions, James Mann in the seventies recommended 12–15 sessions, while nowadays contracts can be as short as 5 or 6 sessions, particularly in primary health care, like GP practices, in the educational sector and in the world of employment assistance programmes where the organizations or corporations fund the treatment, and the clients/patients come in a crisis, with stress- and work-related problems. Assessment for such brief psychodynamic work will not be less rigorous than the psychiatric or psychoanalytic interview, though it will tend to start from the presenting problem and will carefully limit the areas opened up for examination and exploration in order to contain the work to fit the limited time frame. Always essential is a personal and social history and some evidence of how the client relates, reflects on him/herself, functions internally and externally and manages or does not manage anxiety.

Let's take the case of a 19-year-old Asian bank employee who is bullied and beaten by her father whenever she shows signs of independence, as is her 16-year-old sister. The mother is traditionally submissive, housebound and quarrelsome, and hence no support to the girls. The client is fairly new at work, and anxious because she has found herself making many mistakes, a fact which her friendly manager has chosen not to use against her, making her feel that she has a chance of being allowed to stay on. She has a secret boyfriend from a different ethnic background who encourages her to stand up for herself or to leave the house and she is very torn between seeing him and being subservient to father.

But she cannot leave her sister to her father's mercy nor is she ready to fend for herself, while the virtual captivity of the home situation is felt by her as unbearable, to the point of having had thoughts of doing away with herself. The crisis has become more acute because she has experienced a new freedom in the work setting, where she is treated as an adult with rights and responsibilities unheard of so far, and she is now longing to live like other girls of her age with boyfriends who come to their houses and with whom they go out in the evenings. A conflict of duty versus autonomy, of loyalty versus selfishness, has produced a stalemate from which she is struggling in vain to escape, and it has made her take up the free counselling funded by her firm.

When asked the 'miracle question' at assessment – what would have happened if she woke up one morning to a miraculous change in her cirumstances? – she replied: 'My parents would have stopped their noisy quarrelling,' indicating that she craved peace and harmony above all else, but saw no way in which she could change or affect the situation in the family. The assessing counsellor, who was offering five counselling sessions as part of the bank-subsidized employment assistance scheme, and who realized the serious oedipal dilemma the client was in, was aware of the fierce anger that fuelled the anxiety as well as of the lurking danger of self-destructiveness. She began to explore possible solutions to the entrenched problem. How about enlisting the mother as an ally, by giving her a regular monthly allowance from her salary, instead of slipping large sums of money to the sister as she had hitherto been accustomed to do? This could shift forces in the oedipal triangle in terms of weakening the father and strengthening the women, but it might also strengthen the family bonds further instead of paving the way for a separation from home. Why not use the favourable situation at work and tell her friendly manager about the difficult home situation, seeking his advice and approval for gaining some freedom from home, perhaps by initiating some regular course attendance in the evenings, and thus enabling meetings with the boyfriend as well as improving her career prospects and professional independence, which might impress and mollify her father?

By focusing on one and/or on the other strategy, the assessor engaged the client in active problem-solving with her, while simul-taneously gauging the client's developmental stage, her ego strength and her initiative, and finally setting her the task of actively pursuing change in both arenas of her life. A trial interpretation aimed at pointing out the emerging alliance with her counsellor, which received an understanding response, confirmed the counsellor in her assessment that the client was able to make use of psychodynamic linking and led to her decision to concentrate firmly on the two-pronged approach, which meant pursuing the modest goal of encouraging the client to enlist the mother's and the manager's support at the same time.

In the following four sessions the validation of this approach would have to be gathered from how her relations with her father changed, if at all. In case of the latter, i.e. no significant change in the family dynamics, the client would at least have had the experience of being attentively listened to, of being treated as a responsible adult by a parental figure, and of learning how to find solutions to apparently intractable problems, all of which could add up to a good therapeutic experience and inspire her with some hope for the future. In that respect a significant difference would have been made in that the client had learnt to ask for help and found that it was forthcoming and could be internalized, if only in the form of asking questions, devising plans and strategies and believing in the possibility of making changes happen.

This simple example embodies many of the points raised by Malan et al. in that the conditions for Hypothesis B seem fulfilled, while recent onset, precipitating factors, levels of ego strength, a clear oedipal conflict and response to trial interpretation were established. Both the client's high motivation and her good rapport with the counsellor promised cooperation, and the prognosis seemed good provided the client returned with her motivation strengthened and some of the counsellor's suggestions implemented. Also the conditions may have been laid for a 'corrective emotional experience' in that the experience of being bullied, beaten or forbidden to act freely was replaced by attentiveness, validation and support, which could foster hope for change in the future.

An important feature of this assessment would have been the ethnic factor prominent in a case where cultural differences around traditional father–daughter, men–women relationships formed a significant element of the presenting problem. Not to mention nor to explore this 'difference' would be negligent, as the client might feel misunderstood or criticized by the counsellor acting out of white prejudice for 'black' backwardness. Another case in point was the Indian solicitor whose father suddenly died of cancer in India, which meant that the son, who was born and bred in England, found himself called upon to organize a traditional Hindu funeral and observe Hindu mourning rites for the first time in his life. For years he had felt his father had a sad life and was rather estranged from him, and now he was expected to follow the difficult instructions in his last will and to take his place by the funeral pyre, which was frightening. He had returned from this experience shaken and afraid that his mother's demands for male support would be too much for him. The counsellor pointed out to him that it felt as if he had not realized what the traditional role of a son was and that he had now moved up to be the head of his family. He suggested that the work should focus around this issue and be an exploration of what he felt about his father and how he could allow himself to mourn him. Emphasizing that he was going to be helped in this necessary developmental task by a male counsellor who might be experienced as a father, the counsellor attempted a trial interpretation, to which the client responded with relief, indicating that he was ready and willing to use the counselling to complete an unfinished developmental task which his father had been unable to help him with.

Once again, there was recent onset, manifest precipitating factors, a clear oedipal conflict and a sufficient degree of psychological-mindedness on the part of the client, all of which boded well for the time-limited work that was available. Other factors, like starting a new job, an unsatisfactory relationship with his wife, who was white, and general anxieties about his ability to cope (his father had had a 'sad' life), had to be ignored, but eventually they got gathered in at the last session after a series of cathartic dreams about his father's funeral left him strengthened for his new tasks. The counsellor's focusing on the client's ethnic difference in the assessment, and his emphasis on the client's 'neglected' Indianness, which had claimed him with a vengeance upon his father's death, proved the decisive therapeutic factor that eventually worked for change. Already in the initial interview, when his panics were interpreted in the light of this denial, the momentous impact of this first therapeutic encounter proved to be a 'corrective emotional experience'.

These examples of sensitive assessments for brief solution-focused work demonstrate that the experienced assessor will identify relatively quickly a psychodynamic focus that can be worked with briefly when the client presents in a state of willingness to tackle a troubling situation with the help of another whom s/he is prepared to trust. In neither case was there evidence of undue defensiveness that would have complicated or sabotaged the therapeutic task. In cases where it becomes evident at assessment that the client is resistant or ambivalent, the brief therapist will have to overcome this by homing in on an area that increases the motivation to the point that s/he is willing to engage, if only briefly, in working on some of the problems that have brought him/her in. In fact, the promised briefness of the therapeutic engagement may sharpen this appetite as it may seem manageable and bearable, while the prospect of months or even years might be too daunting and make the client decide against counselling altogether.

An example of the appropriateness of brief work was the case of a young woman whose father had recently died and who had suddenly realized that she knew very little about him and, having been at boarding school for some years, had not thought about him very much, hence her surprise at discovering how devastated she was by his sudden death. The therapist had decided that this was a focus that might be worked on productively in three months as it was a traumatic bereavement which had triggered off anxieties about hidden feelings (in terms of Malan's triangle of conflict). Noting that there were eating disorders and a troubled relationship with a narcissistic mother, too, she chose to ignore these in favour of the pressing oedipal issues. By focusing on the loss and mourning she helped the patient pursue the adolescent task of separation/individuation into which the parent's death had thrown her prematurely, and the resolution of which could be achieved by paralleling it in the therapeutic relationship, which was to come to an agreed end after three months. James Mann's time-limited paradigm fitted this case like a glove!

As a rule, oedipal problems are the most suitable for resolution in brief focal work, which is why Sifneos (1979) insisted on excluding all pre-oedipal symptomatology as a waste of time. Of course, oedipal disturbance may mask the existence of more primitive and persistent conflict which can become uncovered in the course of working on the former. In neither of the three cases above did this happen, most likely because the therapists were careful to limit the scope of their work and focused exclusively on the turbulence the clients had come with. Interestingly, loss and mourning or, in other words, separation/individuation were the main themes in all three, and this seems to confirm Mann's theory that the primacy of the time limit produces these fundamental themes in every case. On the other hand, the case for the focus on oedipal problems can be made in terms of the relative ease with which at this developmental stage the management of separation and loss can be facilitated in the brief psychodynamic contract, while issues of fusion and dependence, which in longer therapy would almost inevitably emerge, are not allowed to surface and are thus bypassed. The third client, by allowing herself to grieve for a father she had realized she loved deeply, acquired the strength to face her infinitely more troubled relationship with her mother, without seeking further therapy.

This is a bonus of brief therapy when it is well done. Often, at assessment, the client may present high levels of disturbance which seem to call for long-term intensive work and pluck at the heartstrings of the compassionate therapist, who becomes convinced that only long-term therapy can help. When, on the insistence of a less sceptical supervisor, s/he is helped to attempt a short-term contract in spite of his/her legitimate doubts at assessment, s/he is surprised how much can be done by focusing and containing the area of therapeutic exploration and by narrowing down the focus to a clearly identifiable nuclear conflict. The disturbance seen at assessment tends to recede with the concentration and firm containment of the work, which indicates that even the briefest experience of being contained can have a momentous therapeutic effect. In this concept I want to mention Mark Aveline's essay 'How I Assess for Focal Psychotherapy' (1995) and his ongoing research into the subject based on his NHS work at Nottingham, where he has proved the particular therapeutic effectiveness of the brief intervention which is a result of focal assessment.

There are cases where brief therapy (or any therapy) will be counter-indicated, and the weeding out of these is one of the essential tasks at the initial interview. The woman who insisted that all she wanted was to be instructed in how to influence her colleagues magically, clearly suffered from a thought disorder and could not be engaged in a therapeutic dialogue or alliance. As she had applied at an institution that required potential clients prior to assessment to fill in a detailed questionnaire, in which they were asked briefly to describe their complaint, their family history and their expectations, it was immediately obvious from her garbled answer that she was 'untreatable', to use Malan's word, and she was promptly referred back to her GP for more appropriate treatment.

Some clients are satisfied with the assessment session alone when this becomes a creative consultation in which a form of conflict resolution is achieved. I remember the case of a woman who seemed to have come to the end of her marriage when she discovered that her husband had been unfaithful to her. After listening patiently to the full detail of her story, which included the happy 40-year marriage her parents had had, I came to the conclusion that her husband's affair was of little consequence and found myself saying, 'There is always a second chance.' Pondering it briefly, she took this remark as if it were a revelation, thanked me and departed satisfied. It felt as if all she needed was a push in the right direction. Or, to put it clinically, as if one session presented her in a nutshell with the solution she had been working towards unconsciously.

The lesson to be learnt from all this is that an open and flexible mind at assessment is one of the most important therapeutic tools to bring along. The outcome depends on so many known and unknown factors that for quite a long way into the session the assessor will remain uncertain as to the conclusions he or she will reach in the end (if any). The ability to stay calmly with this uncertainty for as long as possible will be invaluable during the gathering of evidence for a creative reflection on the diversity of clinical material, the identification of the countertransference feelings, the linking of the related bits in the narrative, and the formulation of the working hypothesis which forms the basis for the decisions for or against treatment. The final moments in the process, when an offer is made and accepted or negotiated, deferred or turned down, often have a dramatic quality as they denote the beginning of a relationship and of treatment, or a blank refusal of both, because of an inability and fear to take the hand that is offered. The poignant quality of this moment is often overlaid by the practicalities necessitated by the decision that has been reached together, but it is of great significance therapeutically.

When a decision is made for brief therapy, there is a lot of business to go through: an appointment to be made; instructions issued as to payment for missed sessions or cancellation requirements; false hopes discouraged; and the length of contract confirmed. There may be hints as to what might happen after therapy, and what will not be allowed, like carrying on with the therapist beyond the agreed period of time. The therapist may give the client a task to be achieved, to get used to carrying on the process started and to understand that his/her responsibility for it is to keep it going, like a fire that has been lit. When the door has closed behind the client, it may have opened the floodgates of strong emotion and reflection and started an unstoppable process of change and transformation.

What patients get or do not get in the end depends on many factors: where they apply for help and availability; the assessor's preferences, training and orientation; recommendations by their GP, boss, friends; chance; and, to some extent, their own choice. It may also depend on money, their own financial situation, when they turn to a private practitioner, or the agency's funding situation, and even though their assessment will always be geared to their needs, these can only be seen in context and the contract they will eventually be offered will be a compromise between what is on offer and what they expect.

As Flegenheimer said

the selection of a particular form of brief therapy has to be made either on practical gounds, by what is available, or on the basis of a priori clinical reasoning and judgment. Currently there are few clinics or practitioners who are able to offer more than one form of brief therapy so that, if brief therapy is indicated, the specific form of treatment that the patient will receive is often determined by who makes the referral or what services are provided by the clinic in the area. (1982: 157)

This statement was made some time ago without reference to the boom in and the rise of brief therapy in educational and commercial settings that was to follow, and it is in some respects out of date in the era of employment assistance programmes and of widespread counselling in GP practices, though it is still relevant in that the choices continue to be fairly arbitrary, depending on who is making them, rather than on patient needs or systematic knowledge of what works when.

Some people get started on the wrong foot, are matched with a therapist they do not get on with, are offered too little or have to wait too long, do not understand what to ask for or how to communicate what they expect, and then end up with a disappointing or abortive experience. Though nowadays it is quite easy to get information about available services, and the media, too, however biased they may be, keep the public informed on developments in the field and on the multitude of available services, the public is still dependent on the choices made for them at the places they go to seek for them. Hence, the choice of therapy in terms of number of sessions, frequency and model is still mainly dictated by chance rather than by systematic decision-making, and yet in a culture of diversity like ours this is probably inevitable when the evidence for what works when is still quite scarce.

The NHS, many reputable psychotherapy organizations, and counselling services up and down the UK have been thinking of ways and means to improve their assessment procedures by introducing questionnaires and evaluation forms for patients and clinicians which allow reflection on presenting problems, diagnosis and outcome, and which have become the statistical basis for research and development. These questionnaires are meant to involve the patients, from the moment they apply for assessment, in the process of thinking about their problems and needs in relation to their social and personal history, and to the precipitating factors which led to their seeking help. Balint and Malan were among the first to systematize the therapy assessment procedures by using evaluative forms, and a pre-assessment general health questionnaire has become a standard tool for the induction of psychotherapy patients – a form of homework to start them off in a therapeutic process of self-examination and self-exploration that establishes their suitability, treatability and motivation and helps the assessors prepare themselves for their task on the basis of information supplied by the patient before the assessment session.

Ten years ago, the Westminster Pastoral Foundation, a nation-wide counselling network offering individual counselling and groupwork, on a time-limited and long-term basis, introduced such a pre-assessment questionnaire in order to assist the selection of clients for its diverse services. This was found to be a great help in establishing client suitability for the rigours of psychodynamic work, for groups as well as for short-term work, and the organization has been basing its research for purposes of fund-raising on information gathered from these pre-counselling and follow-up forms. Another purpose of the questionnaire was the brisk induction of clients, who will be offered short-term contracts into the methodology of questioning themselves as to the specifics of their complaint, their personality and psychic functioning prior to the first encounter with a therapist.

In some respects, therapy starts the moment clients pick up the phone, and it gets under way when they begin to ponder the questions in the questionnaire, asking themselves what they want, need, expect and are prepared to commit themselves to. Also, a process of transference starts there and then, and the client's self-assessment sets the ball rolling that may lead to change and an improvement in their situation. Alternately, when they draw back and decide against embarking on a therapeutic venture, they indicate they they are not ready, want something different, or are simply scared.

Assessment is the threshold that needs to be crossed when the choice of coming into therapy has been made, but still needs confirming (or disconfirming) before a final decision is made. It serves as an induction into the 'real thing', and therefore has been called 'trial therapy', but it also serves as a space which allows movement in both directions – forwards and backwards – and is thus essential in the decision-making process of both participants.

5

The Therapist's Task and Roles in Brief
and Focal Therapy

Chosing techniques and styles of implementing the task, the brief therapist operates in various roles

At this point it becomes necessary to discuss the various techniques, the diversity in contract lengths and the fixed and variable styles current in the professional field. These differences were developed for different patient populations and for different developmental stages by different personalities whose personal style and clinical stance is always closely reflected in their variable attitudes to fixing (or not fixing) time limits, to using a strict analytic frame with regularity of sessions or to spacing out sessions over sometimes considerable periods of time, and to terminating as contracted from the beginning (Mann) or when it is considered that the work is done (Malan, Davanloo). Some practitioners permit themselves to carry on beyond the contracted ending when they consider that the patient has more work to do; others always insist on finishing within the time frame initially agreed, because they believe in the primacy of secure frames and the fulfilling of contracts no matter what may beckon away from this rigorous application of rules.

Providing and maintaining the reliable container of a secure analytic frame and establishing a creative working alliance

The task of the psychodynamic brief therapist is different in many ways from the task of the traditional long-term psychotherapist and analyst in that the factor of time (as short, precious and limited) is always crucial and determines the working style, the treatment choices and the speed at which the therapist works. Based in the same theoretical framework, yet confident that with a more active technique some significant therapeutic work can get done in a short time, the goals have changed from gradual change and comprehensive rebuilding of psychic structures to tackling an area of emotional difficulty which the patient has brought and is unable to deal with on his/her own. The aim is to initiate the patient into a new way of understanding and hence of solving this problem, in the light of similar difficulties in the past and of a perceived repetition of unhelpful patterns derived from early relationships, and to help them lay the foundations for change.

By focusing clearly on the present difficulty, which is reformulated in terms of its psychodynamic dimensions, the therapist limits the potential complexity of related problems to an essential core and tailors the brief therapeutic intervention to its intensive exploration and attempted resolution. In the belief that this may amount to completing a maturational task, to facing and overcoming an as yet avoided and feared emotional conflict, to learning how to.express anger constructively, to get in touch with some hidden feeling and to become assertive and creative in adversity, the brief therapist offers the patient a time-limited therapeutic alliance with the promise of cooperative action on a limited aim.

Having established in a thorough assessment the patient's suitability for brief work through testing motivation, ego strength, the ability to relate and to link life events into a personal narrative, the therapist strives to become a reliable enough container that will receive and safely hold the patient's communications, anxieties and distress, and provide the analytic space in which a creative dialogue is possible about the presenting problem and its ramifications in the patient's personal history, about his/her current functioning, and his/her fears for the future. This requires an ability quickly to engage and interest a person who might well be anxious, sceptical or doubtful. It also calls for empathic listening to that person's tales of woe as well as simultaneous reflection on the deeper, clinical meaning of what is said in order to formulate appropriate interventions that grab the patient's imagination and inspire the hope needed to enter a daunting process of self-exposure and to entrust him/herself to a stranger.

For these first moments of the encounter to be successful and to result in an instant working alliance the therapist has to adopt an active stance which conveys the confidence, the good will and the promise that will engender spontaneous belief in a successful outcome, without creating an impression of magical authority or of solutions imposed from above. It has often been said that in brief therapy the therapist's personality is crucial, and that without this matching the patient's personality in some way no work can be done nor significant progress made. It is also essential that the frame and the conditions of work are established in such a way that the patient is made to feel both 'at ease' and invited to take risks in a supportive environment.

Flegenheimer speaks of the 'dramatic' therapist in relation to some of the brief therapy pioneers like Davanloo and Sifneos, and thereby puts his finger on an important aspect of this kind of work. A peculiarly heightened atmosphere is produced in brief therapy by a combination of pressure of time, power of personality and confidence in the method. Compared to the calm neutrality of the analyst, who practises evenly hovering attention for a large part of each session, in brief therapy the stage is set for two protagonists to meet face-to-face in an animated verbal exchange, engaged in the rapid back and forth of a dialogue in which the therapist's constant attention to remain on focus and not to allow any digression into unrelated material produces an energetic quickfire pace quite unlike anything that happens in analysis or open-ended psychodynamic psychotherapy, where time is plentiful and unlimited, and digression can lead to unexpected finds.

Here, the verbal contributions and the quick repartee of the two partners are about equal in frequency and length, contributing to a lively interaction between apparently equally matched speakers which generates ideas and is kept going in a constant flow, without much silence or thoughtful pausing, as both partners remain aware that the clock is ticking and the therapist is intent on pressing on with the task, wasting no time to accomplish it within the allotted span. It is good practice to remind the patient intermittently of where s/he is in the contracted time frame and to mention regularly how many more sessions there are to go. This keeps the adrenalin flowing and puts pressure on the patient to deliver and to think fast. As in normal conversation, s/he feels good when contributions are affirmed, picked up and responded to quickly, and the back-and-forth style of brief therapy dialogue may be more congenial to the beginner (which most patients in brief therapy are) than the analytic technique of lengthy and elaborate interpreting of associative material, which requires acclimatization. There are clinicians who practise successive contracting (Ryle, CiC, some GP or college counsellors), others who permit themselves to convert short-term contracts into long-term work when the patient seems to need this, instead of referring on as a point of principle, and others, again, who transfer patients without hesitation (though not without preparation) from clinic or agency settings into private practice when the allotted and paid for contract has come to an end.

There have been good and plausible explanations for these variations, related to the nature and severity of the presenting problems, the patients' ages, developmental stages, previous therapy experience, and to the individual therapists' personal preferences and temperaments. When the transference is used extensively, as with Malan and his followers, the contract is longer (up to six months) than when it is only monitored or manipulated (as with Alexander), and therapists who regularly use follow-ups to make sure that the patient continues the working through (like Wolberg, Malan, and a number of others) encourage some continuance of transference without necessarily using the follow-up sessions for further therapeutic input. Flegenheimer (1982) contrasts the managerial, the paternalistic, the didactic, the confrontational and the empathic therapeutic stances as embodied by Alexander, Wolberg, Davanloo, Mann, with Malan 'in the middle ground' practising the most purist analytical technique, consistently interpreting transference and resistance and applying his two dynamic triangles to further the patient's understanding of his/her psychic functioning.

The most inflexible technique, and therefore probably the easiest to learn, is the model developed by Mànn, in which the 'central issue' of separation is cast in developmental terms and the tripartite, 12-session structure reflects the Mahlerian sequence of symbiosis, separation and individuation which, theoretically, every individual has to achieve in early childhood. By focusing firmly on this one universal issue, Mann claimed that it was always central to the individual's painfully personal issues and his or her unique intra-psychic world. He thus put brief therapy into a nutshell – you all long to be fused in love, struggle to be true to yourself in relationship and to become unique and free individuals – a complicated developmental task, which everybody is trying to achieve in the early stages of life into adolescence and which is yet failed by multitudes, due to inadequate parenting or traumatic early life experiences.

The empathic therapist who uses this model will help those who failed at it at first go by giving them a second chance to attempt and achieve it. The rich symbolism of Mann's three stages, which echoes the teachings of Jung, Erikson and Margaret Mahler, is a potent tool in the hands of the creative brief therapist, who is able to draw detailed parallels between the patient's life experiences and the current therapeutic relationship, which runs through the three phases of the cycle from symbiosis through separation/individuation to termination. As many patients are suffering from unresolved mourning and are traumatized by early separations and losses, this kind of work is immensely valuable. However, it perhaps does not sufficiently allow for wounds and conflicts which have other pathogenic origins and which also cry out to be healed and attended to.

Mann's insistence on making good use of his prescription to limit the time of the therapeutic encounter, and hence to evoke a panoply of emotional responses to its limitation, the rationing of relationship and the eventual withdrawal and loss of the therapist, has been a major factor in the success, the spread and the effectiveness of brief therapy, equal in importance to the insistence on the analytic frame, as it drew attention to the necessity for consistency and discipline which alone ensure the patients' safety, protecting them from wilful and arbitrary therapists who go back on promises, break contracts and boundaries and contradict themselves at their own discretion.

Mann also introduced a rich philosophical and spiritual dimension into the practical world of short-termism and economizing, and he firmly questioned the validity of extended and potentially interminable therapy, which, considering the powerful forces of the transference, hands almost absolute power to the analyst. By placing time and termination firmly on the analytic agenda, he handed back some contractual power to the patient, and with it the hope that individuation is an ordinary human task, achievable inside as well as outside of therapy.

An equally essential task for the brief therapist is to establish early on where in the life-cycle the patient is and how well s/he has achieved the age-appropriate tasks which Erikson systematized from childhood to old age in his classic *Chidhood and Society* (1950) in terms of polarities and crises which may produce regression to previous stages, temporary identity confusion, permanently arrested development and malfunctioning unless identified and attended to therapeutically. He stated emphatically 'we do not consider all development a series of crises; we claim only that psycho-social development proceeds by critical steps – "critical" being a characteristic of turning points, of moments of decision between progress and regression, integration and retardation' (1950: 262).

The brief therapist may find that the patient presents with failures arising from the inability to move into the next life-cycle stage – from adolescence to adulthood, most commonly – but also with various life tasks not adequately fulfilled – like becoming a parent, separating from grown-up children, acknowledging the onset of old age, etc. S/he may then formulate his/her task as one of facilitating such developmental transitions, and this may well mean successive brief contracts over a lifetime, regular bouts of therapy at critical points in the patient's life story when something has gone severely wrong along the developmental ladder.

Freud (1937) was the first to hint at the possibility of returning to do some more work in the course of time (in 'Analysis Terminable and Interminable'), and to establish the likelihood that patienthood can be lifelong and intermittent, with new problems arising as life circumstances and psychic experiences change. Brief therapy, of whatever length, can thus become a life-line along the way, provided the first therapeutic experience is a good one and helps the patient seek more of it when s/he gets into trouble again. This knowledge is one of the factors which help the humble therapist let go of the patient when the contract has come to an end, without feeling guilt or regret at not having given that patient enough or done everything possible for him or her. It also informs the therapist's choice of referring on or encouraging the patient to seek further therapy him/ herself in future if s/he considers it necessary. This double move of letting go and suggesting there might be the need for some more therapy in time to come is a subtle way of emphasizing patients' autonomy while binding them into a scenario where help is always available. It eases the pain of leaving by assuring and consoling both parties.

Erikson himself was not interested in brief therapy, and it would be too simple to conclude that his view of the lifespan as marked by regular and stage-appropriate crises confines the therapist's task to brief interventions at appropriate times. Many of the difficulties encountered along the line are complicated by multiple failures at various life stages, probably originating in such severe deficit and inadequate parental support at the very beginning of life that the very first task – establishing basic trust – is failed. Where this basic trust is lacking, brief therapy cannot succeed nor even get started, as it requires a good measure of trust to establish the necessary working alliance. Hence the assessment concept of 'the healthy patient', which indicates the existence of some basic trust, namely sufficient ego strength to undertake a joint task, and sufficient commitment, namely basic trust and hope to carry it through to the end.

Applying the 'lifespan developmental perspective' is as useful and necessary as is formulating the patient's developmental stage in terms of oedipal or pre-oedipal conflicts. Neither will indicate *per se* whether brief or long-term therapy is best, but they will help to frame the focus and the aim, and the task is in every individual case to make a choice on the basis of many theoretical and practical considerations.

Holding the focus and monitoring the ongoing dynamic process

Ever since French formulated his theory of the nuclear focus and thereby challenged and modified the analytic concept of letting the patient set the agenda by free association, brief therapy had a chance of being practised successfully alongside the open-ended and free-ranging version, which was based on an assumption of recurring symptomatology, and of a continuing therapeutic process until all underlying pathogenic causes have been analysed and the defences against these have been throughly restructured. The focus gathers the dynamic conflict in the way a boil gathers the inflammation and after being lanced and cleaned will begin to heal. Or, as first defined by French, the focal conflicts are derivatives of deeper and earlier nuclear conflicts which presumably originate during crucial developmental periods in early life. These remain mostly dormant, repressed or 'solved', with one of them becoming activated (or having remained active) and continuously appearing to underlie behaviour in the form of focal conflicts – which can be identified as variations of the same theme. (Balint, 1972: 11)

Balint's description of how a focus is found is based on what he called the 'ten-minute psychotherapy' practised in medical consultation, which

demanded a very high intensity of interaction between patient and doctor. This atmosphere helped the doctor to tune in with his patient's actual mental state which is a conglomerate of hope and despair, trust and mistrust, confusion and clarity. If he succeeds in this task then it will amount to a 'flash' of understanding which usually unites patient and doctor and is felt by both. Another way of expressing this experience is to describe it more poetically as the 'meeting of two minds' or as 'the moment of truth', the closing of a Gestalt or the 'Aha' experience . . . It is sufficient that the event is felt and recognized by both partners and that this recognition is kept alive in subsequent meetings . . . In focal therapy this experience must be expressed by the therapist for his own use in fairly exact ideas, a process that is more or less identical with translating the flash experience into concise words. Without this precise formulation no focal plan can be devised, which means that the therapist will find it difficult to decide when and how to use selective attention or selective neglect. (1972: 151–2)

Where there is no flash of recognition or no instant meeting of two minds, there may instead be the 'crystallization' of a focus, which, in Malan's words, happens more like 'a gradual emergence in the give and take between patient and therapist' (1972: 153).

In psychodynamic brief therapy this focus needs to be formulated dynamically, i.e. in terms of Malan's triangles of person and of conflict, with past, current life situation and present patient–therapist interaction linked interpretatively in the formulation, which also takes note of anxieties, hidden feelings, and defences against these. This is the 'classical' focal technique, devised by Malan and Balint, which became the theme for many later variations, not all as rigorously analytic or concisely delineated, though the limited aim and the methods of selective attention and selective neglect are universally practised. In all of this the therapist's role is to agree with the patient what the focus will be at the start of the treatment and to concentrate on this to the exclusion of other concerns, in the hope that the process of change in one area might translate into other areas by a ripple effect.

It has been said (by Malan and Sifneos in particular) that conflicts involving three people, such as oedipal conflicts and sibling rivalry for primacy with a parent, lend themselves best to resolution through brief therapy, though most therapists would also treat patients whose chief childhood conflicts concern problems of loss, dependency versus independence, or other dyadic situations. A patient selected for brief therapy, according to Flegenheimer, is one of those '"healthy patients" whose major conflicts developed at a rather advanced stage of psychosexual development, or, if the conflicts developed earlier, they did not seriously interfere with the patient's subsequent development' (1982: 164–66).

In other words, as practitioners of CAT or of SFBT would say, patients' presenting problems can become the focus for reformulating or problem-solving therapy work which enables them to change maladaptive behaviour and non-constructive thinking that has become habitual or chronic to the point of sabotaging their adequate functioning in relating and finding solutions to life problems. Insofar as the aim is limited and closely tailored to the limited time, the therapist's activity is geared to involving the patient responsibly in working towards its accomplishment, allowing him/her neither to sit back nor to deviate from the agreed focus in an attempt to hand back responsibility to the therapist or to regress to dependence and hence to demand more than what was initially agreed.

The focus can be a habitual inability to make decisions, a constant need to please and be compliant, an avoidance of conflict or a problem with assertiveness, all of which will show up in patterns at work, in relationships with others and in attitudes to oneself, and need to be tackled and changed in order to establish a modicum of positive self-esteem, a sensible management of aggression, and the ability 'to love and work' – in short, to gain the freedom from neurosis of which Freud spoke as the ultimate aim of therapy. The therapist's task is to home in on areas where s/he is likely to achieve such changes, however minute, and where it is realistic to hope for a significant increase in risk-taking behaviour, in confronting painful issues or in being honest about feelings towards others.

This is similar to the technique practised by confrontational therapists like Davanloo and Molnos whose belief in and experience of 'healing anger' enabled them to open up areas of hidden aggression, by aggressively taking on and breaking down defences against expressing aggression. This paradoxical technique, which aims to 'mobilize affect', can be seen as modelling behaviour – the therapist's fearless confrontation of the patient's fearful ducking away translates itself after a number of offensive thrusts at the defences into trust and confidence in a method that conveys trust in the patient's ego strength while working away at his/her weakness. The major contribution which Davanloo has made to the technique of brief psychotherapy is his gentle but relentless confrontation of the patient, particularly confrontations designed to enable the patient consciously to experience anger. He concentrates on the patient's feelings, especially feelings about the therapist. The main technique used is the repeated questioning of the patient, asking what he or she feels at that particular moment. When the affect can be surfaced, there is a relief of tension and an increase in the patient's motivation. The therapist does not permit the patient to remain vague and evasive and challenges the patient to be more specific as to the exact feelings at a particular moment. The therapist acknowledges the patient's suffering and encourages him/her to be an active participant in the treatment. He relentlessly challenges the patient's resistance, pointing out the patient's characteristic defences against the anger. After repeated repetitions of this process, the resistance 'melts away' and the outpouring of material characteristic of the midphase of the treatment occurs. It is a method that requires the therapist to be comfortable with his/her own anger – otherwise it might become sadistic or retaliatory manipulation – a charge that has been laid at his door by representatives of the caring and nurturing schools who recommend going with the defences and winning over the patient by gratifying his or her needs. Not everybody feels comfortable with the bulldozer techniques Davanloo has successfully employed, while always carefully monitoring the patient's responses to being confronted, in case the therapist's techniques prove too stimulating for the patient or the patient proves unsuitable for this technique. But as a 'dramatic therapist' he is a colourful figure in the wide spectrum and intricate tapestry of brief therapy.

In general, brief therapy allows no time and place for the attitude of patient nurturing, which encourages dependence and regression and may become necessary with very deprived and damaged people whose ego strength is weak. Here patients are given to understand that they will have to take responsibility for and confront their needs without handing them over to another. They are made to realize that in the holding environment and within the boundaries of the therapeutic alliance their fears and their strong feelings can become manageable, can be expressed, discharged and ultimately defused. This makes for a cathartic experience such as Freud's early patients had, but it is necessarily short-lived unless consolidated by repetition, insight and translation into determined action with others in their external environment. The dramatic moment occurs when transference turns into real relationship, according to Molnos, and when the defence has finally broken down, revealing the therapist as trustworthy 'friend and helper' rather than feared adversary. But it takes courage for both players in this particular game, and Davanloo's broad-focused, 'offensive' brief therapy is not everybody's chosen mode, even though he and his pupil Molnos claim that they have used it successfully for almost any condition, as long as the dynamic process is watched carefully and therapeutic interventions are constantly geared to and gauged by the response.

Identifying, monitoring and interpreting the gathering transference and countertransference issues, resistances and defences

The brief psychodynamic therapist needs to be alert at all times to what is going on in the relationship and monitor the dynamic forces which are active and interactive in the therapeutic field, while listening to the patient's communications and responding to these on a verbal level. This involves identifying the development of the transference as well as observing his or her own countertransference responses in order to understand the patient's implicit as well as explicit messages and responses to the relationship, which is allowed to develop so very briefly before it ends as agreed. The art is to make the most of what happens unconsciously between the two protagonists and to interpret judiciously, tailored to the chosen focus, how the patient relates to the therapist in the context of his/her inquiry into the problem s/he has set out to tackle.

As the development of the transference is not a primary aim in brief therapy, and there is not the time for it to develop and flourish, in contrast to its long-term counterpart, it is advisable only to use it actively when it enables the work to be moved on decisively, as when a therapist's clear thinking is obstructed by the neediness of a patient whose demands parallel those of a child on a parent. When named, this can lead the patient to an insight regarding his or her difficulties of relating to others, particularly primary carers.

Otherwise it is most useful to remain aware of the particular way a patient behaves in the relationship and responds to the therapist's interventions positively or negatively and to keep in mind how this resembles his/her relationship to significant others in the past or in current relationships. The way the patient resists or defends against what is said, suggested or repeatedly emphasized by the therapist will find an echo in the latter's countertransference, which picks up unconscious signals relating to the anxiety, aggression or envy activated by the therapeutic process. It is this resonating that enables the therapist to tune in to what is not said but felt and to choose words carefully to become meaningful to the patient, hopefully triggering off memories or other material relating to the focal point.

For instance, there was the client who was anxious about having to address a meeting of strangers in her new job as a senior manager. Her domestic background was dysfunctional: her father, an alcoholic, was unpredictable and fellow family members were always yelling at each other. Her competent voice on the phone had acquainted me with the impressive persona of a performer, while in the session she presented as a quivering jelly with phobic fantasies of becoming speechless and ridiculed as a fool. By making her imagine the meeting and chosing how to dress, practising what to say and where to focus her eyes, she realized that she had often done this sort of thing before and had even felt a buzz once she had a captive audience hanging on her lips. It was the yelling voices that she had to still and pacify in her mind, and my calm voice she had to internalize for the event, which then enabled her to go forward and to address the meeting competently. The split between the competent performing self and the quivering child at the mercy of a difficult father had been stressful to sustain, yet when it was held together by me repeatedly she was enabled to cross the threshold safely. It became the parenting experience she had craved that temporarily banished the phobia. She told me at the end that she was hoping to become a counsellor herself when she had saved enough money to pay for the training. A complex therapeutic process of using an auxiliary ego, of identifying with and internalizing a parent figure had been completed, focusing on a current work situation and relating it to the painful past of the family scenario.

Whether it was enough to see her through future frightening events of a similar kind was difficult to gauge, but it seemed possible that she would seek help again if she faltered. It felt like the beginning and induction into a therapeutic journey. I had used my countertransference hunches to invoke her competent self and to set up an imaginative rehearsal of the feared future event, and in her persecutory anxieties she had forgotten that it had often proved easy in the past. Playing creatively with mother enabled her to face reality.

If the brief therapist is able to apply Malan's two triangles and thus to establish a psychodynamic diagram of each individual case of brief therapy fairly early on in the work, then the patient's material can be processed creatively to focus on and to unravel the problem that has caused him or her to get stuck. Identifying the anxieties, the defences against these and the hidden feelings that cause the anxieties will take the therapist a long way towards working with the second triangle that enables them to relate the past, the current external and the therapeutic relationships in a meaningful enough way to find a solution that may then produce a significant change.

Consider the case of a young man whose presenting problem is pathological jealousy and who remembers that he couldn't bear his parents watching him, because he felt he couldn't be himself when they did. He chooses girls who are attractive and slim and make everybody look when they are seen together, i.e. make him feel envied. It feels as if he cares more about the audience than the girls, and yet obsessive curiosity makes him snoop among their things for signs of other men. How does this relate to his mother, who seems to have been happily married to his father, and to his curiosity about the therapist's new flat? He chooses his girlfriends from among his colleagues – in order to be seen to be a potent and desirable man (which he may fear he isn't). The present five-session contract is the second in two years – like his present girlfriend, who is the second in two years. The solution that offers itself is a referral to long-term work with a woman in order to work out how to relate in a dyad and give himself over to an intimate relationship without an audience or a third party. The therapist's countertransference has alerted her to his fear of being seen and his obsessive curiosity about the inside of her flat/body. Is his jealousy a reaction formation against his incest wishes (to be like father)?

It may be useful at this point to invoke Christopher Bollas' concept of the 'transformational object', which means 'an object that is experientially identified by the infant with the process of the alteration of self experience' (1986: 92). From the first session the encounter with a therapist will set in train such a process, which happens because of the patient's need 'for a prolonged experience of successive ego transformations', which are identified with the therapist and based on 'the object's nominated capacity to resuscitate the memory of early ego transformation'. It is an object that is identified with the cumulative metamorphoses of the self in early infancy, and is sought all through life in order to 'surrender to it as a process that alters the self' (Bollas, 1986: 93). Whatever complicated transferences will emerge in the course of working together, this first object, which Winnicott (1965) called 'the environment mother' and Kohut (1977) 'the self object', will be the template for these. It determines the therapist's faith in the analytic process and facilitates the patient's experience of being held and altered by being in the analytic relationship. However briefly experienced, this 'regression' to a primary relationship will facilitate the first contact that establishes an engagement to undertake the joint task of 'thinking the unthinkable', of 'using the therapist's capacity to bring together hitherto meaningless fragments of the patient's mental and verbal elements into a thinking process, and communicate this back to the patient' (Coltart, 1986: 189).

With this we are in Bion country, and we are talking 'of a form of attention, of an act of faith' that must be, what he calls, 'unstained by any elements of memory or desire or sensation', of 'faith that there is an ultimate reality and truth, the unknown, unknowable, formless infinite, which can become at least partly known through evolution into objects of which the individual personality can become aware' (Coltart, 1986: 189).

Using these currently dominant analytic concepts, I am translating Malan's language and technique of focusing and interpreting with the help of the two triangles into an idiom that is based on meaning and intuition and encompasses the more mysterious and intuitive processes of dynamic therapy which the patient experiences as support and transformation, and the therapist facilitates through faith, attention and thinking. Though there is too little time in brief therapy to 'let the whole pattern emerge' (Coltart, 1986) as the basis for analysis, it seems to be possible with the help of faith and hope to achieve a mini-variation of the extended analytic process in which some of the transformation, metamorphosis and self-alteration can occur that is needed for the patient to 'feel better', i.e. on the way to something significantly changed.

For the brief therapist to feel satisfied with this 'mini-variation', s/he has to be 'unstained by any elements of memory or desire or sensation' in the sense of not regretting what cannot be (i.e. long-term work), for 'if his mind is preoccupied with what is or what is not said or with what he does or does not hope, it must mean that he cannot allow the experience to obtrude' (Bion, 1970: 41). To alter Bion's famous dictum into an exhortation of exercising emotional restraint is not to falsify its message for therapeutic emotional abstinence, rather to translate it from a 'formless infinity' into the time-limited scenario where transformations and metamorphoses cannot be repeated or 'successive', and yet, while limited in scope and extent, they can certainly become qualitative, too, rather than merely quantitative or cumulative. I see brief therapy as a vertical rather than as a horizontal experience, and as such capable of having a powerful impact on the patient's psyche, which will be briefly mobilized to its depths and enabled to release by trigger-effect much withheld material of memories and affect which can be reined into the focusing process.

The first phase

There is a significant link between the patient's search for the transformational object and the 'golden glow' of the 'honeymoon period' which Mann's model emphasizes as the decisive factor when setting up a promising time-limited therapy experience for the patient. His need for symbiotic and fusional experiences echoes the infant's first object-relationship needs, which are to do with his or her early self, ego formation and transformation. Like the environment mother, the therapist is instantly related to as an object that can be used for urgent self-repair, to satisfy a longing for symbiosis and merging, and to counteract anxieties and despair.

If the therapist is aware of this and a follower of Mann's model, his/her initial interventions will be geared to this symbiotic state, aiming to deepen it for a few sessions of positive omnipotent experience in which the patient will be attached to the therapist and transformed into a willing partner in the therapeutic alliance. Using the initial thrust of this 'honeymoon period' to get into a fast pace of therapeutic dialogue, they will be paying close attention to any opportunities for active therapeutic interventions.

If the therapist is a follower of Sifneos, who believed in using anxiety-provoking strategies in order to quickly elicit the patient's oedipal material, the symbiotic state will be cut short and curtailed to make way for the parrying and crossing of swords that induces the patient to become competitive with the therapist and enter into the full-scale oedipal rivalry that was avoided or denied in the primary relationships with father and mother. The aim is this time to arrive at a different, more positive resolution of the conflict and to be enabled to enter the post-oedipal phase in which three-person and other multipersonal relationships are possible and sustained. In other words, the transformational object becomes a challenging oedipal object that demands active and aggressive participation in a competition for first prize and allows no satisfaction of symbiotic or fusional desires for object relating, requiring the assertiveness and separateness that goes with growing ego strength. The therapist is experienced as hostile and demanding as well as someone to be emulated, and this makes for the characteristic oedipal mix, which can lead to a transformational experience of recognition (rather than triumph or defeat) if the therapist can help the patient across the oedipal threshold like the good enough father who claims the mother for himself while allowing the son equal status as a young adult.

In Mann's model there is now the crossing of a threshold into what he calls the 'middle period', when the patient is disillusioned by the therapist's withdrawal from symbiotic support and made to confront his/her central conflict as a fear of ambivalence and separation enacted with the therapist. When this is interpreted, it commonly leads to a flood of new material and memories from the past relating to the central issue and to a deepening of the search for solutions, rather than for the magic cure expected from symbiosis. But this may take some hovering on the threshold, some longing for dependence, even regression, as in Mahler's *rapprochement* phase, which marks a phase of ambivalent vaccillation between sallying back and forth, alternately clinging to and rejecting the mother, who finally should become a separate and whole object of integrated love and hate.

Specific middle period issues

The first stage of the brief therapy is concluded when the two participants have established a viable therapeutic alliance and have agreed to work together for a limited time on a limited goal that appears achievable and desirable to both. The transference should then be positive enough to encourage the patient to open up, confess, remember and reminisce within the focal area to a therapist who will attempt to interpret the material and relate it in meaningful ways to what has gone before so as to produce a fresh understanding. In its turn this will enable a continuous flow of further material, of insight and ideas connected to the focal area, which will thus be mapped out more and more. This is the stage after 'falling in love' in a relationship when an acquaintanceship is deepened with every contribution made by the players, but also complicated by the emergence of hostile or critical feelings, when some of the positive projections and expectations have to be withdrawn, and the experience of the other becomes more realistic, multicoloured and three-dimensional. In the therapy the focal problem is further delineated and elaborated in detail, amplified in its spatial and temporal dimensions, and constantly enriched by further emerging memories, new hypotheses, comments and ideas.

Usually there is a push to widen the focus, leading to dynamic processes of ambivalence, to painful issues of attachment and separation, and almost inevitably to the wish for an ongoing relationship with the counsellor who is receiving so much confidential information, trusting personal revelations and cherished or disturbing childhood material. The therapist's necessary non-gratification of this push and this wish will re-enforce and stoke the ambivalence, the disappointment and the incipient separation anxiety which becomes a maturational task at this transitional stage.

The middle phase becomes usually the provider of invaluable and necessary information as well as the growing point for the patient's autonomous self that will be needed for the achievement of a satisfactory ending. It is the alchemical cauldron in which many ingredients of narrative, fantasy and fact are combined into a fertile mix that can then be distilled into solution, decision, clarity of insight or psychic transformation. It has often been noted that during the middle phase the patient is suddenly enabled to make decisive changes in external relationships or behaviour patterns, will begin to understand his/her characteristic pattern of unhelpful relationships and experience with surprise surges of new energy, self-understanding or constructive solution behaviour unavailable before and indicative of a significant alteration of self-experience and assertiveness which is a sign of the creative changes expected. Whatever the number of sessions contracted the middle session or section is bound to become a decisive turning point, for better or for worse.

An example was the woman who had confessed to her counsellor that she had always been envious of her idealized and hence unmourned dead brother. She had then become able to tell her husband of this admission, whereupon he in turn confessed his own envy and thereby enabled her to become challenging with someone at work too, and resolutely to close her office door, which until then she had compulsively kept ajar as if to be compliantly available to all and sundry.

Another example was the employee who had made his way up slowly from the ranks in his firm, which was now threatening to make him redundant after decades of faithful service. Instead of the feared catastrophe, this became the opportunity for him to claim his independence and to embark on the realization of a long-held dream to start a business of his own. He exchanged boring security with creative self-expression by taking the risk to cut himself off from the parent employer and to try his luck as an adult in the world. A modern fairy-tale of the boy who went out into the world to learn fear!

It is surprising how often the middle section becomes the crystallization point of decision processes that had been long in the making or the clarification of long-standing confused anxieties, as if the anticipation of the approaching ending clears and focuses the minds of both participants to embrace essentials and realities. In the sense of 'something has to happen now', there is a choice – and a change.

If nothing happens and there is no sign of transformation, then the brief therapy may not have worked, as it has not mobilized the patient's rigid defensive patterns, stuck affects or entrenched behavioural positions, and the therapist may have to begin to think of a possible referral to help the patient continue the work that has been started, at a slower pace and with someone else. As the patient is usually told of this possibility in the assessment (or first) session, it is probably wise not to mention referral at this point, in case something might still happen at the last moment or, more likely, in case the patient might become depressed, cling to the therapist or walk out on the therapy, thus spoiling the effect of the planned ending. This might still be creative in the sense of enabling the patient to face the loss and separation experience with the therapist.

The finality of coming to an end of an agreed contract helps in that whatever has happened has to be accepted as the definitive outcome of the joint work. The patient knows that they can do it again if need be, and when they are dissatisfied or disappointed not much is lost except a potential belief in the effectiveness of therapy, i.e. they may not try again. This could be seen as a negative outcome, but it is not necessarily forever and with another therapist it might be different.

6

Ending Brief Therapy

Ever since James Mann (1973) introduced the notion of time-limited therapy, the question of when to end psychotherapeutic work with patients has taken on a new and challenging character. Before Mann, most attempts at shortening treatment adhered to the traditional notion that therapy ends when the work is done, i.e. when therapist and patient agree that they have done together what they set out to do at the beginning and that they have more or less achieved their mutual goal. Whether this was a piece of brief focal psychodynamic work, of cognitive problem-solving or of solution-focused short-term therapy, the required length of time was usually undetermined until the work had progressed to a point when a date for termination could be safely set, and implemented by mutual agreement.

Then Mann came up with the idea of making the ending a planned event and suggested short-term contracts for a specific length of time and for a limited number of sessions, in fact for 12 sessions (a number he says he chose more or less arbitrarily, though it relates of course to the calendar, and divides easily into threes and fours). His idea had the effect of revolutionizing the thinking about when and how to end psychotherapeutic treatment, whether of the long-term or the brief variety, and it also divided the camp of short-term practitioners vociferously for or against him by splitting it into believers and doubters. Mann's rationale for setting time limits was that experience had led him to believe that the longer therapists and patients stayed together, the less productive their work became due to complicated unconscious dependency and transference issues which inevitably develop as time goes on and produce a situation of inextricable enmeshment in which the notion of ending has no place, and in fact becomes frightening to contemplate. There is a strong wish for staying together for ever, and a wish for a perfect ending when all problems would be solved and separation would occur naturally and painlessly. Conversely, the enmeshment can be such that separation is unthinkable, because more and more problems arise, the task becomes circular, Sisyphean and endless. In this situation endings happen too soon or too late, for external or practical reasons and out of necessity rather than choice, and there is no knowing how much is enough and when to stop except abruptly, exhaustedly, or by giving up. Often one or the other partner dies, moves away, retires. Then there is a sense of something unfinished and unfinishable, of profound loss and deep sadness.

Nina Coltart talks about the oddity of ending a therapeutic relationship, of which

> it is said, quite justifiably, to be one of the most important relationships of one's life. All levels of object-relating, closeness, intimacy etc. are at the very heart of analytic therapy. . . . The most casual observer would have no difficulty in noting that here is a relationship of great richness and importance . . . that this absorbing relationship is often experienced as the central feature of the patient's life. . . . So what do we do? We bring it to an absolute end. And it is not an exaggeration to say that although they, the patients, know that this will happen, some patients experience the agreement to end as a death sentence. (1997: 149–50)

'Although they, the patients, know . . .'. Here, Mann and Coltart agree, and both of them insist that it is vital to make an ending total, once it is set, against all resistance, protest, anxiety and acting out. They both believe in the process. They disagree, however, in other vital points, in particular the issue of dependence. For Mann (and many other brief therapists), dependence is something to be avoided at all costs, because it prolongs the therapy unnecessarily. For Coltart and the long-term psychodynamic psychotherapists it is the moment when the patient begins to regress, when the transference unfolds and the transference neurosis has a chance to develop, which then will lead to all the complicated repeating, remembering and working through that is considered necessary to arrive at a resolution of the twisted object relationships and unworkable defences that the patient has been suffering from.

> The patient ceases to suffer in his ways of relating . . . and the acute but passing pains of insight take over from the personality problems presented at the beginning. Defences, of course, may have been taking years to build up and are only slowly dismantled, if necessary, to be supplemented by ego itself and by defences that are more resilient and healthy. (Coltart, 1997: 149–50)

Jeremy Holmes, in his article 'Too Early, Too Late' (1997), also sums up this defence-dismantling and ego-strengthening goal of ending when he says 'only when patients feel safe enough to give up their defences – accept their helplessness and dependence on the therapist – can they begin to progress towards an ending'; and, echoing Bowlby: 'A good ending is possible once a secure base has been established, therefore the process can be relatively brief' (i.e. when the patient's attachment pattern is basically satisfactory – as is the analyst's) (1997: 167).

Through dependence to independence – this traditional and still widely held view of how to bring about deep and lasting changes in the patient's psyche is radically questioned by Mann. His method, which, like all models of short-term therapy, was initially developed in order to cut patients' waiting lists, turned out to have surprisingly good results just because he discouraged dependence and regression, and built on the patient's knowledge of a planned ending from the beginning.

> The knowledge that the treatment will be finite and limited has a profound effect on the course of the therapy. The patient knows that there is little time to waste and this encourages him or her to work hard in the therapy. At the same time the patient knows that the treatment will end in a fairly short period of time and this allays fears of becoming excessively dependent on the treatment and on the therapist. It is the general experience of therapists doing brief psychotherapy that it is a richer, more affect-laden experience for patient and therapist. (Mann, 1973: 10)

This is a fairly dogmatic way of defending a preferred way of working, but the dogma of setting a firm time frame right at the beginning in order to speed up and maximize therapeutic results has been borne out by many experiences of dramatic changes and it was confirmed by Mann's own research findings. The big question, however, remains how lasting these results are, and whether there may not be more likelihood of erosion and tendency for relapse with this method than with the painstaking and repetitive long-term style. All this will require much more quantitative research and qualititative follow-ups before Mann's claims can be fully verified.

Because of this difficulty of quantifying and qualifying outcome in terms of its lasting effects, the validity of Mann's method can only be accepted on the basis of whether it works. Drawing on T.S. Eliot's poetic statement 'in my beginning is my end', it represents a workable hypothesis of psychic functioning based on the realization that separation anxiety is at the heart of much psychic avoidance, malfunctioning and unsuccessful object-relating, preventing, as it does, the establishment of basic trust (Erikson, 1950), and of a secure base (Bowlby, 1988). Focusing on and addressing the separation anxiety in the patient's presenting problems is at the core of Mann's method. He claims that only by setting a fixed time limit will the ambiguity about ending treatment, which he noticed in so many current psychotherapies, be eliminated. This ambiguity can be used as a defence by both patient and therapist in order to avoid confronting the inevitability of separation and death. As a result of the unconscious resistance to termination, the majority of long-term psychotherapies end without a planned and mutually agreed-upon termination and often without adequate working through of the separation.

This then becomes the central therapeutic feature of Mann's method, and its aim is for the patient to 'internalize the therapist as a replacement or substitute for the earlier ambivalent object', '. . . This time the internalization will be more positive (never totally so), less anger-laden and less guiltladen, thereby making separation a genuine maturational event' (Mann, 1973: 36). In effect, unconscious conflicts and anxieties are made conscious and the experience of separation from an attachment object, so far considered unbearable and unthinkable and hence always defended against and denied, now turns out to be bearable and completable. This brave following-through of a feared emotional experience enables the patient to mourn the loss, first in the presence of the object and then on his or her own.

I believe there may be a fallacy at the bottom of this argument in that it skips over the simple and self-evident fact that it is easier to separate from someone after 12 meetings, no matter how rich, than after a relationship that may have been lasting for years. Not everybody will be capable of quickly grasping and experiencing the symbolism on which Mann's method is based. The loss of someone with whom one has been in a long-standing, nurturing and enriching relationship or of someone with whom one has been for years in a rivalrous, competitive relationship steeped in envy and jealousy cannot be equated with the loss of an empathic therapist of three months' duration, no matter how intense and rich in symbolism the brief involvement may have been. And when there is the knowledge that it will end quite soon after it has begun, a defensive reaction of 'I may as well not bother to get involved' can be expected in those people who fear intimacy and are slow to engage or unwilling to commit themselves.

Nevertheless, the strategy of planned endings and time limits has a beauty of its own and it ensures a predictability of outcome that is lacking from most long-term work. The promise of richness and intensity is not vain; it is rooted in the ancient wisdom of *carpe diem*, beautifully illustrated in Andrew Marvell's poem 'To His Coy Mistress':

> Had we but world enough, and time,
> This coyness, Lady, were no crime. . . .
> But at my back I always hear
> Time's wingèd chariot hurrying near,
> And yonder all before us lie
> Deserts of vast eternity . . .
> Now therefore, while the youthful hue
> Sits on thy skin like morning dew . . .
> Now let us sport us while we may . . .

> Rather at once our Time devour,
> Than languish in his slow-chapt power.
> Let us roll all our strength, and all
> Our sweetness, up into one ball:
> And tear our pleasures with rough strife,
> Thorough the iron gates of life.
> Thus, though we cannot make our sun
> Stand still, yet we will make him run.

The comparison of the early stage of a love relationship and its consummation with a piece of brief time-limited therapy is apt, in that it reflects the successive stages and the intense interaction of a rapidly developing and changing relationship, while holding the awareness of passing time sharply in focus. In other words, striking the iron while it is hot, the outcome will necessarily be rapid change. The task completed, there will by necessity be an end and a separation, until the next task requires a new work contract.

Should the difficulty of a task be expressed in the length of a contract, or is there, as Mann assumes, an optimal length of contract tailored to each therapeutic task? Opinions will differ, but the knowledge of a time-limited contract will always influence and shape the expected outcome, the intensity of the therapeutic experience and the nature of defences a patient will use to deal with it.

> As a general principle, the outcome of time-limited therapy is likely to be best if there can be some reaching of the depressive position and the recognition and expression of ambivalence, both in relation to the therapy and to outside life. Idealisation of the therapist or the work is therefore likely to mean that the gains may not be sustained. The ending period will therefore need to work on the themes of ambivalence and separation. (Coate, M.A., 1993, unpublished notes)

This reflect's Mann's theme of disappointment with the therapist and of the necessary progression of the therapeutic couple from symbiosis and omnipotence to ambivalence towards the therapist, which he dates from the second phase onwards, when the patient's habitual relationship problems emerge and his/her working through starts.

Melanie Klein considered that ending therapy is a first step towards maturation, towards the depressive position and the achievement of weaning. It means coping with the rage at mother's capacity to come and go and to wean as she pleases. It also marks the achievement of 'unit status' (Winnicott). And in the words of Bion, the absent breast is a beginning to the stimulus of thought ('A theory of thinking', 1967):

> I shall limit the term 'thought' to the mating of a preconception with a frustration. The model I propose is that of an infant whose expectation of a breast is mated with a realization of no breast available for satisfaction.

> This mating is experienced as a no-breast, or 'absent' breast inside. The next step depends on the infant's capacity for frustration: in particular it depends on whether the decision is to evade frustration or to modify it. . . . If the capacity for toleration of frustration is sufficient the 'no-breast' inside becomes a thought and an apparatus for 'thinking' it develops . . . (1967: 111–12)

In other words, Freud's words to be exact, ending therapy presupposes the capacity to tolerate separation and loss, which also characterizes the resolution of the Oedipus complex. This capacity, whether we consider it the result of a positive experience of weaning, or of the acceptance of the parents as a united couple without feeling excluded and jealous, is hardwon and tends to get lost again and again, whenever regressive longing and unbearable anxieties become overwhelming. Equally, the fruits of a brief therapy might get lost.

Yet once experienced, there is at least the knowledge of its existence, and repeated experiences of facing and surviving separations will eventually establish the mature position of 'letting go' in place of defensive denial or avoidance. The patient who walks out before the agreed ending or misses the last session has not reached the maturity necessary to face the pain of saying goodbye for ever, and does not strive for the courageous stoicism of which Seneca speaks when he says, 'as it is with a play so it is with life: what matters is not how long it lasts, but how good it is. Make sure you round it off with a good ending.' He or she is deliberately leaving a loose end, when avoiding the farewell.

Of course, it takes two to make a 'good ending' in therapy, and the therapist's capacity to tolerate separation and loss is as necessary and as important as the patient's willingness to separate. The challenge for the brief therapist is that s/he needs to make the best use of the short time, in which all sorts of tasks have to be accomplished, while acknowledging the strong feelings due to attachment and loss, and also looking backwards over what has been done (or not done) and forwards into the future. The last session is in some respect of equal importance as the first, in that, true to the motto 'in my beginning is my end', many issues noted at assessment and discussed in the course of the work together will inevitably resurface and will have to be dealt with for the second time, hopefully with a more lasting effect and better understanding.

It is inevitable that during this ending previous experiences of endings and loss are remembered and emotionally reactivated, which is a chance to compare and contrast situations in terms of unfinished business, painful memories, regret, remorse and relief, and then to establish what can now be done to make amends or to work through emotions so far avoided. Often there is also a realization that ending is not as difficult as feared and that it can also become energizing and clear the way to new beginnings.

Another part of the wrapping-up process is the need to think about what has been achieved as well as what has not been achieved in terms of goals set at the beginning and of pressing issues that may have emerged in the middle period and had to be set aside to keep going with and concentrate on the work in hand. Rather than considering it a failure, the realization that there is further work to be done can be flagged up as a future objective, as a task to take away and complete in the hereafter, or as a pointer to the desirability of referral for further work, with another therapist. There is the option of deferment, and this may lead to a discussion of what the patient can do now, whether s/he feels strong enough to leave, fortified with the results of good work done, and can be left to ponder the options on their own, making independent choices, autonomous referrals or enquiries, even give the changes achieved a chance to permeate as if by osmosis into the psychic system and activate the natural self-regulatory forces of the psyche, due to the inevitable internalization of the therapeutic process.

In reviewing the work done together, the therapist will look out for signs and glimpses of the depressive position, of individuation and of the psychological-mindedness that will enable the patient in future to self-analyse emotional difficulties and conflicts as and when they arise, and to persist in working through these by linking experiences dynamically and thinking about them analytically. In the course of such reviewing, many a patient will indicate that their brief thera-peutic experience has made them realize that they can have more of the same when the need arises, and this thought will be like a talis-man to carry with them into the future. I would call this experience the priming function of brief therapy, the induction not only into a new way of thinking, but also into a new willingness to seek help and contemplate further therapy as and when the need arises.

Referring on

After the priming, the referral-on! If it is not immediately apparent at assessment, in the course of brief therapy (whether the contract is for 5 or 10 or 15 sessions) the patient's level of disturbance will become apparent to the experienced therapist, who carefully consults his/her countertransference for signs of increasing defensiveness, anxiety or confusion in the patient resulting from the pressure, pace and emo-tional demands of focusing, probing and interpreting. The therapist will decide to use the available time for a thorough ongoing assess-ment rather than for active uncovering and interpretative therapy, and will carefully monitor the development of regressive transference phenomena with a view to what might become necessary in the long term. The question arises whether the brief contract should be honoured even if little constructive work can be done apart from the 'priming' that will hook the patient into a therapeutic dialogue about the fears and symptoms which characterize his/her disturbed mental functioning and also to make the patient experience a containing therapeutic relationship. Depending on the severity of the condition and the rigidity of the defences exhibited by the patient, an instant referral-on (without completing the contract) might produce a panic reaction of traumatic intensity or increase the existing sense of futility, disconnectedness and hopelessness, while the experience of therapeutic interest may produce curiosity, a sense of containment, even incipient hopes, and can then pave the way for a successful referral – provided the therapist manages the existing transference so that it functions as a stepping stone rather than develops into an attachment that becomes difficult to let go of when the transfer to another therapist for longer-term work is attempted.

Referral-on can, of course, be experienced as being rejected, passed on, or declared difficult rather than feeling cared for and wanted. Therefore it needs to be well prepared for and mutually agreed, so that the patient really wants it him/herself rather than merely appeasing the therapist by being compliant. Quite often a referral may be set up and then is not taken up, or just used by the patient as a splitting device. Then the sense of disappointment can be great, for all concerned, including the putative referee. Delicate transference issues abound, connected with parenting or authority problems, with matching and resistance, and the crossing of a referral threshold will always require hand-holding and good anxiety-management. It is a journey into the unknown for all participants, akin to adoption or fostering, fraught with feelings of anxiety, abandonment and anger.

When brief therapists declare that they have achieved significant results even with very severe conditions, they may be saying many different things. By discouraging dependence, they are careful not to get near the patient's main areas of disturbance and focus on their ego strength rather than their unconscious anxieties and defences against these. By 'mobilizing affect' Davanloo encourages the patient's aggression and then contains it firmly by his own aggressive interpretations in a parenting sort of way. This is cathartic, but is it also curative in the long run, i.e. will it enable the patients in future to contain and manage their anxieties, aggressiveness and destructiveness themselves? Facing them once with the therapist will certainly be salutary, but is this enough to establish a truly integrated mode of conflict resolution and anxiety management, and does it take into account the powerful forces of erosion and repetition compulsion which operate in the unconscious? Quite possibly, the brief therapist often ends his/her work before s/he uncovers the depths of a patient's disturbance, by avoiding the intimacy of a relationship that most likely is the painful source of that individual's pathological mental functioning, and, in other words, by not heeding or interpreting the transference in which we believe that psychic disturbance manifests itself. This avoidance tactic allows an affective therapeutic intervention based on cognitive, problem-solving strategies, which may make a temporary difference to the patient's behavioural functioning, but will not touch the deeper levels of his/her psychic world which may be crying out for help.

On the other hand, it may well be a therapist's unconscious anxiety which triggers off a patient's disturbed behaviour in the therapeutic interaction, and the former's inability to offer containment will mean that the patient is not helped to metabolize his or her overwhelming fears. I am thinking of a supervisee with whom every patient showed disturbed behaviour as if they took on or anticipated a behaviour pattern from her, and for whom the containment both of supervision and of a circumscribed focus was essential to get some helpful therapeutic work started and done.

Am I saying that both the therapist and the patient have to be sufficiently 'healthy' to engage in the demanding task of a brief therapeutic contract, and that the more disturbed personalities, with little ego strength and a weak sense of self, should not be treated in this mode? Yes and no. Yes, in that a brief therapeutic involvement may never touch the parts which other, more intensive and ongoing therapies are often able to reach, and thus may not achieve any meaningful and truly lasting change. No, in that any therapy, however brief, has a chance of reaching a patient and of establishing a therapeutic contact which might produce results, if only to open a window into a closed and haunted world which will throw some new light, dispel some old fears and enable the sufferer to open up some more later or begin to hope that s/he can get help, after all.

Successive contracting

I have talked before of successive contracting, of what one might call 'intermittent therapeutic life support', which could be shorter or longer periods of therapeutic intervention whenever living becomes difficult and the patient once again requires a helping hand, a listening ear or an understanding companion temporarily to share and exchange experiences beyond their own capabilities. If this remains a

genuine future perspective, then any remaining doubt, disappointment and inconclusiveness will be easier for them to shoulder and to
take away with them for further reflection on parting. Patients
should be given the opportunity to discuss this possibility and take
away with them the hope that they can repeat or renew the therapeutic experience they have just ended.

Follow-ups

There remains the possibility of a follow-up, which would enable both
participants to check out after a suitable period of time what effect the
therapy has had on the patient's ongoing life and how s/he has been
able to use the insights, exploring, reminiscing, problem-solving and
unburdening in the intervening time. As far as I know, the therapeutic
follow-up (though, of course, a well-known tradition in medical
practice) was introduced into psychotherapy by the Balint–Malan
team and has since been used extensively in the field of brief and time-
limited therapy for the conduct of outcome studies, to establish the
lasting or proliferating effects of changes achieved during therapy and
to enable the patients to monitor themselves in the presence of their
erstwhile therapists, who on this occasion will function as observers
rather than therapists. They would look out for evidence of continued
working through on the part of the patient, of progress in the focal
area, of increased ego functioning and of lessening of symptoms,
while any recurrence or relapse into previous complaints and conditions would necessitate the cautious reassessment of any hopes or
fears expressed when the therapy ended. Further follow-ups at regular
intervals can be helpful; though probably prolonging the transference
involvement, they often strengthen the patient's resolve to sustain
their self-analysing mode of working through the material that might
be emerging in the wake of their therapeutic experience, and they can
become a positive supportive system, as long as dependency or
addictiveness is avoided.

There are some therapists who have no scruples about transferring
patients into long-term work after the time-limited contract is ended
if they feel that the patient is ready for this and that his or her welfare
is at stake. Their arguments for this action would be cogent if some
new problems had arisen that absolutely required a continuation of
the work, e.g. when there is renewed trauma, or when a new deadline
has been set for something that was part of the focal area of work
and hence requires finishing. An example of carrying on beyond the
agreed deadline is the transfer of patients into a counsellor's private
practice from the GP surgery which only funds 5 or 6 sessions per
patient at a time. With adequate preparation and review of the

original assessment this can be vital and successful, depending, of course, on the therapist's real and acknowledged motives (in particular, a thorough self-examination of these in the light of a possible need to keep one's practice going). After obtaining the patient's agreement, the ongoing transference situation will have to be taken into account, as there may be a serious loss of authority, due to the inconsistency in contracting, and a noticeable change in pace, style and venue. The ending of the transference to the doctor and the practice will also have to be noted and addressed.

Finally, it is essential to treat the ending phase of the time-limited therapy in the manner of an accelerating countdown and to remind the patient from session to session how many more times they are still going to meet. By clearly marking the approach of the end, the patient's emotional responses to the impending separation will be sharpened to the point of snapping, which can make the actual ending a relief all round, expressing itself in tears, the sharing of most precious confidences, or the determined bracing of oneself for the solitude to come.

Patients are often anxious and impatient to know what happens in the last session. How will it be different? What can be done? What else can be said? This anxiety seems to be about a fear of becoming speechless, embarrassed, tongue-tied, as much as of losing control and of being overwhelmed by emotion. And it can be a denial of the particular pain of ending therapy, of losing a valued relationship and of crossing a threshold into the unknown rather than merely ending a session which promises continuation. But mostly it expresses the extent of one's disbelief that it is humanly possible to face with adequate means an experience which comes close to abandonment, annihilation and falling forever, and provokes the most primitive and archaic fears.

7

Case Studies

Making a difference

I was referred a young woman by an agency which provided counselling to companies. The client was impatient to be seen instantly, and rang back as soon as she had been given the counsellor's phone number, indicating that she was in a crisis and desperate to get help. After some negotiation she agreed to come before work the very next morning. Her American voice sounded competent and fierce on the telephone, very much in contrast to the wisp of a woman who turned up in a taxi, on the dot and immaculately dressed in a power suit, who sat down and instantly talked about overwhelming anxiety, panic attacks and sleeplessness caused by her being in between jobs and having to meet a group of 20 people in a few days who would be reporting to her in her new capacity as head of human resources.

The contrast between competent persona and anxious young woman afraid of losing control and of disintegrating was the main theme of the assessment. This established an early history of being the youngest of three daughters of American parents who was always 'trying to be good' to appease her irritable father and getting her parents' approval, and had become a professional highflier while living in permanent self-doubt and anxiety of not being smart enough, of being made a fool of, or failing at important tasks. It also established that this 35-year-old successful manager of people (in her last job she was responsible for 3,000 people, in her future job there would be 1,700) was very clinging and needy in her sexual relationships with men, and that her present affaire with a divorced top executive of the firm she was leaving was in the doldrums because he wouldn't 'commit', i.e. was resisting her wish to get married and settle down together.

This precarious existence on two levels and the habitual splitting of professional competence and personal insecurity was generating high levels of persecutory anxiety and had apparently reached a crisis point because she was waiting in between jobs for the new one to begin, and had become overwhelmed by fantasies of failing because she was temporarily unable to use her habitual defences of gratifying busy-ness and hard work. I picked up an urgency and appeal to be looked after, held together, given the ego strength she lacked, being supported and comforted in a situation of intense anxiety in which she was afraid of breaking down.

Interestingly, she had decided to leave the present job because she wanted to get away from a woman who had dominated her professional life for 10 years, who had been difficult to work for, but had also got her the job in the first place, thus suggesting that she believed in her on condition that she was good. She had now come to another woman for counselling, though briefly, from whom she hoped to gain the strength needed to get into her new job, but, as I pointed out, we could only meet five times 'on the firm'. It emerged that in New York she had had a therapist for five years, which explained her instant linking of childhood anxiety with the present situation, her willingness to be open to probing questioning and the technical language she used when she spoke about the 'phobias' (of being in groups and committees, of flying, driving, heights, etc.), which she wanted us to focus on.

In terms of psychodynamic assessment, there was recent onset, some psychological-mindedness, evidence of persecutory anxiety, splitting, defensive activity, longing for validation and for being taken care of. I saw two warning signs: the propensity to become clinging in an intimate situation and the defensive compliance in order to be liked. In her question: 'What shall I do?' I sensed surrender to parental advice, and the difficulty I had in formulating an intervention seemed to indicate a difficulty in thinking due to the anxiety projected into me. I decided to try an exercise of imaginatively preparing for the dreaded event by going over her worst fears and making her imagine the specifics of the meeting, memorizing her five-minute talk, what she was going to wear, where she would sit or stand, and this guided imaginary enactment of the anticipated group meeting seemed to give her relief as an experience of jointly holding and facing the persecutory uncertainties which had tortured her so obsessively.

Focusing squarely on the phobic anxiety – an echo of fearing to fail her stern parent – and on concrete ways of overcoming it – i.e. on successful solutions to past dilemmas – enabled her to commit herself firmly to the brief contract with me, as an immediate solution to the situation in which she was floundering, though she tried to persuade me to take her on for longer work when I suggested she might well need some more therapy after ending our work together. She dropped this suggestion quickly when I said I would have to refer her on, and then she compliantly added that she was thankful for my help, agreeing to honour our contract for four more sessions, which would see her firmly into her new job and thus become a piece of crisis management.

My assessment hypothesis was of a schizoid young woman who was trying to manage high levels of anxiety by desperately proving to herself and others that she was competent, in control and capable of managing other chaotic lives, while secretly yearning to be recognized, looked after and allowed to hand herself over to another. The brief therapy could only name her dependency and attachment pattern, while enabling her to survive and manage a temporary crisis with the help of therapeutic containment, and finding a temporary solution by talking about her fears in order to manage them sufficiently to face and go through what she so dreaded. The uncertain relationship with the reluctant boyfriend became the subsidiary problem, as did the decision about buying a house, which would have meant committing herself fully to her adopted country and finally separating from a family which had always withheld support unless she was 'good' and managed their chaos.

I was of course aware that her condition was quite serious in that the splitting of manic performance and psychological dependency needs was a fragile defence that periodically broke down to give way to persecutory anxieties of phobic intensity, thus necessitating avoidance of situations of physical and psychological exposure that repeated infantile experiences of abandonment and helplessness.

Believing that an experience of surviving unscathed by being lent my auxiliary ego would amount for her to a confirmation of her own strength in adversity and reduce the clinging onto the boyfriend, I entered quite confidently into the brief therapy with her with the limited goal of focusing on the triangle of conflict and addressing some of her hidden feelings behind the sky-high anxieties that made her feel mad when she was alone. In the following sessions she explored her ambivalent feelings about her family, whom she had way outstripped in terms of professional performance and yet secretly envied because they were still together, all married and constantly yelling at each other, making her feel guilty for going away and earning lots of money.

She described her feelings of exclusion and loneliness when she was away from them and of exasperation when she was with them (as during a short holiday in Florida which she funded for her mother and sisters in order to feel one of them), and the perennial fear of not being good enough in spite of vast efforts at pleasing and getting approval for her achievements. It emerged that life had always been an effort for her, being good, the peacemaker in the family, the academic achiever, and that work was a repetition of this. She was longing for a less stressful life, and had a fantasy of becoming a counsellor, like me, working from home and doing what she wanted. I was aware of the idealization and identification with me and of the complexities of her emotional conflict, torn between regressive long-ings and age-appropriate wishes for stability and mature relation-ships. In the third session she was still racked by nocturnal panic attacks and made me feel called upon to comfort and hold her. She had found herself envious of her sisters and the apparent closeness of her family, from which she felt excluded away in England, wishing that she could resolve her stressful personal situation and lose her fears. There was the theme of impossible ambition, which produced a constant sense of failure. The fear of failing this therapy was as palpable as the anxiety about starting the new job, in which her two predecessors had failed.

This was a typical middle-period situation, struggling with issues of attachment and separation, of autonomy, ambivalence and insecurity, which had revealed their origins in parental neglect, in the impossibly high demands and expectations to perform felt by the child and the young woman in order to be acceptable. However, there had been a change: the reiteration of her dream of becoming a counsellor now felt more like a competitive challenge than like compliance, and the firmly expressed knowledge that she would be able to do her new job indicated an emergence of self-assurance that implied the possibility of separation from me.

By the next session she had crossed the difficult threshold into the new job successfully, though with an enormous effort, and was now afraid of managing the three-month probation period, in which she had to build up a new team, sack some old and employ some new assistants, and get on top of a backlog of work while being observed and assessed. There was a new note of almost pride, of 'I can manage this', mingled into the excitement and anxiety, of rising to new challenges, though it was not the managing of people or tasks but what might be thought of her that had always been the issue. The return to brisk activity had brought with it a noticeable change to self-confidence, though now I felt anxious as if she had saddled me with something unwanted, and as if I was one of her new employees who had to show what she can do. I also caught a glimpse of something fierce that had been regained, and identified the off-hand manner as a workable defence that strengthened her determination to be tough and succeed.

No more panic attacks, no suicidal depression or sense of failure, but competence and determination, and while asking me for strategies to deal with the ongoing uncertainty this was no longer done in the appealing girlish manner but in a more professional, businesslike way as if a request among equals. The crisis over, her ego strength regained, she faced the knowledge of one more session calmly, as if it were another piece of difficult, but manageable business. This attitude made the ending a gratifying experience of having achieved what we set out to do, and of reviewing where she was now – with me, with the job, in her personal life. The latter had not been the area of focus, yet there was also a marked change in her dealings with her boyfriend, who had revealed his own anxieties and was showing a willingness to move in with her, which seemed a function of her recovered self-control as much as of the weathering of the anxiety crisis which had made him anxious about committing himself. Whether this was an example of flight into health or of bouncing back into equilibirum after a wobble remained a question on my mind.

I had previously suggested referring her on for further work on her anxieties and childhood issues, and once again she seemed interested in this, though again regretting that because of the agency policy, I could not remain her counsellor. She had found herself talking to me when she became anxious and had found this very helpful, which made parting difficult and tinged her compliance with regret. I realized that the idealization had given way to ambivalence, and though having become reliant on me and identified to the point of some incipient internalization, she also was determined to let me go without betraying her true feelings about this brief and containing intense relationship. Interestingly she wanted to finish early in the last session, ostensibly because she was getting uneasy to get back to work and prepare for a meeting, but more likely because she wanted to cut short the unease and anxiety about parting. This was formal and polite, always the good girl.

I had an indication of her real feelings when I heard that she had not taken up the referral that had been arranged for her. Probably she was angry or felt rejected by me and expressed this by rejecting the referral. Also, she must have found herself able once again to use the frenetic work activities and the work satisfaction as a defence to manage her obsessional anxieties. Moreover, she had completed the therapeutic contract – whatever positive or negative feelings she felt for me could be shelved.

As a piece of solution-focused brief therapy, the work was fairly successful – helping the client manage her phobic anxieties by seeing and holding her through a work and personal crisis, exploring some of the hidden feelings behind the panic, the fear of failure and the obsessional worrying, enabling her to regain her professional equilibrium and to make a new start in a high-powered job, which she had dreaded to the point of panic. As a piece of brief psychodynamic counselling it may have made a meaningful difference in that the client had an opportunity to link her severe persecutory anxiety state with childhood experiences of abandonment and her professional highflying with her life-long attempts to get her family's approval, and to understand the ensuing tensions as the product of this defensive 'good girl' behaviour. Considering the severity of her anxiety state, the five-session contract provided the necessary containment to see her through this paranoid episode and into calmer water, but there was no guarantee that it had equipped her with enough ego strength to weather the next potential crisis, to manage her anxieties by herself in future and to hold the tensions creatively.

As so often in brief counselling, the counsellor felt sad about not being able to take the client further, that she had to let go without knowing the outcome and wondering whether there was a transferential issue in the client's not taking up the referral suggestion. However, the knowledge that she had found therapeutic help twice and would be able to find it again eased the parting, and it felt that this therapeutic chapter in a life had ended promisingly, though it could be no more than a stepping stone towards continuing individuation.

A case of successive contracting

A client asked for a second five-session contract three years after her first brief therapy within the context of an employment assistance scheme, and requested to be seen by the same counsellor, which was granted.

She was a Canadian woman in her fifties who had worked for many years in the information technology department of a worldwide charity organization, work which she found stressful and not always validated. The first bout of counselling had focused on her tendency to sabotage herself and never to complete any task. This had led to criticisms at work which she experienced as 'attacking', and which was making her feel insecure and depressed. She had come full of suicidal thoughts and fears of breakdown, no longer able to hold herself together, appealing for what she called 'cognitive therapy', by which she meant an understanding of what was going on in her inner world. The counsellor encouraged her to tell her story, which was a relief as telling it, apparently as if for the first time, made her realize how the dramatic events of her life linked up and why she had always felt so insecure. Sexual abuse in early childhood had started her on a pattern of promiscuous, short-lived or perverse sexual relationships, moving from country to country until she settled down in England with a husband whom she had met in South Africa, by whom she had two children and who left her after a few years to fend for herself. After some more short-lived relationships she eventually found herself alone, with her children grown up and departed and work becoming the centre of her life. Always insecure, prone to recurring depressions accompanied by suicidal thoughts and one unsuccessful overdose, she had sought psychiatric and therapeutic help before, once in an analytical group, but she had never stuck to anything for long, while finding temporary relief in complementary medicine of different kinds.

Obviously quite disturbed, there was a toughness and tenacity about her which enabled her to carry on working in the same organization, though often feeling paranoid when she felt 'attacked' or militantly defending herself against all comers. She carried on a vendetta against her daughter, who had come out as a lesbian and lived in Paris with a woman of whom the client felt fiercely jealous. Relations with other members of her family were fraught or had been cut off, underlining her pervasive sense of being abandoned, which had its roots in childhood.

The work in the first bout of counselling had focused on her sabotaging herself and on her inability to complete anything. Against the odds, she managed to complete the contract, aquiring some understanding of her self-destructiveness and of her tenacity to survive on her own. There was an attempt at referring her on, which was not taken up, and yet also a sense of completion, as she had for once not sabotaged an offer of help, and gained some self-confidence as a result.

When she availed herself for a second time of her organization's free counselling scheme for employees, she indicated that her first experience of brief therapy had been positive and that she wanted another instalment of a treatment which had helped her solve some of her problems. This time the focus was agreed to be work-related, as a situation had arisen in which she felt paranoid and afraid of being made redundant because her job description had been significantly changed in a recent organizational restructuring to include tasks she was not equipped to perform, and this required her to undergo a skills test which she was afraid of failing.

Once again, she felt depressed and suicidal, afraid of breakdown and full of persecutory anxiety, appealing to be held together and helped to acquire a 'positive mindset' which would see her through the time of uncertainty until a decision was made on her professional future. The counsellor acknowledged her anxiety and decided to encourage her to think constructively about the options she had in terms of attempting to retain her job, of asking to be redeployed, or of using redundancy to try something new. This suggestion worked extremely well, as she realized how reluctant she was at her age to retrain or to leave the work she had done for so long and felt she was best at.

Having initially sabotaged the homework she was given at the end of the first session, she became keen to work in the next sessions on the various options she had and on actively pursuing a strategy to fight for her rights and for her job. But she also discovered that with luck the situation could be used to implement a plan that she had been hatching for some time and that was now taking clearer shape as a result of talking to her union and to some visiting Canadian cousins who encouraged her to return to her homeland. She would be turning 60 at the end of the following year and realized if she played her cards right she could retire on the basis of redundancy money and the sale of her house, settle in Canada, where housing was cheaper than in London, and apply for the course in social anthropology which she had been dreaming of doing for years. This would mean returning to her roots in more than one sense of the word – returning to the country of her childhood and researching actively into her family history as the descendant of a Native American tribe which after a century of persecution was now finding its voice and taking its place in the politics of its country. It would certainly involve facing memories and regrets, tying up loose ends and mourning losses she had run away from and defended against up to now.

From the third session onwards this plan was slowly taking shape, implying a careful consideration of its consequences for her children (for whom she wanted to obtain Canadian citizenship), and for herself in terms of leaving her country of choice to return to the country she had fled as a young adult. It would be an opportunity to reclaim and mend her broken life in a meaningful way, and perhaps to repair some of the early damage she had been suffering from for so long, and had been avoiding to face squarely for fear of breaking down irretrievably. A homecoming of a special kind, promising integration, reconciliation and understanding.

As we were talking about all this, always carefully considering the realities of the plan and the possibility of it not materializing, I kept an eye on what was going on in the present, at her workplace and between us; and in the final session, when she reported the death of a person with whom she had been in a therapeutic group years ago and the imminent departure of her most supportive work colleague, there was a poignant sadness about our ending before she had had a decision about her job and had not had time to make a definite commitment to her retirement plans.

But some things were definite. She knew that she did not want to have more intensive therapy at this time as she was lacking the support network she knew she needed to sustain such an undertaking, while having a realistic knowledge of her underlying depression and 'insecurity', of which the persecutory anxieties relating to the job situation were a clear sign. She also knew that our work together had strengthened her resolve to pursue an active course of finding a positive solution to the work situation she found herself in, which was not of her own making, but might somehow be turned to her advantage.

In this respect the work fulfilled the main conditions for solution-focused brief therapy, where the client is encouraged to activate solution behaviour and enabled to find her own solution to a presenting problem that she had found intractable on her own. As a short piece of psychodynamic counselling it demonstrated that some significant change can be brought about by focusing on a defined work problem which had produced fear of breakdown and led to suicidal ideation, a recurrent condition which had occasioned a previous request for help four years ago that had successfully contained similar paranoid anxieties. This time, while linking with but deliberately not addressing the depressive anxieties due to early abandonment and abuse, the work consisted in thinking about possible options, i.e. in mobilizing ego strength and encouraging imaginative playing with ideas in the safe therapeutic container. This led to the reconnecting with and attempted integration of the client's troubled origins as well as a constructive perspective on her future, a major step forward in the therapeutic individuation process that may have been started by the first therapy instalment when the spectre of breakdown had also been banished and containment of persecutory anxieties achieved.

In terms of the transference situation, the counsellor seems to have been remembered and carried over internally from the previous meetings, indicating positive experiences of her as a 'self-altering transformative object' (Bollas) which could be used as support and thinking aid at a time of crisis, while feeling attacked and helpless in the face of imagined and real persecution at work. While somewhat contemptuously dismissing the five-session employment assistance programme model as 'sticking plaster', and also unwilling to attempt any long-term therapy, the client demonstrated the existence of hope that a brief therapeutic intervention of the same kind as last time might be helpful again in overcoming a crippling depression and paranoid fears of being got at. The repeated request was 'to change my mindset', i.e. to be enabled to think constructively, to overcome the persecutory anxieties and the self-destructiveness which had bedogged her life and once again threatened to lead to sabotaging herself. Turning this around in five sessions was an example of therapeutic containment, i.e. of transformation and change while interacting creatively with another.

As an example of successive contracting, this case could be looked at as one more piece in a chain of fruitful therapeutic interventions which helped the client weather recurrent life-cycle crises. The first time there was a difficulty of separating constructively from a grown-up child and accepting her life as a single divorced woman. This time, the life task was getting used to the approach of retirement, letting go of her self-definition as a competent working woman and finding a creative solution to an insecure and uncertain work situation. Using the counselling as a secure base from which to explore realistic ways forward and to manage crippling persecutory and depressive anxieties affirmed the resourcefulness and tenacity of a personality who had learnt to survive, with the intermittent help of others and despite her quite severe emotional disturbance. It could be said that the psychodynamic input acted as a reinforcement of the good internal object that had been established as a result of the first contract and with its help some change became possible, a move from depressive and paranoid destructiveness to constructive planning and facing of the future.

At the end of the contract the parting was for good, but the client indicated that she knew where to go if she ever experienced another crisis and that the possibility of coming back had been a ray of hope in her often turbulent life. This did not seem a jumping of the gun of ending, but rather a reaffirmation of the value of brief therapy – grasping a hand when there is a danger of drowning. That it was my hand was a bonus, but she would have taken another hand, too. To the charge of a 'quick fix' I would reply that it felt like a cumulative progression, like a further stage in an ongoing therapeutic journey. Though some of the symptoms were similar – the paranoia, the sabotaging, the fear of falling apart – the developmental issues were quite different, and the work carried on from where it had been left off. What was done this time could not have been done last time; indeed, the components of the situation were completely new and the solutions found came from a more mature understanding of herself. She might be back in a few years, but most probably with a new agenda, and if not in this country, then in Canada and with a new counsellor to tackle the next life phase. Meanwhile she would be safe in the knowledge of her own independence and self-sufficiency, which was a kind of strength acquired early on as a defence against feeling she could not depend on anyone else, and a weakness that could turn into angry sabotaging when it came to turbulent patches in her life beyond her ego strength.

A case of brief focal psychotherapy based on Malan's model

The client, a 52-year-old woman who described herself as a counsellor, had applied for counselling at the agency on the suggestion of her daughter, who was training there. She was assessed as suitable for brief Malan-style focal therapy on the basis of her comprehensively completed questionnaire and agreed to a six-month contract of weekly counselling after telling me her history. Psychological-mindedness, the recent onset of her presenting problem and the ability to respond to trial interpretations were the positive indicators for the choice, while among negatives were noted hysterical defences of seductiveness, false independence and some suspected high disturbance levels related to a two-year separation from her mother in early childhood due to war-time separation by evacuation.

The anxieties she came with were described as experiencing her house as haunted and encountering a ghost on the landing. This was consciously put down to a projection of fears when she was alone in the house which produced nightmares of being possessed by ghosts. She had recently moved back into the house after 10 years away in the country following the break-up of her marriage, which had led to her abandoning her three teenage children and setting up alone as a counsellor. Her manfriend, an ex-client who had become a lover, was living with her, but she was uncertain as to her commitment to him, for fear of becoming dependent and of losing the treasured independence she had struggled for since her separation and divorce. Also there were issues around troubled relationships with her mother and with her grown-up children and a general sense of fear about the future with approaching menopause and ageing.

The assessment hypothesis of being haunted by her past while running away from it into a defensive imagined independence led to the formulation of an agreed focus defined as 'laying the ghosts of the past and healing the splits', which the client seemed well motivated to tackle, though initially showing some resistance both by competitively choosing to sit in the counsellor's chair and by seductively asserting her independence whenever an opportunity for this offered itself. Her need to sparkle (as a manic defence) was apparent, and it expressed itself in colourful verbal and visual presentation, in playful painterly imagery and dramatic anecdotes about her daily life which often seemed to owe as much to fantasy as to reality and reflected a strong need to draw attention to herself.

After the assessment she returned with a dream in which we were together in the counselling room with another woman leaning on me and her watching jealously, feeling excluded. She interpreted the dream as her being two people, one fiercely independent, wanting to go it alone, the other one wanting to lean on somebody, very needy and wanting to be special. She had also bought a large mirror for her house in which she could see herself full-length. This set the tone for the therapy, relating obliquely to the focus as a warning to expect resistance to the joint task as well as neediness and a desire to be special and admired, both of which were consistently interpreted and related to her narcissism. So, too, was the constant bid for independence, which from early on in therapy was linked with the poignantly remembered experience of being sent away from home, to Wales, aged 4, with a name tag round her neck bearing the description 'bedwetter', an experience which was unforgettable as a brutal rejection by an insensitive working-class mother who was pregnant with the next baby and unrelenting when tearfully appealed to.

Though the evacuation experience was altogether a good one of being fostered by a loving childless couple whose superior education and class instilled in the client a life-long longing to become educated and better-class, it ended abruptly in her return to London and to a mother who was preoccupied with her younger children and to a father who was mostly absent or desultorily flirting with her. This set the example for the flirtatious manner with which she latterly conducted all relationships, while making her suspicious of men and constantly expecting rejection. It also probably explained her pervasive anger with and ambivalence towards her mother, whom she alternately despised and pined for, and who had appeared in a dream as the ghost on the landing who scared and haunted her and was a constant irritant in family affairs which required their meeting.

As for the matter of the ghost, this was part of the client's New Age presentation, related by her to her grandmother, who was a spiritualist medium, and to other colourful witch women in her family and among her acquantainces. It was both magic and metaphor, a manner of speaking which she had adopted in the sixties, and half believed in, half flirted with in her characteristic manner of both trying to impress and to distance herself, which became a running theme of the therapy. We treated the 'laying of the ghosts' as the task of facing the guilt, shame and anger about her own bad mothering of three children as well as her mother's bad mothering of herself which had produced the problems around dependence and independence she was now so hopelessly struggling with, and had in the past firmly defended against by either ignoring or running away from into acting out dramatically.

The fact that she had become a counsellor after leaving her family was one of the most telling choices of her life – she had been dealing with other people's problems rather than facing her own (though she had had some therapy while she was training). During our work together she gave up the counselling altogether, realizing that it was she herself who needed to be counselled and that it had been a desperate displacement activity serving the illusion of omnipotence and independence. This omnipotence was still evident when she talked about starting her life again on a blank screen or of giving up her present live-in relationship, which required her to make compromises, and allow herself to be dependent, physically and emotionally, which produced rejection fears. There was a persistent romantic fantasy about a house in the country, about being in nature with animals and flowers and of fusing with the universe, narcissistically inflating herself, embracing and dissolving into the whole. On the other hand, going from one extreme to another, there were fears of ageing, of losing her sparkle, her attractiveness and her popularity, and becoming a bag lady rejected by everybody. Her children made fun of her, her partner ignored her hysterical and melodramatic play-acting, while admiring the liveliness and seductiveness that had made him break the boundaries with his ex-counsellor and enticed him into her orbit.

After the difficult first part of the therapy, which consisted of patiently interpreting her resistance to dependence, her hysterical acting out and her flights into omnipotent phantasy, the fear of the ghost lessened, and in the middle period she became gradually able to take true responsibility for her life and for her children, to link her anger with her mother to her anger with her husband, who had tried unsuccessfully to be mother and father to her and whom, like mother, she could not disown as they shared the children. Finally she learnt to accept that in her relationship with her partner, who, as her oldest daughter reminded her, was her 'bread and butter', she had to yield and adapt to the realities of ordinary life in which she was neither princess nor bag lady, and had to pull her weight sharing his work and his bed.

She was trying to make amends for the mistakes of the past, particularly in relation to her youngest daughter, whom she had abandoned aged 14, and who was as angry with her as she had always been with her mother for abandoning her as a child. There were two persistently painful memories, often repeated: one of sitting on her mother's bed, on the evening of her departure for Wales, imploring her not to send her away and being sternly told that it was impossible; the other of tidying up her house together with her youngest daughter just before leaving London 10 years ago and finding a toy frog in the garden she was about to abandon. They both made her cry pitifully, as they linked together her abandonment and her abandoning, her anger and her guilt, indicating that wounds inflicted can never be forgotten, though they may eventually be forgiven.

While she never came to a loving acceptance of her mother, who was still tantalizing her by preferring her brothers and whom she could never forgive for inflicting the narcissistic wound of rejection, she learnt to forgive herself for her deficiencies as a mother and to live with her daughter amicably in the house from which the ghost had been exorcized. The older daughter trained as a counsellor at my agency, to whom she had sent her mother. This seemed meaningful as she had been mothering her mother, my client, during the marriage break-up and the difficulties with her father/my client's ex-husband. The client was gradually able to relinquish the notion that her much flaunted independence equalled maturity rather than being a competent performance of the real thing, and this went hand in hand with a lessening of her dramatic and attention-seeking manner-isms as well as with a loss of her sparkle and frenetic seductiveness. She never became actively depressed, but the change in her indicated a move into the depressive position, a remarkable transformation which deepened as we neared the end of our six-month contract.

This was characterized by some acting out – two missed sessions when she took time off just before the last session as if to demon-strate her still cherished independence. She talked about leaving me in her habitual colourful way as if it were an adventure, with her setting out on safari, well equipped with antidotes against snakebite and sunstroke which I had given her. I suggested that we might supplement this fantasy by discussing our ending in terms of her separation from her second mother, the foster mother in Wales, which had been tearful but well managed and had enabled that woman to become an internalized good object, an experience which she might now want to repeat with me becoming the internalized therapist who had taught her how to observe and analyse herself. In one of the last sessions there was talk about death and growing old, and she also developed a severe rash of acne, which was interpreted as an adolescent condition! A week before our last session there was the Great Storm of 1987, and soon after came the Stock Market Crash – as if she had to take leave against a big dramatic backdrop. All these were useful as signs of a well-sustained separation and of parting on a note of mutual agreement, but there was no denying the fact that much remained to be done of the task of stabilizing her emotional reactions, of banishing her grudges (particularly with mother and husband) and of maturing in her relationships with others and with herself, which we both acknowledged.

This being a Malan-style therapy, we were able to arrange for a follow-up in the last session, which would take place six months later and allow us to take stock of how she continued to benefit from the therapy and made use of the changes which had occurred. There were two more follow-ups spaced out over a year, in which it became obvious that she had continued the self-reflective work we had done together. At the third follow-up she asked for a referral into twice-weekly therapy, after I had to turn down her demand to be taken on by me. Apparently her mother had reminded her of some forgotten abuse in her childhood and memories of this had come flooding back – by then, I think, the interest in child sexual abuse had become widespread in therapy circles and somehow it seemed characteristic of her that she was climbing on the band-wagon.

When all is said and done, I think this case was a relatively successful example of the brief focal therapy model developed by Malan and Balint. In retrospect, however, I have some reservations and doubts which still nag me as they flag up some interesting aspects of brief therapy. For one thing I notice reading through my notes that this case seems almost too good to be true, and that in spite of all the scrupulous interpreting and analysing I may have been seduced or even led astray by my client's unconscious compliance, her colourful clinical material and lively story-telling, and by a collusive need to bring this therapy to a successful, almost text-book-like ending. Furthermore, the follow-ups demonstrated an ongoing process of the repairing and relating characteristics of the depressive position, yet there always remained a wish to resume work with me. Was this indicative of success or failure, a healthy sign of using an internalized object, or a continuance of the transference? By eventually asking for a referral, she stated that she was still troubled, though now by a different childhood trauma which had not been part of our agenda. Once again, one could thus speak of a case of successive contracting, and recall Freud's remarks in 'Analysis Terminable and Interminable' about new matter and symptoms emerging in the aftermath of analysis. One thing leads to another. While we deal with what is there, we cannot anticipate what is to come!

8
Different Contexts and Treatment Settings for Brief and Focal Work

I have concentrated so far on what happens in the consulting room between the two participants of brief psychodynamic therapy, and have merely mentioned the contexts or settings in which such treatments happen. This was done deliberately, working from the inside, so to speak, towards the outside, leaving to the last the envelope and the container within which the therapeutic couple are held and function: the hospitals, clinics and general practice surgeries, the schools and higher educational establishments, the voluntary agencies and charities, and last, but not least, the employment assistance programmes, all of which offer free counselling and psychotherapy to members of the public and for whom the various models of time-limited and brief therapies have been developed in the course of recent decades, implementing Freud's post-World War I vision of a 'psychotherapy for the people' (1919). Of course, not all of these are based on the psychodynamic principles developed by him for the – mostly quite brief – analyses he conducted with his early patients in his private practice setting, yet they are all profoundly influenced in their dynamics by the various contexts in which they take place. How and why this happens will be one of the themes of this chapter, which will draw on three classic organizational studies: Isabel Menzies-Lyth's *The Functioning of Social Systems as a Defence Against Anxiety* (1970), Elliott Jacques' 'Social Systems as a Defence against Anxiety' (1955), Robert de Board's *The Psychoanalysis of Organizations* (1978), and other more recent papers on organizational issues and how these influence the analytic frame and dynamic processes in contextual therapy.

The figure of the 'clinical rhombus', developed by R.E. Ekstein and R.S. Wallerstein (1958: 11) to describe the characteristic four-cornered field arising in organizations where patients are treated under supervision, demonstrates that the quality of relationships between administrators and clinical staff can affect the patients for whose treatment the organizations have been set up, and that the levels of cooperation and/or competition are equally indicative of the dynamics and effectiveness of therapeutic work done in organizations, often poignantly reflecting the conflicts and anxieties brought by the patients themselves. While the therapeutic couple reproduces the one-to-one relationship between mother/parent and child, the organizational context represents the social system in which this primary relationship takes place, is held and develops. The powerful reciprocal influences and group processes active in this dynamic field can be both helpful and destructive to the therapeutic work.

The pioneers of brief therapy like Alexander, Malan and Mann developed their various models because of the increasing numbers of patients with emotional problems, who could not be given lengthy and expensive conventional analytic treatments due to lack of hospital resources. Surprisingly, they took little account of the medical contexts in which they worked and they remained focused in their theorizing on modifications to the analytic frame and on the interaction between the therapeutic couple without considering other influences potentially acting on and influencing this work. It is only in recent years that the analytic studies of organizations, systems, and groups have been brought to bear on the therapeutic work done in such contexts, clearly distinguishing therapy work done in private practice from work happening in organizational contexts where group processes and patient pathologies are interacting in complex unconscious ways furthering and/or obstructing effectiveness and outcome. While these writers still describe their work as if it happened in private practice, more recent studies and evaluations in the field are directing their attention to organizational interactions and contextual factors influencing clinical processes.

Possibly the first of these was Tom Main's 'The Ailment' (1989), an examination of the disturbing effects a particularly disturbed patient could have on the hospital staff group as a whole which was studied in terms of the splitting transferences, the projections, acting out and depotentiating of the professionals by the patient and the powerful defences created in reaction to this. Like Menzies-Lyth, Main stresses the need for the helpers to monitor themselves and their unconscious interactive processes in relation to the patient's pathology, which is the object of their clinical efforts, and emphasizes the insuperable difficulties of identifying and treating large group pathology.

Most brief therapy at the moment is done in organizations, and in the context of primary health, of education, or at the workplace. The various social and administrative configurations in these fields profoundly influence the therapeutic work that is attempted, and the systems in place to support and service the therapeutic couple are decisive for what happens or does not happen to the patients. It is reasonable to assume that some brief models are better suited to one or the other context. For instance, Malan's brief focal therapy and Ryle's cognitive analytic therapy were developed specifically for the clinic and hospital setting where doctors, psychiatrists and psychotherapists co-exist, and the organization acts as a container. De Shazer's solution-focused brief therapy, meanwhile, matched a stress- and work-centred environment with its pragmatic emphasis on competence and effectiveness. Finally, Mann's time-limited model confidently straddles a wide field because of its universality, adapting to various and diverse contexts and carrying the promise of good use being made of sparse resources as well as of being easily taught.

After the similarities, the differences, of contexts, client populations, goals, etc. The intention is to focus on the three main sectors and fields where nowadays brief and/or time-limited therapy is offered to members of the public – GP surgeries, education and corporate business. The different divisions of the British Association for Counselling clearly reflect these distinctive settings, all of which offer brief or time-limited contracts of free counselling to those who qualify as clients.

GP surgeries

The pioneering work of Michael Balint, particularly his paper 'The Doctor, his Patient and the Illness', emphasized the simple idea or paradox that

> by far the most frequently used drug in general practice was *the doctor himself*. It was not only the medicine in the bottle or the pills in the box that mattered, but the way the doctor gave them to his patient – in fact the whole atmosphere in which the drug was given and taken. (1955: 199)

But what, he asked himself further, were the factors that determined the doctor's responses?

> When we [i.e. Balint and his research seminar at the Tavistock Clinic] examined this response we found that much of it depended on what might be called his 'apostolic function'. By this we meant that every doctor has a set of fairly firm beliefs as to which illnesses are acceptable and which not; how much pain, suffering, fear and deprivation a patient should tolerate and when he has the right to ask for help or relief; how much nuisance the patient is allowed to make of himself and to whom in his environment . . . (1955: 204)

By emphasizing the importance of this function, and of the doctor–patient *relationship*, Balint claimed that interaction and understanding are as crucial to healing and to the treatment of physical symptoms as are drugs, and that, therefore, in his view, soma and psyche are indivisible. More and more, the general practitioner is taking on board these ideas (nowadays called holistic), and the increasing use of counselling and psychotherapy in general practice is evidence of the medical paradigm shifting from the purely somatic to a more all-embracing psychosomatic belief which implies an interaction of body and mind and an integration of the body/mind split. In other words, in many cases the psychological factors determining people's health or illness need examining as much as the physiological factors, and there is an area where, putting it crudely, the doctor's work ends and the psychologist's or psychotherapist's begins, though almost always the two will need to interact and hence manage their patients' care together.

Nowadays, many doctors and medical staff are equipped with counselling skills, yet the cautious practitioner would always ponder carefully, as Balint wisely states, 'when to start and when to stop'. As with serious physical conditions, so with critical psychological complaints – when the doctor has reached the limit of his/her competence and resources, a specialist is called in to take over and do the job s/he is better trained for and experienced in. These specialists are no longer only medical experts or technicians, but also psychologists and counsellors. These days, the general practice relies for its effectiveness more and more on the multi-disciplinary approach as the patients' demands become more complex and the knowledge of psychosomatics increases.

There is also a financial aspect to this shift, as general practices have become fund-holding and are able to employ paid counsellors rather than, as in the past, referring patients out for psychotherapy. This has the advantage of speedy referrals, better communications among professionals, and a combined holding of patients. Money is saved because of this, most importantly, on the drugs bills as patients are encouraged and enabled, with the help of counselling, to give up their reliance on pills and to face their worries, their pain and suffering rather than relying on tranquillizers and anti-depressants to take it away.

An example of this was the project designed to reduce patients' dependence on drugs with the help of some counselling, described by Mark Heal in 'Introducing a Counselling Culture to General Practice' (1997), which showed impressive reductions in the numbers of prescriptions over a short period and a marked change from the 'culture of prescribing' into an approach in which the patient was helped, in Balint's words, 'to change his symptoms back into the severe mental suffering which he tried to avoid by a flight into a more bearable physical suffering' (1955: 209). This kind of change is the goal of much of the brief counselling done in GP practices, and it requires a well-functioning collaboration between the GP, the counsellor and the rest of the practice team which enables the patient to drop his/her somatizing defences and take responsibility for their emotional reactions, exploring and reflecting on what lies behind the symptoms which brought about a visit to the doctor in the first place.

This collaboration has its problems, as the patient's relationship with the doctor can conflict and clash with the patient's relationship with the counsellor and lead to situations where two transferences create a split which is then used destructively by the patient (Jones et al., 1994) unless monitored and interpreted as a defence against anxiety.

It can also conflict with the counsellor's ethical stance and the need to preserve confidentiality, which is the basis of trust in the counselling relationship and essential for the containing and uncovering work to be done between the two participants. In contrast to Bollas and Sundelson (1996), who plead for the 'absolute privilege of confidentiality', Murphy (1997) asks whether this 'purity' can ever be preserved from 'intrusions' in settings where the impingement of 'the outer world on the inner world' is inevitable, where responsibilities for patients are shared, and where some communicating about them is necessary in the interest of the patient's welfare and the functioning of the practice. She states that patients need to know that 'there is no such thing as absolute confidentiality because of the clinical responsibility of the doctor', and that 'it has been my experience that patients are grateful for the distinction made and there is every indication that transferences which communicate disturbed parts of the self are possible under these conditions particularly when the therapist's anxiety may be lessened because of the containment of the setting' (1997: 21–2).

There are two interesting points to this argument. On the one hand, the importance of ground rules, of what the patient is told at the beginning of therapy and of what s/he can reasonably expect. In sharing the care for the patient, doctor and counsellor can be experienced like mother and father, a couple united in their efforts to facilitate the patient's physical and psychological well-being and to contain his/her anxieties and suffering. On the other hand, the counsellor, in receiving the support and interest of the doctor, is strengthened and contained during the difficult and emotionally demanding work with the patient. Depending, of course, on the quality of collaboration, there can be a containing within containment that benefits all the participants concerned, and the counsellor can rely on the fact that the patient's ongoing transference on doctor or GP practice is bound to be a healing and containing factor in the overall process.

Furthermore, and this is the gist of much of the literature on organizational settings, the opportunity for disagreement, competition, splitting and defensive acting out is immense, and no GP practice is immune to this, even if the doctors are positive and well inclined towards the counsellor and the administration is running fairly smoothly. As one of the essential guarantees for effective psychodynamic work is the establishment and upholding of the analytic frame, factors working against this – like lax appointment systems, inefficient room allocation or gossiping about patients, which are not in the power of the counsellor – can create havoc in the counsellor's work.

Hoag (1992), writing about the difficulties of maintaining a secure frame in the GP practice, is eloquent about her collaborative efforts to establish a presence while securing the practical and emotional framework in which to attend to her therapeutic work. Like Heal, she points out that within months her measures to tighten up appointments, time-keeping and boundaries led to a marked increase in kept appointments and attendances. She quotes optimistically Jones' statement that the structure of the GP surgery 'reinforces professional independence and responsibility while encouraging maximum contact' (1986: 200), adding that the therapist in a GP practice is presented with a challenge continually and repeatedly to reassert his/her position with an attitude of 'seriousness, straightforwardnesss, compassion, and restraint' (Langs, quoted in Hoag, 1992: 428). There is a hope that her example of maintaining security of frame will prove catching, as the therapist who is 'adhering to the ground rules rather than altering them' will 'provide the GPs and surgery staff with a structure and means of understanding what the therapist has to offer that is unique and valuable in itself and also different from the medical model' (Hoag, 1992: 417).

Investigative studies on the whole confirm this optimistic hope, though there is still much disagreement about the usefulness and advisability of maintaining counsellors in GP practices at all (see e.g., Corney, 1998). Issues of sensible fund allocation, fragmentation of services, communication difficulties and referral decision-making are balanced against patient preferences and uncertain statistics. But on the whole, the climate is counsellor-friendly, particularly in large practices where GPs' workloads are heavy and patients can easily feel depersonalized.

Counselling contracts in GP practices vary, but tend to be on the short side: between 6 and 12 sessions on average. Because of the relative independence of the counsellor, this is mostly left up to the individual, and to an extent so are the assessment and evaluation of referral needs. A good example is John Lees' (1997) description of his flexible approach, which indicates a freedom from constraint that allowed him to work with his countertransference in a creative way while leaving the patients a relatively free hand to attend and conform. This contrasts with Hoag's very frame-conscious and orthodox therapeutic stance, while paralleling the GPs' almost absolute power to set the pace. Another experienced GP counsellor has learnt to work a system of successive contracting (6 + 6 + 6) which helps even the most disturbed patients achieve some therapeutic benefit and get a better understanding of their condition, prepares them, if necessary and possible, for more ongoing therapy or to make enough changes in their external lives to function better on their own. In the intervals between contracts the patients are encouraged to maintain a self-reflective stance, and as they remain as patients on the doctors' list this will continue the holding achieved by the brief therapeutic contract after its ending. This method of contracting is an idiosyncratic version of brief therapy which can be very beneficial (and is also practised in a modified form in CAT), but it may also prolong and complicate the attachment to the point of becoming dependence (see also Pietroni, 1999).

Of course, there are endless frustrations because of time constraints, waiting lists and inconclusive contracts, but on the whole the work is productive and rewarding to the counsellor, because of its variety, range of clinical experience and interest, and because of the colleagueship, when it works. Jones et al. (1994) paint a fascinating picture of the dynamic interactions and criss-crossing transferences in the multi-disciplinary team. They illustrate how these tend to block and interfere with the ongoing work and need to be harnessed as reflective processes in the interest of the shared patients. This presupposes that things are honestly talked about (see also Lees, 1997, as above), and that they are processed in a psychodynamic way which requires regular staff meetings and adequate joint staff time. It is also essential that there is ongoing, preferably external supervision (see the next chapter), and training updates, as matters are moving fast in the field.

What has given GP counselling a bad name in some quarters is the fact that far too much counselling is done by inexperienced counsellors or by trainees who use surgeries for their placements and are hired by these because they are unpaid and promise savings, which can be misplaced and unethical. The disturbance levels they are on the whole confronted with would often daunt even very experienced therapists, and many trainings do not prepare the beginner for what their clients present with. There is a difference of opinion about the level of experience required to do good brief work, as most people willy-nilly get thrown in at the deep end and learn to swim quickly, but on the whole the brief counsellor will need a solid foundation of training, skills and experience to survive the rigours of surgery counselling, with the rapid turnover of patients, the diversity of ages, gender, ethnicity, and the wide spectrum of baffling symptomatology – from the chronic patients who use the practice for lifelong maintenance to the worried-well and the 'heart-sink' patients whom the doctors are keen to pass on, but who may not always respond to brief work, which requires good motivation, ego strength and a strong desire to get well, rather than the passive-aggressive or compliant dependency attitudes which characterize the majority of GP surgery patients.

Both Balint and Bion talked about the need to help patients develop a capacity to think about mental pain, instead of automatically asking for a pill to ease their physical pain. This is the difficult, but paramount, duty of today's GP counsellor, who has been brought in to relieve the busy doctor who struggles with enormous caseloads. As vital as this is the ability to understand the physical symptom as communication, as resistance and as attempt to escape unbearable mental pain which has been repressed and displaced into the theatre of the body (McDougall, 1989). In order to do this counsellors need to be able to symbolize and learn to translate from the code language of symptomatology into the verbal form of communication, and in each individual case to unravel and interpret the meaning of the particular illness they may be confronted with (Groddeck, 1977). Then patients, instead of being dependent on the expert's opinion to be cured, can be helped to understand what makes them ill and, in chronic cases, what keeps them ill. If counsellors and patients can do this transformation work together in a few sessions, then patients may be able to drop the somatizing defence, the crippling hypochondriacal fears and fantasies and allow themselves to have emotional experiences and to have their emotional needs met instead of asking for another quick fix of medication.

Hence, counsellors will look behind the illness to identify patients' ways of handling anger, dealing with loss and mourning, and generally managing unpleasant, conflictual and painful experience which involves depressive and persecutory anxiety. This process includes an understanding of their own way of handling anxiety, conflict and pain, and of the particular defences they may have developed against these, which implies that they have willingly undergone some self-reflective work themselves, have learnt to use their counter-transference experience and feelings, and to place and observe their clinical work in the particular context in which it happens and is shared.

It is not unusual for the counsellors to experience themselves as marginal figures in the practice, at times being scapegoated or feeling like an 'enemy within' (MacKenzie, 1996), with the doctors perhaps threatened or threatening, exposed to the splitting and projecting that constantly goes on behind the surface in organizations, particularly when they are under stress, negatively affecting and infecting the work in obstructive ways. This happens partly because they are relative latecomers in the field – still suspect because of lack of sufficient evidence of their usefulness and because their ground rules and procedures are so different to the medical ways and conflict with the prevailing culture. Co-existence needs to be won and constantly rewon, as much in personal terms as in terms of clinical effectiveness, and the ability to work in a team, as equal and interdependent with others, is therefore a necessary precondition for working productively in the tension-prone multi-disciplinary environment of a GP surgery and of primary health care.

The need for shared decisions about referrals (internal and external to the surgery) necessitates a reasonably functioning relationship between doctor and counsellor and is dictated as much by financial as by clinical resources, by patient psychopathology and patient suitability to be treated by practice personnel. As long-term work is rare in GP practice and psychiatric or social work services are often indicated, decisions, even if they are made by the counsellor and not in tandem, will involve the practice as a whole because of the joint responsibility and accountability in case something goes wrong, which can be both daunting and reassuring. The problem is that referrals are often made against a background of not knowing, or a desire to dump problems in somebody else's lap.

Brief therapy has often been prescribed on the basis of 'something is better than nothing', and this can only be justified if it is not considered second-best or done as a 'plastering over the cracks'. When administered in the GP practice, whose whole culture is geared to short interventions and brief meetings, it is often experienced as a first time, rather than as a one-off – an introduction into an alternative way of being seen, listened to and talked with (rather than to), and this in itself is revelatory and healing. Much depends on how the doctor makes the referral to the counsellor and how s/he introduces the patient to this new need to be counselled, of which s/he has so far been unaware. The phrase 'You may find counselling helpful' rather than 'You need counselling' can ease the transition from one consulting room to another, as the patient who feels 'sent' may become resistant, as every counsellor knows from bitter experience. Linking back to the doctor and indicating that there is agreement on why the patient may find counselling helpful is another essential ingredient

of the atmosphere of shared care which is the strength (and occa-
sionally the weakness) of GP work. Bridge-building and confidential
attention to sensitive personal matters require the empathic negotiation skills of both partners in the exercise and the well-coordinated
letting go and receiving of the patient.

Many counsellors working in GP practices have been trained in
long-term work and may therefore feel unconscious resistance to the
medical culture in which the short-term approach predominates.
Fantasies of not giving enough or of actively harming the short-term
client can interfere with their effectiveness and produce an internal
tension between the medical model and their preferred counselling
mode. These fantasies may be of promiscuity, of brief unions, adop-
tions and abortions and prompted by parental longings for attachment, completion, slow maturing and gradual growth of their
charges. In reality brief counselling in this context usually happens
against the background of the patients' long-term attachment and
transference to the practice and to individual GPs which provide the
safe containment over time that the counsellor cannot provide (Brave
Smith, 1996).

Educational settings

Counselling in the context of edcuation, whether in schools, colleges
or universities, has been as long (or short) in coming as counselling in
medical settings and shares with this the necessity of brevity,
economy and collaboration with other professionals while having
distinctive features of its own. The goals and tasks of counselling are
determined by a context where all groupings are impermanent and
where the patients represent certain age groups and common
interests. The didactic or academic background is another distinctive
feature of this context, as it has its own values concerning intellect,
hard work and the bearing of anxiety, and its own structure of
repeated beginnings and endings. The existence of long summer
breaks and course endings limit and concentrate counselling work,
like teaching, to certain set times, semesters or seasons of the year.
The prevailing culture in educational institutions is one of
achievement, competition, assessment and judgement which produces high levels of depressive and persecutory anxieties, particularly
at certain times of the year, when exams loom and end of year
reports are due and when the whole college or school assumes a
paranoid atmosphere that puts enormous strains on students and
teachers and is crying out for therapeutic containment. Students are
facing crucial questions about their future while struggling with
issues of identity, relationship and sexuality.

In further education and university student counselling, these contextual issues are parallelled by the developmental issues of adolescence, which have to do with the separation from parents and family, with the formation of personal identity, and with the growing need for autonomy, prone to lead to developmental crises which often cannot be managed without outside help. On the other hand, the young adult, on the point of leaving the long-term relationships of the family, which may still exert a strong regressive pull and interfere with the completion of adolescent tasks, will not want or be helped by offers of a regressive therapeutic relationship and is best served by precisely focused therapy which makes use of the 'triangles of insight' and is time-limited, leaving the student to choose how regularly to meet. This is what Alex Coren writes in defence of brief counselling for college students, based on Erikson's definition of the adolescent life stage as a crisis of intimacy and isolation:

> At a time in their lives when they need to go out and face and actively master the world we run the risk of encouraging them to enter into a long-term regressive relationship which might be experienced . . . as a tyrannical demand that can be met only by a defeated or hostile compliance. However difficult it is for us as therapists to accept, real life happens outside the consulting room. (Coren, 1996: 29)

And further:

> Brief consultations are the most productive use of the adolescent/young adult's developmental drive. They may need a haven away from the intimacy of the family which they have only just left as well as from the intellectual intensity of the tutorial or teaching relationship which can be experienced as particularly intrusive. (1996: 29)

Hence much student counselling averages four sessions and closely resembles crisis management in that the counsellor may lend auxiliary ego strength for the completion of a maturational task like cutting off the strangling umbilical cord, making and changing course choices, sitting exams, writing theses and crossing the threshold of graduation. It has been found that these tasks can successfully be tackled in short-term psychotherapy groups focused on the issues of dependency, procrastination, perfectionism and fear of graduation (Fredtoft et al., 1996). This method is not only economical and cost-effective, it also allows and encourages identification with peers, prevents isolation and suicidal fantasies, and ideally liberates the compulsive, superego-driven students from their fantasies of failure towards a playful enjoyment of their study tasks and will lead to the realization that 'being good enough, accomplishing something rather than everything and letting go of the extreme involvement and demands of the family in favour of an involvement in their own growth' is possible and desirable (Fredtoft et al., 1996). Altogether, there can be a shift from the paranoid-schizoid position, in which harsh inner voices demand perfection and produce guilt, to the depressive position, where a dialogue with benevolent internal objects develops and a pattern of interdependence of parents and children emerges which is the goal and essence of maturity.

As with Balint's brief focal and Mann's time-limited therapy, in this modified group-analytic framework,

> the group sets off knowing that within four months it will stop. This makes for a speeding up of the process of revealing therapeutic material and at the same time delivers some kind of security, as the group members do not need to fear becoming swallowed up by the therapists or the group, knowing all along that the group will eventually end. This is especially important when the material is about separation, individuation and dependency, because these themes might provoke anxieties. At the same time, it is important that the clients do have time to get in contact with feelings of dependency. (Fredtoft et al., 1996: 483)

For these short-term and focal analytic groups the therapists select the members on the basis of certain criteria in order to achieve homogeneity in the group. These criteria include

> the necessary ego strength to tolerate the anxiety that will arise during the therapeutic process, the ability to engage in and disengage from interpersonal relations without collapsing, the capacity for self-reflection and to form relations with others. . . . This means that we exclude clients with personality disorders, with any kind of psychosis as well as clients suffering from severe depression, severely narcissistic clients and clients with addictive problems. (Fredtoft et al., 1996: 482)

In fact the therapists favour the so-called 'healthy patient' who is favoured by all brief therapists as capable of instant engagement and disengagement, as tolerating frustration and selective attention, willing to learn from his/her experiences with others.

There remains the question of how to help the students excluded from the groups and from brief therapy because of their weak ego strength, the severity of their pathological condition and their urgent need to work through very deep-seated anxiety-provoking emotional problems of addiction, depression, attachment and integration in the safe and containing presence of another. As long-term therapy is rarely an option, and money constraints will exclude referral-out into private practice, the only solution is 'referral-in', i.e. to other student services. As in the primary health context, educational institutions usually maintain a referral system which involves youth and social workers, GPs, psychiatrists and other medical staff who can administer medication, prescribe occupational therapy, offer practical or statutory support. The student counsellor in these cases will need carefully to assess, induct and refer clients to the appropriate channels, ensuring their safe passage and arrival and preventing their slipping through the net.

This is one of the more anxiety-provoking and hazardous tasks of the educational counsellor, especially in institutions where these support services do not work hand in glove and suffer from lack of coordination. But the worst nightmare is the scenario where a student is found dead in his/her room, days after having committed suicide in desperation and isolation – alone in the crowd and far from home. There will be massive guilt and blaming surrounding the inquest and the inquiry, and the institution will be thrown into turmoil and upheaval, affecting students and staff alike, not least the counsellor, who 'ought to have known better'.

The fragmentation, the unconnected and uncontaining structures, the confusion of programmes and choices existing in many educational institutions easily create situations where isolated individuals lose their way and are lost sight of, and this will be resonating with universal experiences of feeling abandoned and producing a response of 'there but for the grace of God go I'. Reviewing Elsa Bell's book *Counselling in Further and Higher Education*, American university counsellor Robert May comments on this problematic positioning of counselling services with educational institutions as follows:

> As the student counsellor inevitably is involved in multiple roles and complex dealing with other parts of the institution, maintaining useful liaison relationships is a crucial aspect of the work. A counselling service in an academic setting is never at the centre of the institution's function. Our role is at best supportive of the primary function of the institution, at worst it may be seen as peripheral or unnecessary. There is also always some degree of institutional ambivalence towards our presence, since we represent disorder and disability and our existence can be, more or less consciously, an embarrassment. Combined with the unusual degree to which our work happens behind closed doors, this puts us constantly up against the question of how we demonstrate our usefulness to the institution. (May, 1997)

As student counsellors are sometimes expected to do advice work as well, they find themselves placed uncomfortably close and next to tutors, career counsellors, religious advisers and health service staff, trying to carve out a distinctive niche for themselves and to educate staff and students as to what counselling is and what it has to offer to the students, in terms of enhancing their study skills, their personal functioning, and their sense of belonging in an often vast, dauntingly anonymous place where they may feel like birds of passage.

The college counsellor's room can become a refuge and a safe place in which to explore and take care of emotional problems arising from stresses and demands created by the external environment. In order to be such a safe place, it needs to have a 'secure analytic frame', in terms of Langs' criteria of privacy, confidentiality, consistency of contract and therapist neutrality (quoted in Hoag, 1992: 428). To safeguard this in the busy and chaotic context of an educational institution can be even more difficult than in the GP practice, where privacy and flexibility regarding attendance and keeping of appointments are part of the culture.

Another context of educational counselling is the school sector, where the need for a secure frame in which to do the work has been emphasized in a recent paper by Steve Seaton (1996) which describes the setting up of a counselling service in a secondary school following the painful expulsion of a pupil. The author points out the specifically complex issues arising for the school counsellor as:

- the clients are legal minors
- schools must work with parents
- schools have a multitude of legal responsibilities towards students under the in loco parentis banner
- schools have specific responsibilities under the Child Protection Act. (1996: 510)

He also discusses the developmental problems relating to the age group of pre-adolescents and adolescents

> who may find it more difficult to find their way into counselling than adults. . . . Boys, in particular, have shown a marked tendency to regard counselling as a threat to their autonomy and . . . hence to their pride and dignity. Some have registered anxiety about peer group ridicule, and others have expressed a sense of shame that they are seen as being needy or lacking in 'independence'. (1996: 511)

This lies behind much acting out (as with the boy who was expelled) and also behind the somatizing which Seaton registers as more characteristic of Asian students, who find their way to the school nurse rather than the counsellor. Methods of referral are carefully considered, ranging from self-referrals and referrals by tutors and teachers to involving the pastoral system of the school. And so are ways of publicizing and recommending counselling as a 'normal and healthy resource with which to tackle problems, explore difficulties and gain support, not only during these crucial years, but for life' (1996: 513).

The following is an example of the particular difficulties of school counselling in which the need of informing and involving the parents has to be balanced against the child's need for privacy, echoing Courtman's comment that 'we need to remind ourselves that we are working with an immature population, young people in a stage of becoming, in the process of developing personal and social maturity' (quoted in Seaton, 1996: 512).

The client was a GCSE student who was severely depressed, unable to do his home- and schoolwork, and in an emotional crisis triggered by his uncle's terminal cancer diagnosis, which had revived memories of his mother's death of cancer, when he was 6. He had reached an impasse in his life with his father and stepmother, who were trying hard to be supportive, but also putting on pressure for him to perform in his exams, and did not trust his school counsellor, who was struggling to contain his suicidal fantasies and to hold him over the long summer break. The lack of parental cooperation which was fuelled by distrust of the efficacy of counselling put her in a severe dilemma regarding confidentiality and contracting: his strong transference to her showed features of dependence which required a long-term therapeutic relationship in which to face the issues of life and death he was struggling with, while his oedipal conflict remained unresolved.

In view of the pressures on her time and availability to the institution the school counsellor's recommendation was for him to receive ongoing therapy outside of school, which would require the active and positive involvement of the parents, who themselves seemed to be in need of therapy to sustain a precarious relationship. This was a situation where the counselling had uncovered a plethora of problems which could only be tackled by strengthening the boy's resolve to receive further therapy. If ever there was a case for the transferral of a client from brief focal work into long-term intensive psychotherapy, this was it. But how would this change of contract satisfy the ethical code of the brief counsellor? In view of the dead mother and the dying uncle, should the counsellor be left alive, albeit operating in a different analytic framework?

Seaton does not address the issue of referring out disturbed students like this client whose counselling needs go beyond the brief management of an adolescent crisis and may have breakdown dimensions. I assume they would be handled by the school's pastoral system in consultation with the parents, but they would also involve the counsellor in a breach of confidentiality and make her feel like an 'informer'. I have previously mentioned Bollas and Sundelson (1996) in the context where the GP counsellor recommended collaboration with the doctor (Murphy, 1997). The ethical conflict between being *in loco parentis* and honouring the Child Protection Act can become severe for the counsellor, as can the responsibility towards the school which operates its counselling service with scarce resources. It is a case of serving two masters.

The counsellor's skill is to assess the difference between crisis and breakdown, which is particularly valuable and necessary when working with adolescents, whose volatile emotional life is characterized by extreme states which can take them to the brink and back from it in quick succession (Laufer and Laufer, 1984). When the parental containment is lacking, as in the case mentioned, the counsellor's containing function is essential, and this in turn needs the support of the institution.

Let's hope that the days are over when a disruptive child is expelled from school rather than given sustained support, and that severe acting out is seen as a request for emotional containment and understanding, which, for lack of parental support and ego strength, has not been available to the child. It is useful to consider that, in developmental terms, the child client may not have reached the stage where a reasonable ego is able to enter into a working alliance with the therapist, and that, in contrast to the adult client, s/he is bringing the inner child and the outer child into the therapy as one. This may require a different, less verbal and more playful technique, and it will certainly need an empathic understanding of the child's particular ways of thinking, symbolizing and relating, including that child's perspective of his/her own parenting and the problems s/he experiences as connected with this. It may be invaluable to help the child put these into words for the first time rather than compulsively acting them out in terms of truancy, poor school performance or difficulties in peer relationships, and equally important to involve the real, 'outer' parents in some way in the therapeutic exploration.

As our example has proved, issues affecting learning are closely related to family nexus and personal functioning in this age group, and the school counsellor has an important role to play in improving the integration and management of these.

Employment assistance programmes

In recent years another context for brief psychotherapy and counselling has developed and rapidly gained ground in the field, which is allowing ever larger numbers of the public access to therapeutic services: employment assistance programmes (EAPs). Pioneered in the United States as part of personnel and human resources departments in companies and corporations, the idea of sponsoring counselling for employees suffering from stress and emotional problems whch affect their performance at the workplace has also been adopted in the UK and has led to many firms setting up or buying in counselling services in an attempt to improve the health and welfare of their employees and to reduce the alarming increase in absenteeism, the rising level of error and personal conflict, and of excessive drinking and drug-taking.

As most companies now restructure on a continuous basis, fear of redundancy and lay-off produce constant high stress levels which affect and unsettle whole organizations, making it necessary to support the affected and confused employees and to help them face and adjust to their tough new employment conditions. Supporting those who buckle under conditions of permanent stress to get back on their feet has become an imperative corporate strategy which is dictated more by necessity than by kindness. It has therefore been described as a patching-up exercise and compared to a field hospital service which attends to the casualties and the walking wounded severely affected by the managerial revolution that is happening at the workplace, and then sending them back into the warzone, where the conditions remain unchanged, to resume their work.

While assuming parental responsibility for their workforce and offering a counselling safety-net, the corporations are admitting to the battering force of their withdrawal of workplace security and are seeking to make up for this by guaranteeing a minimum of professional support, just enough to mend the fences and prop up the tottering structures, with a recommendation that if further help is needed, it will have to be provided and paid for by the employees themselves. In many cases the initial brief counselling, if it is well done, opens up new vistas for employees on how to manage stress, to use their own inner resources and to find their own solutions through a deeper understanding of their problems, greater insight and a sense of control. In this respect it is a welcome new trend in employee care and corporate management. Yet in other respects it suffers from the vices of short-termism, from the same diluting of scarce resources which we have already discussed in relation to the NHS and to educational institutions.

There are also important questions about boundaries and confidentiality which crop up in this context; and the handling of the initial contact, whether it should be done by the employer or left entirely to the employee, is another particularly sensitive issue. For the psychodynamic counsellor, this is a situation full of new challenges. The maintenance of the analytic frame, so difficult in the two other settings, suffers another twist in that on the whole the work is done in the counsellor's private setting, yet the referral arrives through a complicated organizational system in which the employee's firm is the starting point, followed by the service provider, who will be processing the request, and, if advisable, choose and match the counsellor, who, in turn, will then set up an assessment session in which to discuss what is troubling the client, and to decide whether the client is ready and willing to engage in a brief counselling contract.

The clinical rhombus mentioned above is thus enriched by another corner, and now forms a pentagon. To chose another metaphor, there are five principal actors on this stage: the employer, the client, the therapy provider, the counsellor, and the supervisor.

There are ten possible pairings, some of which are taboo. Thus the employer and the client have an ongoing relationship, as does the employer and the therapy provider, but the counsellor and the supervisor are prohibited from talking to the employer and the client may not speak to the supervisor. The therapy provider speaks to everybody. (Kutek, 1999: 8–9)

Understandably, this is a scenario in which fantasies and projections abound, in which clients can get lost, wires get crossed and where speed and efficient administration are essential, as clients are promised instant access to a counsellor and expect no less. The counselling work, however, which goes on in the privacy of the counsellor's consulting room, is boundaried and safe as long as the counsellor observes the psychodynamic ground rules and scrupulously implements the contract that s/he sets up with the client once they have agreed to work together for the number of sessions they are allowed by the particular 'employment assistance programme' they belong to. This gives the counsellor relative freedom of action and a fairly secure frame in which to pursue the goal and the focus chosen to work on. But this precious container is hedged around with paperwork and administrative detail of payment, claim forms, questionnaires, assessment notes and closure documentation which reminds the counsellor of his/her own rigorous employment conditions and contracts with the service provider.

Counsellors are usually not guaranteed work on an ongoing basis, but are asked to work in an open-door fashion, i.e. to wait and hope for a reasonable flow of referrals, which is dictated by supply and demand as in the commercial sector, where free market conditions reign. In my experience one needs to be fairly flexible and keep open a number of likely slots for EAP referrals, best in the early mornings or evenings before or after work. This requires a constant juggling of the schedule and careful diary-keeping and -checking, because in this commercial context there is none of the regularity of the analytic routine.

There are numerous other frustrations which complicate the counsellor's work. Often referrals do not get beyond the clinical administrator and the counsellor waits in vain for the promised client who is dragging his/her feet or has simply decided against taking up the offer because of anxiety or indecision. In other cases the client cannot get settled into a regular pattern of sessions and demands that appointments be spaced out over a period of time, which has become an EAP custom, probably approximated to corporate appointment styles of meetings or due to work pressures. Some clients 'bank' their sessions, in an attempt to spread out what is their due, or to save a session for a rainy day – interestingly the phrase again reflects the commercial context.

To ensure a reasonable measure of containment is a fraught business and yet an essential precondition for successful brief work. It is essential for the counsellor to bracket out fantasies of what goes on behind the scenes between employer and therapy provider. As there are always anxieties about getting enough or the right kind of work, reasonably good relations between the counsellor and the provider are important, and this area often needs to be discussed in supervision as rivalry and jealousy of colleagues who seem to be getting more work and anxieties about empty slots and lack of referrals can affect the process of work, get transmitted to the client unconsciously and then get entangled with his/her anxieties, which may be similarly focused on job insecurity and rivalry with colleagues. Sorting this out in supervision in terms of a parallel process can be immensely valuable as an exercise in empathy.

Working in this context, the counsellor needs to know something about managerial styles and will soon learn what goes on in large organizations in terms of job structures, workplace protection, appraisal procedures, etc., as the particular problems EAP clients bring always reflect the culture and atmosphere in which they are required to work. It is interesting to find out how they came to work in their particular sector in the first place and how this might fit into their patterns of having been parented, their expectations of and problems with authority and their need for security: For instance, clients who worked for a human rights charity seemed on the whole to be more emotionally disturbed than clients working in a bank: the former had childhood backgrounds marked by violence and injustice, while the latter, having gone straight into the bank as juniors after school and working their way up into managerial positions, had transferred their dependency needs from parents they had never managed to separate from to the firm, which became their substitute parent and family. In both cases work restructuring and fears of redundancy had increased deep-seated persecutory or depressive anxiety, shattered fragile defences and brought about crises of confidence and relating which affected work performance and personal relationships and brought the clients to counselling to restore their equilibrium.

Noting these differences determined by parenting and workplace choice, the counsellor will be attentive to both in the endeavour to bring about a change and a solution. S/he will also keep an eye on all the parallel processes operating within the clinical pentagon and on the transference where the particular conflicts with and anxieties about authority are likely to be played out, without necessarily having to be addressed or interpreted.

The pentagon in which the EAP counsellor works is particularly sensitive to issues of confidentiality in that:

(a) the client does not want the employer to know what is being talked about in the counselling sessions;
(b) the therapy provider will be hard put to resist the employer's pressure to disclose information about the client; and
(c) the counsellor is ethically bound to curb his/her desire to share interesting titbits about the firm they have been made a party to and thus to observe strict commercial confidentiality as well as the usual personal confidentiality, with the exception of
(d) the supervisor, who in turn is ethically bound not to disclose to third parties confidential material that is discussed with the supervisee.

The brief EAP counsellor is bound by her/his terms of engagement to work with clients in accordance with the particular brief therapy model that the employer and their therapy provider have agreed to implement. In the case of CiC (WPF) this is the five-session solution-focused brief therapy model, which means that clients referred to the counsellor are offered the same five-session contract, which is rarely extended or modified to suit a particular client's special needs. In my experience as a supervisor quite a few counsellors find it difficult, particularly in the early stages of doing this kind of work, to accept this tight schedule and they rebel against it at times, arguing that the client needs more. They may be expressing their own need for more time or, in the countertransference, their client's wishes, but either way there is a protest against time limitations imposed from above which, on the one hand, go against the grain of the nurturing, allowing therapist and of the dependency-craving client while, on the other hand, producing an ambivalence about authority that is endemic to the corporate sector, where authority is wielded and experienced as autocratic.

In a recent article 'The corporatization of psychotherapy', David Pingitore (1997) describes the finance-driven EAP scenario in the

United States where cost-effectiveness demands quick results and positive outcome, where short-termism is ubiquitous, where there is talk of treatment goals, symptom removal and behavioural adjustment rather than of growth and sharing of pain. The therapeutic paradigm has changed and the clinical language has become technological when talking of therapeutic techniques, objectives and diagnostic concepts, and non-clinicians like insurers, care managers and occupational health and human resources departments have a decisive say in the allocation of therapeutic resources. There has been an energetic push into the UK and the American EAP approach (which includes special trainings, degrees and certification of counsellors who become Certified Employee Assistance Professionals) may well become more widespread there, though other, more indigenous forms of 'counselling in companies', like CiC, which is a subsidiary of the WPF, may be more suited to English temperaments and needs.

My supervisees' rebellion is directed against this trend and against the high-tech mindset that divides reality, time and process into bites, as if for entry into an accountant's spreadsheet and related to time and motion studies. But they may also be resistant to the inevitability of change and throw out the baby with the bath-water, when they could make a virtue of necessity, could set the obvious gains of short-term therapy for the multitudes ('something for everybody rather than a lot for a few') against its losses in terms of length, breadth and depth and get on with the exciting brief work in a spirit of experimentation and curiosity. Once again my experience as a supervisor has taught me that after their first few cases of SFBT most counsellors admit that they are amazed what can be done in a short time and how much they have got to know about their client's inner and outer worlds. They may not shed their political reservations against the employers' 'band aid' approach, nor their fears about its effect on the survival chances of long-term therapy, but they almost universally learn to enjoy the quick-pace, fast-thinking and pragmatic approach which is accompanied by high spirits, optimism and positive outcomes, though of unknown duration.

The psychodynamic approach to brief counselling and psychotherapy is becoming established in this field through initiatives like CiC which combine it effectively with a solution-focused module and offer a thorough clinical assessment and referral service alongside the five-session counselling option. This distinguishes it favourably from many less professionally run EAPs which employ voluntary or inadequately trained counsellors, though increasingly selection procedures everywhere are becoming more stringent and professional.

The particular advantage of the psychodynamic approach to counselling at the workplace is the theoretical perspective of human development as an ongoing process prone to recurrent crises and reparative needs when interrupted by traumatic events or cumulative stress conditions, which produce high levels of anxiety. For the adult the work environment will often present situations in which his/her 'core complex' or childhood traumata become reactivated, assume crisis proportions and require instant therapeutic attention.

The psychodynamic assessment in the first session will establish the extent of the problem, its probable roots in infancy, ways of tackling it briefly through focusing on how the client's inner resources and problem-solving capacity can be harnessed and can lead him/her towards a temporary solution, thus re-establishing a measure of psychic equilibrium and increased ego strength. The assessment will also establish, beyond the client's expectations and fantasies, whether this crisis is a one-off or part of an ongoing critical situation that might require more therapeutic input in the future or other types of help, like group work or couples counselling, a psychiatric assessment, a prolonged rest or vacation, a change of job or the move to another country.

The latter options may become an important part of the five-session search for a solution, but these sessions may also become an ongoing assessment period in which, with the help of Malan's triangle of conflict, the therapist will attempt to establish the gravity of the client's emotional and pathological condition and enlist his/her help in reaching a decision to carry on in long-term therapy, with another therapist and at the client's own expense, of course. The therapist will also attempt to help clients understand fully why they need more exploration and working through of their emotional problems and induct them into the way of thinking about themselves psychodynamically, i.e. in terms of the clinical triangles: how they relate to others, to themselves, to significant figures from their past, and, tentatively, to the therapist. This kind of brief therapy experience, prolonged assessment, is a form of 'trial therapy'.

An example is the workaholic father whose relations to his small son are severely strained and who is encouraged by the therapist to go on one outing a week with him – to the playground in the park, to a football match, to the swimming pool. He recognizes that his own experience of an absent, workaholic father conditioned him to neglect his son, too, and that the new weekly schedule creates a growing bond between them the like of which he never had, and that this also allows him to relax his compulsive overworking. It is a revelatory insight and a kind of solution is reached at the end of five sessions, but this has also opened up depths of pain he cannot cope with on his own. A referral to long-term work with a male therapist is agreed and managed. This case demonstrates how a work problem can be identified as a home problem and as a psychodynamic conflict that can be tackled in both areas, which in turn will lead to changes at home and at work.

Like all referrals, it involved contacting the therapy provider, who was clinically responsible for referrals and took over (or back) the client to implement this procedure, which requires great care, good matching and the sensitive management of a transition which is difficult for all concerned, particularly the client and the counsellor. For the former, because s/he will have developed a transference to the counsellor which, even when it has not been actively interpreted or used during the work, will need to be resolved before s/he can actively engage with another strange therapist. The latter because s/he has probably become attached to the client, which makes it difficult to let go at the moment when the referral decision has become a reality.

Many a counsellor will be tempted to hang on, and intuitive clients may become aware of this conscious or unconscious twitch of emotion in their counsellors, may become affected by it, perhaps to the point of wavering in their resolution to take up the referral or to put it off. This is a critical moment, as it may muddy the waters for the referral or complicate the transition. In my experience clients complain most often because of ill-considered contract extensions or mismanaged referrals. Both of these situations should be discussed carefully and clarified in supervision, as they involve serious unresolved transference and countertransference issues and can be damaging to clients.

In my three case studies (Chapter 7) the first client asked to be referred out and was assigned to a new therapist, but she did not take it up and disappeared from sight. In the second case, the client was referred to another therapist, did not take it up and reapplied for another stint of five sessions after a couple of years. The third client, who had been treated in the 30-session Malan model, was seen for a number of follow-ups and finally went into long-term therapy. These outcomes may be typical, though they were not predictable. They indicate, however, that on the whole a brief experience of therapy sows a seed, and enables the client to have another go at it or even to contemplate a more intensive therapeutic involvement at a later date. Which means that it is always worth our while to give everybody something even if it may not be enough the first time round.

The question of what happens to clients after therapy, in the months and years to come, is too rarely asked by brief therapists or by researchers of brief therapy outcome, unless they take a long-term view (which is a contradiction in terms) and are applying a psycho-dynamic perspective which, on the point of assessing a client for brief or long-term psychotherapy and counselling, helps them make a rough prognosis and form a clinical hypothesis. I was surprised and disappointed about the first client's disappearance as she seemed to be so motivated to continue, but her disappearance does not con-clusively prove either a total recovery or a turning away from therapy altogether, rather, I would venture, it indicates a decision not to pursue the option at this time. She was, after all, on the point of becoming engaged in a long-term relationship which, ironically, might have been another kind of solution to the brief therapy she received. And she was also becoming involved in a more than full-time new job – another valid distraction from therapy, ironically.

Referral-out is an offer and an invitation to enter into a new relationship. This is inviting and tempting, particularly when the brief counselling was a good therapeutic experience, but it is also difficult because it involves the loss of the first therapist, and the crossing of this daunting threshold is very similar to the crossing of the first threshold when the client takes up the offer of counselling. Many waver at this first threshold, and do not cross it beyond making the initial telephone call, receiving the papers to fill in and the name of a counsellor to ring. Having experienced drop-outs at both thresholds I reckon that the wastage is about 30 per cent. This causes bad and guilty feelings in three of the participants – the client, the counsellor and the therapy adviser – and the management of these, at least with the counsellor, can be facilitated by the super-visor, the fourth player in the pentagon. But the fifth player, the employer, is also involved, though at one or two removes, and perhaps only cost-wise, though the success of the scheme as a whole depends on the active take-up of the employer's generous offer.

For the brief counsellor, early drop-outs and unsuccessful referrals are quite serious set-backs, the former because they mean loss of earnings and painful feelings of rejection (even when the referrals did not get beyond the call from the therapy provider), and the latter because the counsellor's well-considered plans for the client were thwarted, and this can be felt like a slap in the face after the work one has put into it. But drop-outs are an inevitable part of the job and they indicate clearly that the client is free to choose, even if it may not be in his/her immediate interest (or so the counsellor thinks). There are so many uncertainties to bear in this kind of brief work and so many stories are apparently inconclusive or unfinished. It is absolutely essential that counsellors are able to manage negative feelings, have learnt to manage grief and to allow mourning take its full course. This is one of the reasons why counsllors need supervision for their work, if for nothing else. But that will be the subject of the next chapter.

Charities and voluntary organizations

There is another context in which much brief therapy happens, though again this is not all of the psychodynamic kind: the voluntary sector and the charities. Many counselling agencies are theme-centred, staffed by voluntary or unqualified counsellors: bereavement counselling, alcohol counselling, counselling of drug users, victim or rape support, abortion and pregnancy advisory services, women's centres, youth drop-in centres, prison visitors and a whole plethora of services for sufferers from particular illnesses like MS, Alzheimer's, AIDS and HIV, where counselling is also available for relatives. When, after a rail or plane disaster, the media report that survivors have been given counselling, this must be brief counselling of some sort, though probably support and crisis management rather than exploratory interaction. I have often wondered who the counsellors are who do this job and whether their work is done 'on the hoof' rather than in a structured, planned and properly ended way. People tend to sneer and doubt the motives of the helpers, instead of distinguishing this necessary first aid, pastoral support, from other forms of counselling done by people who are supervised, have received some training and are allocated clients who have been assessed by experienced therapists.

Nowadays much of the counselling in voluntary agencies is done by trainees who are on placements for their training and need to fulfil their training hours under supervision. They have almost wholly replaced the charitable ladies from the past who gave some of their free time to help others less privileged than themselves, and they now counsel the bereaved, visit the sick and support the suffering in return for supervision and some often quite rudimentary training. There is no saying which of the two categories do better work; yet nowadays counsellors are probably safer, more self-aware and more knowledgeable than their lay predecessors. The short-term nature of their work is often dictated more by the length of their training than by the clients' needs, and while they are learning from the clients they may also be making their beginners' mistakes.

It is an important and undoubted fact that most of the free counselling on offer through voluntary agencies like MIND and CRUSE is only possible because there are now such hordes of counselling trainees who need clients to become qualified, and that these trainees are often confronted with situations and with clients whose conditions and severity of symptoms are way beyond their competence. In a way this would be more worrying if one didn't know that the majority of clients are sensible enough to vote with their feet when they do not feel satisfied with the service they are getting, and that all the trainees are obliged to be in supervision, which is more than charitable ladies used to get or what many qualified therapists consider necessary. Once again, the quality of the organizational set-up is important, how it enforces ground rules and secure frames, contracts, confidentiality and the observance of endings and referrals.

The work of CRUSE and MIND has in some respects fulfilled Freud's vision of a 'psychotherapy for the people based on the pure gold of psychoanalysis' in that this has now become truly available to everybody in general and in critical life situations which cannot always be managed by people on their own. It is very important to note how many of these organizations were founded by clergy, starting with the Samaritans, CRUSE and, *nota bene*, the BAC, the British Association for Counselling, and are now clearly doing the pastoral work for which people used to go to their priests and ministers, many of whom have since been trained in counselling (or at least in counselling skills) in order to improve their traditional skills of pastoral care. One could consider the snowballing of counselling in recent years as an outcome of the continuing movement of 'secularization', and the 'faith of the counsellors' (Halmos, 1965) as a sign of what Dietrich Bonhoeffer called 'man's coming of age' (Mander, 1998), which created this 'religionless religion'. In this context of faith in a personal commitment to help others charitably, of 'care in the community', the psychodynamic counsellor believes, like his/her predecessor, the priest, that everybody in need is entitled to receive some counselling help and makes him/herself available for this, if necessary for a low fee or none. This kind of counselling will at times of necessity be brief and pragmatic, though anyone who knows something about the history of the WPF (Black, 1991) will remember that this clergy-founded training and counselling charity offers the majority of its clients in its nationwide network long-term counselling on a sliding fee scale, and is financially kept afloat mainly by its wealthy subsidiary, CiC, which generates its wealth through its successful scheme of SFBT for corporate employees.

The psychodynamic counsellor who believes with Freud that as many people as possible should be helped to 'transform their neurotic misery into common unhappiness', and that they can thus be helped to 'love and work', will endeavour to do this in any context, and in relation to any psycho-somatic symptom that causes people suffering. Many of us are or have been involved in the running and staffing of voluntary counselling agencies to which the whole public has access; we have been involved in fund-raising, training and supervising in such centres and have found the work rewarding and stimulating, provided the agency was properly constituted, structured and boundaried, in other words, safeguarded by a reasonably secure frame with ground rules which allowed its participants to feel safe in their practice and in their therapy. There are voluntary agencies, on the other hand, which have been started with good will and enthusiasm without being based on firm managerial foundations. These will make clients and counsellors feel insecure, unheld and uncared for and not much good may come of them in the long run, unless the profession keeps up its vigilance and enforces its codes of ethics and practice.

Conclusion

Contextual and organizational factors will inevitably influence therapeutic work. I hope I have been able to show this in this chapter by briefly pointing out how the goals and the structures of different organizations impinge on the clinical work and how the unconscious and ubiquitous fantasies, projections and anxieties operating in these environments interpenetrate, parallel and reflect each other to the extent of creating sometimes unbearable levels of stress for clients, staff and management. That this needs constant observation, vigilance and supervision in order to be managed and contained has been described in the classic studies by Elliott Jacques (1955) and Isabel Menzies-Lyth (1970), both of which used Kleinian concepts of defences against anxiety to analyse unconscious processes underlying organizational interactions and hierarchical structures. Organizations are a large-group experience for the individual in which it is a balancing act to establish the sense of security necessary for reasonably good work. They have been compared to halls of mirrors, entities in which unconscious processes are transmitted and reflected in complicated and replicated ways, affecting and obstructing as well as facilitating tasks and working relationships. The apparent purity of work possible in the private practice context which generated much of the psychodynamic theory that informs and supports the practitioner has been expanded, enriched, complicated and modified to suit such contexts, and it is always necessary to be mindful of their pervasive influence on what goes on in the therapeutic dyads operating within them.

9

Supervision and Training in Brief Therapy

Supervision

From the beginning, supervision has been an important aspect of the training and practice of brief psychodynamic therapy. In the Tavistock workshop in which Balint, Malan and their colleagues developed and tested their brief focal model, they supervised each other's cases from session to session and practised painstaking self-supervision with the help of the verbatims and process notes with which they documented their cases from assessment to closure and follow-up (see Balint, 1972). Supervision was one of their primary research and training tools for the practice of brief therapy. It has remained so ever since, as the careful reflecting on and close monitoring of the interactive therapeutic processes, of the therapeutic relationship and of the patients' material is of the essence for the effectiveness of this approach, which relies on a methododology of making economical use of limited time and selected material. The training in both the Malan and the Ryle model consists chiefly of close, session-by-session supervision of training cases in training groups. There supervisees are encouraged to contribute actively to the discussion and evaluation of each other's cases and to develop supervisory and self-supervisory skills while doing so which sharpen their knowledge and understanding of the model, enhance their own practice, their assessing, interpreting and processing of patients' communications, and their technical skills in using the model with ease and confidence.

The supervision of brief work requires the generic supervisor to adapt his/her style to suit the specific requirements of work that is done briefly, actively and fast and that may therefore not offer the opportunity for much supervisory input between beginning and ending, assessing and wrapping up a case. There is little room for sitting back and waiting for things to happen and to develop, for a second chance or for a rethink. While the clock is ticking it is imperative to think fast and to formulate one's supervisory feedback quickly, to comment succinctly and to rely on one's intuition and on one's countertransference responses absolutely in order to contain the supervisee's anxiety, uncertainty and hesitation which prevent the firm decision-making, the accurate hypothesizing and the conceptualizing that is always necessary while working in the brief focal mode. In this respect the supervisor models for the therapist a particular stance of working and invites the supervisee to imitate the speed, observe the technique and introject the decisive thinking which underpin the confident supervisory hypothesizing, the playing with ideas, and the fluent associating of information that is necessary to fulfil the envisaged therapeutic goals of problem-solving and change within a contracted time limit.

For the supervisor as for the counsellor, the constant pressing in of time, with the end always in sight, as the sessions diminish in number, gives the process an urgency that makes for inventiveness, that produces quick responses, initiates solutions, suggests ways forward and keeps one on one's toes mentally and emotionally. It is equally essential to hold the frame firmly all through and to insist that the basic tasks of assessing, focusing, structuring and being mindful of the ending, of the limitation of time and space, and of the countdown of sessions are scrupulously observed.

To start with it is necessary to hear about clients immediately after the first contact and to process the supervisee's assessment session carefully in order to help her/him focus on the problem brought by the client, to understand its psychodynamic implications and to hypothesize about the goal and possible solution that might be reached in the short time allocated. After making a contract, for supervision as much as for the therapy, it is important to look at first impressions and monitor the countertransference in order to learn as much as possible about the client and to identify early on what might be difficult for the counsellor in terms of his/her expectations and fears relating to the particular client under discussion.

The supervisor assists the counsellor in the scanning of the client's personal story for the turbulence and discomfort that prompted the search for help and in the formulating of a diagnosis which tracks down a core problem, reads the symptoms in the light of his/her professional knowledge and experience of pathology, and makes a decision about how to tackle and to contain the disturbance and how to involve the client in the task for the period of time at their disposal. This includes the establishment of a working alliance, the testing of the client's suitability for therapy, of his/her ego strength, his/her ability to relate, to cope with strong feelings, to sustain the unfamiliar and intense experience of exploring a dilemma that has seemed insoluble, and to separate at the end of this endeavour without harm to either participant.

The supervisory task after the initial assessment is to help the supervisee deepen the findings, to monitor the decisions reached, confirming or adjusting the focus envisaged and preparing carefully for the next and the following sessions. The counsellor may be overwhelmed by the wealth of material and therapeutic possibilities, longing to offer long-term work and worried about the lack of time, and all this demands a challenging and supportive supervisory experience in which the counsellor's belief in the method is firmly held and his/her vigilance and imagination strengthened.

I maintain that it is best when there are three supervisory inputs during brief work: the first one straight after assessment to formulate a focus and plan strategies which can bring about a solution, make a significant difference or lead to a desired change; the second one in the middle stage when there are anxieties and disappointments for both partners relating to separation and attachment, when the view forward and backwards allows review, prediction and an interim assessment of what has been achieved and what still needs to be and can be done; and the third one before the last session, when this can be planned in the light of what has happened so far and when the question can legitimately be asked whether the client has benefited, has been helped towards understanding and tackling his/her problem, whether s/he could do with more therapy and has been initiated sufficiently into clienthood for this to be possible, and whether to offer follow-up, in order to establish whether s/he has learnt to self-analyse and continue the working through begun with the counsellor. If they have become able to think in a psychological way, the counsellor's anxieties about perhaps not having given them enough can be allayed and the process of separation can be initiated, take its course and be completed satisfactorily, usually involving some regret and strong emotions relating to loss and disappointment, all of which could be seen as a reaching of the depressive position and of a realistic sense of loss and ambivalence.

Ongoing supervisory tasks are as follows (see Mander, 1998b):

- Concentrating on the intense countertransference experience, the counsellor's and the supervisor's, which will reveal diagnostic clues, ethical dangers and needs for emotional containment.
- Guarding the focus and reminding the counsellors when they wander off or stop keeping the ending in mind. Remaining mindful of the organizational context and structures in which the counselling happens and of the complex psychodynamics of splitting and projecting this may produce for all participants in the joint endeavour and that may become reflected in the process of supervision too.
- Modelling a particular relationship, the brief model's active style of intervening, questioning, decision-making, of constant alertness, quick-footedness, preparedness and firm resistance to seduction,

elation, dejection – not to forget abstinence, and a stance of remaining realistic in one's goals throughout.

- Ongoing assessment of the counsellor's ability to implement the model. Not everyone can do it. Beginners invariably mistake flight into health for change and mishandle the onset of ambivalence. The supervisor has to supply the experience when it is lacking in the counsellor and teach the rudiments of the brief technique by constantly reiterating the basics and rigorously holding the counsellor to the task. If necessary, the counsellors have to be told in supervision that they haven't got it in them to do brief work, which can be due to an inability to let go, to contain the transference, to curb the client's desire for dependence, or simply to make quick decisions, to think on their feet and to scan qantities of material for relevant detail. This is not surprising. Not every client benefits from brief therapy, and equally not every counsellor is able to work in this mode. It follows that not every supervisor can or wants to supervise it.
- Finally and very importantly, assistance in the necessary brief mourning, grief work and any other finishing business after the end of each contract, clearing the ground and the memory for the next beginning, attending to issues of referral, follow-up and feedback. (1998b: 303)

Whether it is done in a group or individually, supervision of brief work demands that often more than one client is discussed in a session, and this means a supervisory style that is flexible and focused. It does not mean hurried or superficial supervising, rather a more concentrated and alert approach that will enable both participants to let go and to move on quickly and willingly. The secret is to remain focused on the counsellor and on the countertransference, and not to feel undue regret about missing things, trusting that an unconscious process of reflections and parallels will guide and activate one's intuition and thinking. Of course, much will have to be left out, and once chosen one has to follow an avenue of thought to where it will take one. The maxim in brief work is that there is only one chance, for the counsellor and for the supervisor.

Supervising brief psychodynamic work usually involves a form of irregular scheduling which mirrors the counsellors' uncertain working conditions and their relationship to an employing organization which supplies the clients or refers these to them on an irregular basis (which is particularly the case with EAPs). The supervisor is either employed and paid by the organization and hence clearly accountable to this (EAPs like CiC operate in this way) or s/he is freely chosen by the counsellor, who may work in a GP practice and take responsibility for his/her own supervision needs. In the latter context, issues of clinical responsibility can become complicated by the doctor's involvement and this means that the supervisory contract needs to take this into account, in particular in relation to endings and referrals. It has been said (Roberts, 1997) that too much of the counselling in or for organizations is done without proper professional contracting, particularly in relation to payment and fees and to conditions of employment, and that counsellors are on the whole lax in these matters and careless of the necessity for firming up working conditions and for looking after their own (and hence the clients') interests. In many situations (particularly EAPs), nobody is guaranteed ongoing work (including the supervisor), and this hand-to-mouth existence and ad hoc environment create an uncertainty about supply and demand which may mirror the client's employment situation while emphasizing all the difficulties the self-employed counsellor in private practice experiences at a time when the profession is unable to balance supply and demand for all its members.

As a CiC supervisor of brief counselling work, I never know from one week to the next whether my services will be called for. Sometimes there are so many cases to be supervised at once that I feel overwhelmed by the demand; at other times, there is an ominous lull that makes me feel redundant. All this is part and parcel of doing brief work, where numbers constantly fluctuate, where beginnings and endings overlap, and where generally free market conditions prevail which are characteristic of our age and which have given rise to a situation where brief therapy is in the ascendance at the expense of the long-term and intensive therapies favoured in the past. All this has made it imperative that the brief supervisor possesses a more than average capacity to contain strong anxieties – the clients', the supervisees' and their own – and a robustness which supports the ability to remain hopeful, creative and confident in conditions of uncertainty.

Training

The training in brief focal therapy initiated by Balint and Malan at the Tavistock Clinic has been fairly unique in the field, and in my opinion there is still not enough systematic training of counsellors and psychotherapists for the qualitatively different work that is time-limited, focused and brief. For a long time the assumption has been that any reasonably competent counsellor and psychotherapist could adapt their long-term practice style to a 'shortened' version, or that it would be natural to start off beginners doing brief work, as their clients initially do not stay very long. This is and was a fallacy as there is obviously a decisive difference between stopping when clients say they feel better (which as often as not is a resistance to the difficulties of working on painful internal material or of allowing themselves to become dependent in the transference) and stopping when a significant change has occurred in their life circumstances or in their emotional functioning that indicates a qualitative shifting of the problem presented or of the mood that has made them seek help. In fact there is now general agreement that it may well be more difficult for the novice to work briefly than for the experienced practitioner, who can be taught to assess and to process clinical material with a view to the different goals and techniques of brief focal therapy and to become versatile in another mode of working without feeling compromised, provided s/he believes in the usefulness and effectiveness of it as a viable alternative and as another leg to stand on when the circumstances demand this.

In many medical, educational and business contexts, time-limited or brief counselling and psychotherapy is becoming the preferred option. Consequently, and as with other relatively new areas of training – for supervisors, for instance, or for trainers, assessors, accreditors, etc. – the training for this kind of work is gradually becoming more of a requirement for increasing numbers of practitioners. Some training institutes, like the Westminster Pastoral Foundation, are offering courses specifically designed to teach the various models and techniques of time-limited work. These lead to certificates and diplomas qualifying graduates (who are usually trained counsellors) for this kind of counselling and usually also offer an element of supervised practice to equip them with some experience. The Association of Cognitive Analytic Therapists specializes in trainings teaching Dr Ryle's particular model, mostly through theoretical seminars, supervision groups and work with a specified number of training patients. Characteristically, much training for brief or time-limited work is itself brief and often consists of weekend or day courses, which may be geared to EAP counselling, be offered as in-house courses in voluntary counselling services or as a regular section of general counselling courses which have become aware of the new trend in employment opportunities for brief counsellors.

The very latest development in the field is training for Counselling in Primary Health Care, which is intended to equip the new armies of GP counsellors up and down the UK with the skills and the knowledge needed to assess, treat and appropriately refer on the increasing numbers of general practice patients who are referred by their doctors for short contracts of emotional problem-solving or for the psychodynamic assessment of their psycho-somatic disorders. Not to mention the numerous brief courses sponsored by the

Association of Student Counsellors, by bereavement services and by various charities catering for specific illnesses like AIDS and eating disorders, for ethnic minorities or for victims of rape, violence and torture. As most of the more specialized counselling of our age is publicly funded, it has become short-term and therefore requires most practitioners to be trained and experienced in short-term work, even if they are volunteers.

It is probably safe to predict that sooner or later all counselling and psychotherapy trainings will include a substantial module of time-limited training alongside the more traditional long-term or intensive varieties, and that these will consist of experiential, theoretical and clinical components, including supervision and research work, as pioneered by Balint and Malan. I envisage and believe in a future in which a plurality of treatment choices will be available to all and practised by many, in a diversity of public and private settings.

10

Post-Therapy Issues: Questionnaires, Research, Evaluation

In the preface to his book *A Study of Brief Psychotherapy*, David Malan states that

> the original aim of the work which was initiated by Dr. Michael Balint, was to explore Brief Therapy, in an attempt to reconcile the 'clinical' and the 'objective' approaches to psychodynamic material, by treating clinical judgements exactly as rigorously as is appropriate, no more and no less.

The study is based essentially on the therapies of nineteen patients and is largely retrospective, but it is designed to fill some of the important gaps to be found in the literature:

1. Detailed case histories are given of all patients treated;
2. Particular attention is paid to long follow-up;
3. A method of assessing therapeutic results has been developed which is regarded as psychodynamically valid and is based on published evidence;
4. The relation is examined between outcome and
   a) the characteristics of patients,
   b) the characteristics of technique.

The methods used are clinical or statistical, where appropriate, and for b) include a quantitative analysis of the case records, which were dictated from memory. It is shown that clinical judgement and quantitative analysis often support each other.

The results are as follows:

1. The widely held conservative view that it is the 'mild' illnesses of recent onset that are the most suitable for brief therapy is not supported.
2. On the contrary, there is strong evidence that other factors are more important, and that quite far-reaching and lasting improvements can be obtained in relatively severe and long-standing illnesses.
3. The cumulative evidence is very strong that a) interpretation of the transference is general, and b) interpretation of the link between transference feelings and the relation to parents in particular, not only carried few dangers in these therapies, but also played a very important part in leading to a favourable outcome.

In short, the results of our work consistently support the radical rather than the conservative view

It is finally shown that, in almost all the hypotheses reached, a single unifying factor can be found. It is suggested that this may be one of the important 'non-specific' factors common to many forms of psychotherapy. (1963: v–vi)

I have quoted Malan in full because he raises most of the points which are still fundamental and relevant to psychotherapy research, then in its infancy in terms of the quantitative and empirical approach chosen by the team and badly in need of painstakingly systematic work carried out convincingly to support the statement: brief psychodynamic therapy works.

As a pilot study and a forerunner of many subsequent attempts to prove that evidence-based research can be conducted into the clinical work done by psychotherapists and counsellors with individuals suffering from emotional stress and conflict, this classic work boldly stepped out of line by enriching the qualitative format of the single case study, favoured by the traditional analyst since Freud, with the more strictly scientific inquiry using statistics, summarizing evidence and evaluating findings in order to establish empirically the validity and effectiveness of a revolutionary new treatment method.

Following in the footsteps of his medical predecessors, Malan tackled the difficult problem of successfully submitting to scientific scrutiny clinical material from the team's practical work with individual patients, and single-handedly took on the pervasive antagonism of his psychoanalytic colleagues to research methods which to them seemed to threaten the essential elements of the psychoanalytic process. By persisting in writing up assessments, brief case histories and subsequent follow-ups, he laid down a blueprint of how to conduct valid research into the interactive world of dynamic therapists and how to compare and measure the complex outcomes of this endeavour in a way that might give his study a predictive format on which future practitioners could base their clinical work and plan further developments.

In the 20 years since then, the resistance to psychotherapy research has been lessening significantly due to the establishment of psychoanalysis and psychotherapy departments in universities, colleges and medical centres and to a profusion of new MA and MSc courses which now offer interested students ample research opportunities in the field. It is a field, however, that has been dominated for too long almost exclusively by the practitioner and, following Freud and his disciples, has derived its main theoretical base from nineteenth-century-style hermeneutic criteria applied to clinical experience, and from the classical single case study through the precision of analytic inference and interpretation in the 'laboratory of the consulting room' (Rustin, 1997). Target puts her finger on this complex situation when she writes:

> It seems there has long been a reluctance among most psychodynamically orientated psychotherapists to use audit and empirical research methods to record their activity or investigate the effectiveness of their work. This is partly because these therapists have tended to believe that their results are best demonstrated by individual and clinical case reports, presented . . . to support a theoretical perspective, a procedure followed by Freud . . . and only recently strongly challenged within psychoanalysis itself. . . . This is also because many practitioners . . . are not inclined to carry out empirical, quantitative studies which are commonly demanded by both journals and consumers or purchasers of services: these ask for evidence that people get better, and if so, in what ways, how long it takes, whether this is the best way of help that is available for these problems, and so on.
>
> My experience has been that some psychotherapists and counsellors have no training in these evaluation methods, others are refugees from these approaches. . . . It can be a confusing field of jargon-ridden methodologies, in which advocates of quantitative methods tend to denigrate people who try to develop qualitative studies and vice versa. . . . The best-known research methods for describing presenting problems such as symptom checklists or structured diagnostic interviews are often seen as inadequate or even irrelevant measures of problems or outcomes thought to be too individual or complex to be captured by standardized assessments. And many would go further and maintain that any attempt to describe either the process of work or outcomes in standardized terms is misguided and fruitless.
>
> There is an issue of principle and professionalism involved in questions of whether therapeutic approaches can be evaluated in terms of effectiveness. . . . In an era when paternalistic attitudes are being questioned and issues of professional power and the desirability of consumer choice are taken far more seriously, I think it is entirely legitimate to ask what evidence we have that our form of help actually does help. . . . There is at present no methodology which exactly fits the psychotherapeutic focus on the individual and at the same time maintains internal and external validity; compromises are therefore necessary. The same question can be gradually answered using more than one design and a picture can be pieced together of how and when a therapy is helpful. . . . These approaches complement each other and begin to provide answers to the questions which clinicians ought to be asking themselves. Am I doing the right thing for this client? Why does this therapy help or not help in this type of case? Can I show other people that this treatment is effective or cost-effective? Are there ways of adapting what I usually do which will help some clients more? Where should scarce resources be used and are there cases where less help is more help? . . . Just as the clinical disciplines we practise have grown through asking new questions and looking at the evidence through fresh eyes, so it is with evaluation, and each can stimulate the other to remain creative. (1998: 79ff)

Target has summed up the situation masterfully.

I think it is legitimate to say that the recent advent of brief and time-limited therapies like the focal, the cognitive analytical and the solution-focused approach may also have something to do with the decisive and noticeable increase in evidence-based research and outcome studies by academics and clinicians in a concerted effort to prove the effectiveness and validity of all forms of therapeutic intervention with larger numbers and wider groups of people in need of psychological help and better self-understanding. Organizations like the British Association for Counselling and the United Kingdom Council for Psychotherapy are systematically stepping up the promotion of empirical research, and there is a shift from qualitative to quantitative-based research, with prestigious professorships and research fellowships increasingly being bestowed on the best minds in the profession. Pioneering researchers like Peter Fonagy (Freud Professor at University College, London, and Director of the Anna Freud Centre in London) and his assistant Mary Target (Fonagy, 1996; Fonagy and Target, 1986) have been conducting complex scientific inquiries into the no-man's land of psychotherapeutic processes, frequencies and psychopathologies, applying quantitative and statistics-based methodologies retrospectively to the Anna Freud Centre's rich archives of clinial material in order to establish the accurate validation (or falsification) of hypotheses demanded by strictly empirical scientific research methodology. This was definitively formulated by the Viennese philosopher Karl Popper (1967), who had once so mercilessly condemned Freud's 'unfalsifiable' theories that psychoanalysis received a decisive blow and is still trying to recover from the attack.

What now goes on in university research departments and is taught in research seminars to MA and MSc students is an embodiment of the 'university spirit' that was so well defined in 1912 by Professor E.H. Starling in a statement to the Royal Commission on University Education in London, the Haldane Commission, as

> not simply diagnosing a patient and deciding what we do for him in order to earn our fee, but what we can get out of this case in order to do better next time. The question is: How can we get some knowledge out of this patient in order to have more power when we have another man in the same condition?

Writing about 'psychotherapy research: psychological research and intra-psychic events', Porter (1986), from whose work the above quotation is taken, supplements this question with others:

> There are many research questions to be asked, such as: How can we make use of individual case studies for research purposes? How can the accumulation of clinical impressions be used to increase our knowledge

and improve our practice? How can observational data, even anecdotes, be formulated in such a way that assessments and comparisons are possible? And one particularly fundamental question that is now increasingly being put: how can we prove which therapeutic approach and model is effective and when? (1986: 257)

Mary Target (1998) states that conclusive research projects are always costly and complex to design as they require control groups and volunteers, while the average MSc thesis, which is based on surveys or questionnaires and on relatively small numbers of returns, is difficult to execute efficiently and to interpret accurately enough for it to become statistically significant. Most of these isolated research efforts never see the light of publication in the professional journals and they moulder away in obscure archives without further use.

To go on asking fundamental questions with Porter may be more fruitful than to bemoan the wastage of academic research efforts which may do no more than earn degrees and awards for their authors and establish their professional credentials. There is now no longer any chance of turning back the clock, and a whole diversity of research methods, of both the qualitative and the quantitative kind, is being practised up and down the UK under the banner of evidence-based research which attempts to provide plausible answers and to pose further questions, contributing to the accumulation of a body of knowledge. The most urgent questions are still these: 'Do the results of psychotherapy depend on specific therapies and therapists? Do patients with a particular psycho-neurosis respond better to one form of treatment than to another?' (Porter, 1986: 260). Or is it sufficient to know that, according to a number of important research papers, a major factor in all the exploratory psychotherapies is the establishment of a therapeutic relationship in which the patient can feel safe and be listened to, regardless of the therapist's theoretical background, interpretative skill and technical knowhow? This may indeed be the 'single unifying factor' that Malan found in almost all the hypotheses reached by his teamworkers and that he suggested might be one of the 'non-specific factors' common to many forms of psychotherapy.

How can clinical concepts be tested and validated in the Popperian sense? It is possible to establish the physical correlates of emotion, heart rate, blood pressure, skin disturbance and muscle activity. But how can the meaning of feelings and of intrapersonal events – conscious and unconscious – be assessed, compared and measured? How do we evaluate intrapersonal change and events that carry personal but not universal conviction? In answer to these as yet unanswerable questions Porter quotes John Keats' 'negative capability' cited in

Chapter 2 above: 'when a man is capable of being in uncertainties, mysteries, doubts, without any irritable reaching after fact & reason' (letter of December 1817). 'In psychotherapy research', she states,

> we reach after fact and reason, but not irritably and not to the exclusion of mysteries and the denial of our own uncertainties and doubts. We work with Starling's research spirit, 'what we can get out of this case in order to do better next time' but without losing sight of our sense of mystery and wonder. Objective measurement and the 'capability of being in uncertainty' are, together, the subject and object of psychotherapy research. (Porter, 1986: 260–61)

All too often, however, there is irritable reaching after fact and reason and researchers' bias in favour of their model which can lead to what has been called 'allegiance effects'. This is also true, in the field of brief therapy research, where practitioners (like Davanloo, Ryle) have been eager to prove that their particular treatment version has been found to work for most conditions and severities by quoting verbatim material from their own clinical practice, which some would consider a scientifically controversial and dubious research procedure.

Another example are the often quoted research findings by Garfield and Kurtz (1952) relating to length of attendance and stating that in excess of 40 per cent of clients discontinued psychotherapy prior to the fifth session. Feltham states: 'These data suggest, according to Barkham (1990), that many people seeking help do not wish or cannot afford long-term therapy' (1997: 141). Consequently, it is thought that there seems to be an overwhelming need for brief forms of therapy. This is supported by another argument based on the finding that there is a course of 'diminishing returns with more and more effort required to achieve just noticeable differences in patient improvement' (Howard et al., 1986), and this apparently recommends 'a model of therapy which provides a closer match between the findings of the research literature [i.e. the dose–effect curve] and client expectations and service delivery needs'. I think this is a debatable point, in particular because there is no definition of what constitutes improvement. Feltham buys Barkham's argument regarding the dose–effect curve and concludes that

> what can be inferred from these figures [14 per cent of clients improve even before attending the first session, 24 per cent are likely to have improved by the end of the first session, 30 per cent by the second session, 41 per cent by the fourth, 53 by the eighth, 62 by the thirteenth, 74 by the twenty-sixth, 83 by session 52 and 90 per cent at 104] is that two-thirds of clients are helped significantly within 13 sessions or so. Certainly a great many people can be helped within a relatively short time, whereas there are diminishing returns after a certain period of therapy. (1997: 140–41)

From these findings it is a short way to concluding that short-term therapy could be as effective as long-term therapy, as happened in an analysis of outcome studies (Smith, 1980). Feltham provides supporting evidence from another study which calculated the mean length of therapy as actually experienced by clients as being around six sessions (Garfield, 1995). This sort of statistics-based argument in favour of brief therapy is quoted frequently. It sounds to me, however, like special pleading, as there is no attempt made at finding out what people mean by improvement or help, nor are they being asked whether a few sessions is all they expected. The statement about diminishing returns is equally bald, and no distinction is made between quantity and quality. 'Overall a large amount of data suggest that short-term therapy is wanted and preferred, is appreciated and perceived as successful. . . . We ignore such findings at our peril' (Feltham, 1997: 141). The questions Feltham asks after making this apodictic statement in support of short-term therapy instantly undermine and contradict it, however, as they address issues of quality and individuality which cannot be quantified. So much for the apparent conclusiveness of scientific truths that have been arrived at statistically and are bandied about carelessly.

Interestingly, Malan's quantitative study was followed in 1972 by a retrospective and posthumous study based on Balint's work with one patient from the Tavistock research team: *Focal Psychotherapy: An Example of Applied Psychoanalysis* (Balint, 1972). The reader is taken through this one case from beginning to end, and as an illustration of the method and the clinical procedures, including the meticulously filled-in interview and session reports and the therapist's ongoing comments, this 'qualitative approach' demonstrates the validity and effectiveness of the treatment method as graphically as does the multi-person research written up laboriously by Malan a few years earlier. By presenting one sample, Balint wished to point to one area that 'claims some priority over the others in our minds, namely the technique of therapy. . . . Without a clear link between the techniques and processes of therapy and the specific outcome, both the teaching and the researchability of psychotherapy is hampered if not made altogether impossible' (1972: 158–9).

This complementarity of approach established an evidential base for the Balint–Malan experiment that combines traditional and contemporary research methodology and sets an example for the validity of an And/And approach over the Either/Or of much later brief therapy research that is guided by therapist bias and special pleading for a preferred technique. Both Balint and Malan aimed to practise the empirical objectivity they had been taught in their medical training.

Leppar quotes an interesting statement by Jung (1909) that succinctly compares diametrically opposed research attitudes:

> The scientific needs of the investigator prompt him to look for rules and categories in which the most alive of living things can be captured. The analyst and observer, on the other hand, must eschew formulas and let the living reality work upon him in all its lawless profusion. Thus I shall present this case in its natural setting, and I hope I shall succeed in showing you how differently an analysis develops from what might have been expected on purely theoretical grounds. (Leppar, 1996: 219)

Researchers nowadays describe their methodologies with the help of adjectives like objective-empirical, phenomenological, hermeneutic, heuristic, inductive, etc., and as long as the reader is told and the research design is careful in the sense of Keats' 'negative capability', this is as it should be. Ever since Kuhn published his seminal book *The Structure of Scientific Revolutions* (1962) it is known that no scientific paradigm is absolute and that ages and personalities favour a diversity of mutually exclusive perspectives. What is scientifically objectionable is the 'irritable reaching for fact and reason' that leads to bias, dishonesty, wishful thinking and false conclusions like 'brief therapy works as well as long-term therapy' or to competitive scoring like 'my way is better than yours'. Jung clearly favours the second of his paradigms but does not claim exclusivity for it, and Leppar, by recommending a 'discursive approach' to clinical analysis instead of the hermeneutical method of interpretation (which she calls the 'taken for granted method of creating meaning'), is stating her preference by arguing its pros and cons. Objectivity is a scientific ideal which we cannot ever reach fully, only try to approximate to.

In the brief therapy field, objectivity has sometimes been flaunted when claims made for its superiority and effectivity have been supported by skewed evidence or have been based on insufficient evidence. There are, however, many other instances of brief therapy research that are backed up by convincing proof and reach conclusions free from wishful thinking. For instance, Roslyn Corney's (1998) study into the usefulness of counsellors working for GP surgeries, 'A Counsellor in Every General Practice?', ends on a note of open verdict after conscientiously reviewing the research literature and covering every aspect of the important topic: 'More studies are needed, particularly those which measure long-term effects', such as reduced visits to the doctor after cessation of counselling, reduction of psychotropic and other drugs prescribed, and fewer referrals to psychiatrists. 'Clinical trials have yielded very mixed evidence of the cost effectiveness of counselling', however, and yet the final recommendation is that more emphasis is necessary on the development of the communication and counselling skills of all the primary care team members, including nurses and doctors. . . . The high proportion of GPs employing counsellors is proof indeed that this is what GPs want. . . . Users of psychiatric services repeatedly demonstrate their desire for counselling. Counselling has been shown by population surveys to be the treatment of choice for depression, indicating that clients view it as an acceptable or even preferable alternative to medication . . . and a study of patient satisfaction found that 85 percent of clients agreed that counselling should be available in general practice. (Corney, 1998: 17)

This may mean that the question in the title can be answered in the positive, but also that much more research is needed to establish the general effectiveness of counselling, particularly its brief focal version as pioneered at the Tavistock.

Questionnaires and follow-ups: research and evaluation

Balint and Malan used some valuable research tools with which to gather evidence for their research, in particular the pre-assessment questionnaire and the follow-up interview. The former has become standard practice at many NHS psychotherapy units (see Aveline, 1990) and at counselling services like the Westminster Pastoral Foundation, where it was introduced in 1986 in order to assess clients differentially for brief focal as well as long-term work and to start up a process among prospective clients of thinking about themselves before they presented for assessment. In conjunction with the General Health Questionnaire, in which clients are asked to ring a series of multiple-choice questions to establish their present state of psychic and physical functioning, prior to assessment and once again after they terminate their counselling, this form provides material on which to base longitudinal and quantitative research into the reasons for seeking counselling and the results as seen by the clients. Supplemented by follow-up reports, this evidence can easily be interpreted in terms of client expectations, client improvement and lasting effects, and Malan's book constitutes the blue print for such much-needed research.

My own experience of preparing a limited study (which has remained unpublished), based on four cases seen in 1986 for 25 sessions each and followed up for 18 months, established that three out of the four cases showed extensive improvement and ongoing 'working through' on the part of the clients. This outcome convinced me and my colleagues of the effectiveness of brief focal work, though at the time the institution could not find a practical way of using it as a basis for selecting and allocating clients for brief work. This required the establishment of a Training in Time-Limited Counselling some years later, whose trainees work with selected clients under supervision, and this has led to a steady stream of clients suitable for and benefiting from time-limited work, though so far no empirical research study has been designed to supply the conclusive evidence for the long-term benefits of this, nor for those of the extensive solution-focused brief therapy work done over the last five years by Counselling in Companies (CiC), which is affiliated to the WPF and employs many counsellors.

It is clear that more and better designed research is needed to back up the 'counsellors' faith' in their work (Halmos, 1965), which is not always shared by the media, which influence the general public. Yet this is a profession of practitioners and pragmatists whose training (as Target bemoaned) does not usually equip and motivate them to do research into their activities, as this seems to go against some of their fundamental principles (to do with confidentiality, non-directiveness and a non-judgmental attitude). The more the pity as the general public is increasingly being influenced by the media to distrust counsellors because a minority of them are not always as ethical and conscientious as they should be nor as well trained and supervised as their professional Code of Ethics and Practice requires them to be. As the numbers of people who receive counselling, and particularly brief counselling, increase exponentially, the push from the universities and research committees of the professional bodies for more evidence-based research is becoming more urgent and will hopefully bear results in the near future.

A recent guest editorial in *Counselling*, the journal of the British Association for Counselling, commented on the fact that counselling is slow in generating the body of applied theory which is vital if it is to be taken seriously.

> Counsellors must analyse their practice so that underlying trends and insights may be identified and quantified. In short, it must play the academic's game. Psychiatry did. Look where it is now. . . . If counselling is to be taken seriously, it must generate valid research which will stand interrogation, provide plausible answers and pose further questions. (Hall, 1997: 242)

It is an important task for the future.

11

Summary and Conclusion

I have tried to cover as many aspects of my subject as I could think of and fit into the format of the series. I hope that I have managed to convey my strong belief in as well as my persistent doubts regarding the uses of brief psychotherapy, both of which are based on years of experience and practice as a therapist and supervisor in the context of the Westminster Pastoral Foundation, where I trained and was a trainer for many years.

I have been exercised by the ethical problems besetting the brief practitioner, who is constrained by necessities and pressures arising in the contexts where brief therapy is offered to a clientele largely ignorant of what therapy is about, what it is likely to lead to and will be able to deliver, in contrast to their vague expectations and hopes for relief and solutions. I have been worried, too, by some of the developments in the field which are finance-driven rather than based on sound empirical outcome studies, and particularly by claims that most problems and conditions can be tackled successfully by brief interventions, as these relegate the traditional long-term approach to the dustbin and belittle the importance of a holding and nurturing therapeutic relationship over time, where change and healing are given a chance to develop slowly.

I have also pondered the fact that the staggering increase in NHS and corporately funded time-limited therapeutic assistance, while fulfilling Freud's hope of a 'psychotherapy for the people' (1919), constitutes in some way a return to the traditional brief intervention by doctor or priest in their medical and pastoral roles which predated the offer of privately paid-for long-term involvement in therapeutic treatment as recommended by psychoanalysis. From being a privilege available to the few, therapeutic help has now become available to the many, as befits a democratic age and a mass society whose demands and aspirations often produce emotional stresses beyond the power of individuals to manage and require a publicly responsible attitude from state and employer for the health of citizens and employees.

This increase in 'managed care', as the Americans are fond of calling the free provision of health services by corporations and in industry, has required the thinning and spreading out of resources to a point of minimally reliable availability which is reflected in careful calculations of cost-effectiveness that parcel out so much to each and everybody as is considered enough for the purpose of achieving set targets and desired goals. Some of this smacks of the time and motion study – e.g. the 12 minutes allotted per patient in the GP surgery, as well as the 6 sessions allowed per contract lasting 50 minutes each, which are becoming the norm in many contexts. Practitioners who are able to perform well within such constraints have to be quick at making decisions, good at finding solutions or at formulating accurate hypotheses, and easily able to establish rapport, whereas those with a slower and more reflective temperament can find themselves at odds in a world where the pace is fast and relentless and where there is no time to wait and see how things develop.

The world of brief therapy is hence peopled by a type of personality who is self-confident, extrovert, articulate, optimistic, fearless and above all determined to produce results, all of which is likely to inspire the patients to cooperate and be optimistic. When Freud mentioned 'suggestion' as a likely component of the envisaged 'psychotherapy of the people', he may have thought of the persuasive and charismatic temperament rather than of hypnosis and manipulation, which he had abandoned as dangerous and unlikely to produce insight. In working briefly, what matters most is to make an impact and to use this impact to make something happen, by harnessing the patient's initial startled response to the thrust and surprise of the therapeutic encounter. By the time this has worn off and produces resistance, the therapy is probably over and has done the work of achieving a limited goal. Striking the iron while it is hot is therefore all that needs doing in a piece of brief work to make a lasting impression. The passive, neutral or invisible therapist is unlikely to get there. Hence, brief therapy requires supervision and an effective training in the specific skills and attitudes that promote speed and decisiveness when time and the goal are limited. It also requires a firm belief in its effectiveness and a steadfast adherence to its principles and ground rules, an endless ability to hope and a capacity to wonder at its infinite possibilities, in particular when a psychodynamic formulation opens up a problem to a satisfying solution.

At the time of writing, brief psychodynamic psychotherapy is still gathering momentum and is practised widely in the UK, contributing actively to a situation where the majority of the population now has free access to brief therapeutic help through various public, corporate and charitable channels. Recognized by the NHS, by universities and schools and by the providers of EAPs, the brief psychotherapist and counsellor can have influence and a busy practice providing help to distressed GP patients, students and employees, apparently appreciated by consumers and providers alike for cutting waiting lists and drugs bills. Within a few years the therapy scene, from being dominated by long-term practitioners and predominantly middle-class fee-paying patients, has been transformed into a dense spectrum of diverse therapies, differing in length, frequency and style and offering choices for many needs. While there is still a hierarchy in status ranging from lofty analysts to humble telephone counsellors, the gradient is becoming less steep and improvements in training and professional standards have helped practitioners move into close-knit professional groupings which practise self-regulation and vigilance through codes of ethics and complaints procedures in order to offer their customers a safe and reliable service.

The advent of brief counselling and psychotherapy has had another important effect in that the profession has now seriously begun to ask itself questions about contracts, lengths and criteria for ending therapy, has started to put its house in order regarding abusive therapists and lax counsellors, and has finally become properly research-minded, which may lead to the improvement of its reputation in the eyes of other professionals, the public and the media. By emphasizing the importance of secure frames, of consistent ethical-mindedness and ongoing supervision, the psychodynamic therapist is working towards gaining the professional status due to his/her important person-centred activity.

Another consequence of the brief therapy boom is a redistribution and rethinking in the whole field concerning claims made for the superior curative powers of analysis and intensive psychotherapy. Brief therapists have no ambition to cure all and everything; in fact, curing is not a word in their vocabulary. The modesty of their claims is attractive, and, of course, one of the main reasons for their ability to shorten and complete their contracts. The brief practitioner works within known limitations and is therefore more likely to produce results, limited as they may be. The modest proposal of limited help is a promise that is more likely to be kept than the promise that long-term and intensive therapy will produce definite and significant character changes, will lead to permanent relief and to a lasting conflict resolution. Making a difference, however small, is an achievable aim, and it is always rewarding for both participants, when it happens. When it doesn't, the failure is less severe, there is less guilt than regret, and the small investment can be overcome. Instead of omnipotent hope, there is likelihood and a realistic expectation of desired results. We remain in the realm of the modest and of the possible, which is a good and affirming place to be, though rarely world-shaking.

Bibliography

Alexander F. and French, T.M. (1946) *Psychoanalytic Therapy: Principles and Application*. New York: Ronald Press

Aveline, M. (1990) 'Psychotherapy and the NHS: Developing a new NHS Psychotherapy Unit in the provinces', *British Journal of Psychotherapy*, 6 (3): 312–23

Aveline, M. (1995) 'How I assess for focal psychotherapy', in *The Art and Science of Assessment in Psychotherapy*, ed. C. Mace, London and New York: Routledge

Balint, M. (1955) 'The doctor, his patient and the illness', in *Problems of Human Pleasure and Behaviour*, London: Maresfield Library

Balint, M. (1968) *The Basic Fault: Therapeutic Aspects of Regression*, London: Tavistock/Routledge

Balint, M. (1972) *Focal Psychotherapy: An Example of Applied Psychoanalysis*, eds P.H. Ornstein and E. Balint, London: Tavistock Publications

Barker, P. (1991) *Regeneration*, Harmondsworth: Penguin

Barkham, M. (1990) 'Research in individual therapy', in W. Dryden, *Individual Therapy: A Handbook*. Milton Keynes: Open University Press

Barkham, M. and Hobson, R. (1989) 'Exploratory therapy in two-plus-one sessions', *British Journal of Psychotherapy*, 6 (1): 79–86

Bateson, G. (1978) *Steps to an Ecology of Mind*, London: Granada Publishing

Bell, E. (1996) *Counselling in Further and Higher Education*, Buckingham: Open University Press

Bion, W.R. (1962) *Learning from Experience*, London: Maresfield Reprints

Bion, W.R. (1963) *Elements of Psycho-Analysis*, London: Heinemann, reprinted Karnac Books, 1984

Bion, W.R. (1967) 'A theory of thinking', in *Second Thoughts*, Selected Papers on Psycho-Analysis, London: Maresfield Library

Bion, W. (1970) *Attention and Interpretation*, London: Tavistock

Black, D. (1991) *A Place for Exploration*, London: The Westminster Pastoral Foundation

Bleger, J. (1967) 'Psychoanalysis of the psychoanalytic frame', *International Journal of Psychoanalysis*, 48: 511–19

Bloom, B.L. (1981) 'Focused single-session therapy: initial development and evaluation', in *Forms of Brief Therapy*, ed. S.H. Budman, pp. 167–216

Bollas, C. (1986) 'The transformational object', in *The British School of Psychoanalysis: The Independent Tradition*, ed. G. Kohon, London: Free Association Books

Bollas, C. (1999) 'The goals of psychoanalysis?', *The Mystery of Things*, London and New York: Routledge

Bollas, C. and Sundelson, D. (1996) *The New Informants: Betrayal of Confidentiality in Psychoanalysis and Psychotherapy*, London: Karnac de Board, R. (1978) *The Psychoanalysis of Organizations*, London: Tavistock Publications

Bowlby, J. (1988) *A Secure Base*, London: Routledge

Brave Smith, A. (1996) 'The shadow in short-term counselling: An exploration of resistance in the counsellor using a Jungian perspective', *Psychodynamic Counselling*, 2 (4): 533–5

Casement, P. (1985) *On Learning from the Patient*, London: Tavistock Publications

Coltart, N. (1988) 'Diagnosis and assessment for suitability for psychoanalytic psychotherapy', *British Journal of Psychotherapy*, 4 (2): 127–34

Coltart, N. (1986) *Slouching towards Bethlehem*, in *The British School of Psychoanalysis: The Independent Tradition*, ed. G. Kohon, London: Free Association Books. pp. 185–99

Coltart, N. (1996) 'Endings', in *The Baby and the Bathwater*, London: Karnac Books

Coltart, N. (1997) *How to Survive as a Psychotherapist*, London: Sheldon Press

Coren, A. (1996) 'Base metal or pure gold?', *Psychodynamic Counselling*, 2 (1): 22–38

Corney, R. (1998) 'A counsellor in every general practice?', *European Journal of Psychotherapy, Counselling and Health*, 1 (1): 5–20

Courtman, D. (1995) *Considerations and Guidelines for Introducing a School Counselling Service*, University of Hertfordshire School of Humanities and Education

Davanloo, H. (ed.) (1980) *Short-Term Dynamic Psychotherapy*, New York: Jason Aronson

East, P. (1995) *Counselling in Medical Settings*, Buckingham: Open University Press

Ekstein, R. and Wallerstein, R.S. (1958) *The Teaching and Learning of Psychotherapy*, New York: Basic Books

Erikson, E. (1950) *Childhood and Society*, Harmondsworth: Penguin Books

Eysenck, H. (1985) *Decline and Fall of the Freudian Empire*, London: Viking

Feltham, C. (1997) *Time-Limited Counselling*, London: Sage

Fisch, R., Weakland, J.H. and Segal L. (1982) *The Tactics of Change: Doing Therapy Briefly*, San Francisco and London: Jossey-Bass

Flegenheimer, W.V. (1982) *Techniques of Brief Psychotherapy*, New York: Jason Aronson

Fonagy, P. (1996) 'The future of an empirical psychoanalysis', *British Journal of Psychotherapy*, 13 (1): 106–18

Fonagy, P. and Target, M. (1986) 'Predictors of outcome in child psychoanalysis: A retrospective study of 763 cases at the Anna Freud Centre', *Journal of the American Psychoanalytic Association*, 44: 27–77

Foulkes, S.H. (1975) *Group-analytic Psychotherapy: Method and Principles*, London: Gordon Breach

Frank, J.D. (1982) 'Therapeutic components shared by all psychotherapies', in *The Master Lecture Series, Vol. 1: Psychotherapy Research and Behavior Change*, ed. J. Harvey and M.M. Parkes, Washington: APA, pp. 17–39

Fredtoft, T., Poulsen, S. and Bauer, M. (1996) 'Dependency and perfectionism: Short-term dynamic group psychotherapy for university students', *Psychodynamic Counselling*, 2 (4): 476–97

French, T.M. (1958) *The Integration of Behavior*, Chicago: University of Chicago Press

French, T.M. (1970) 'The cognitive structure of behavior', *Psychoanalytic Interpretations: The Selected Papers of T.M. French*, Chicago: Quadrangle Books

Freud, S. (1893–5) *Studies on Hysteria, The Standard Edition of the Complete*

Psychological Works of Sigmund Freud, ed. J. Strachey, Vol. 2, London: Hogarth Press

Freud, S. (1914) 'Remembering, repeating and working through', in *The Standard Edition of the Complete Psychological Works of Sigmund Freud*, ed. J. Strachey, Vol. 12, London: Hogarth Press

Freud, S. (1917) 'Mourning and melancholia', in *The Standard Edition of the Complete Psychological Works of Sigmund Freud*, ed. J. Strachey, Vol. 11, London: Hogarth Press

Freud, S. (1919) 'Lines of advance in psycho-analytic therapy', in *The Standard Edition of the Complete Psychological Works of Sigmund Freud*, ed. J. Strachey, Vol. 17, London: Hogarth Press

Freud, S. (1937) 'Analysis terminable and interminable', in *The Standard Edition of the Complete Psychological Works of Sigmund Freud*, ed. J. Strachey, Vol. 23, London: Hogarth Press

Garfield, S.L. (1978) 'Research on client variables in psychotherapy', in *Handbook of Psychotherapy and Behavior Change: An Empirical Analysis*, eds S.L. Garfield and A.E. Bergin, New York: Wiley

Garfield, S.L. (1995) *Psychotherapy: An Eclectic-Integrative Approach*, 2nd edn, New York: Wiley

Garfield, S.L. and Kurtz, M. (1952) 'Evaluation of treatment and related procedures in 1216 cases referred to a mental hygiene clinic', *Psychiatric Quarterly*, 26: 414

Gray, A. (1998) *An Introduction to the Therapeutic Frame*, London: Routledge

Green, A. (1975) 'The analyst, symbolization and absence in the analytic setting (on changes in the analytic practice and analytic experience)', *International Journal of Psychoanalysis*, 561–22

Greenson, R.R. (1967) *The Technique and Practice of Psychoanalysis*, London: Hogarth Press

Groddeck, G. (1977) *The Meaning of Illness*, London: Hogarth Press

Guggenbühl-Craig, A. (1971) *Power in the Helping Professions*, Dallas & Thalwil: Spring Books

Guntrip, H. (1992) *Schizoid Phenomena, Object Relations and the Self*, London: Karnac

Haley, J. (1963) *Uncommon Therapy: The Psychiatric Techniques of Milton H. Erickson M.D.*, London and New York: W.W. Norton

Hall, E. (1998) Guest editorial, *Counselling*, 9 (4): 258

Halmos, P. (1965) *The Faith of the Counsellors*, London: Constable

Heal, M. (1997) 'Introducing a counselling culture to general practice', *Journal of the Institute of Psychotherapy and Counselling*, 6: 15–19

Heimann, P. (1950) 'On countertransference', *On Children and Children No Longer Collected Papers 1942–80*, ed. M. Tönnesmann (1989), London, New York: Tavistock/Routledge

Hinshelwood, R.D. (1991) 'Psychodynamic formulation in assessment for psychotherapy', *British Journal of Psychotherapy*, 8 (2): 166–74

Hoag, L. (1992) 'Psychotherapy in the general practice surgery: Considerations of the frame', *British Journal of Psychotherapy*, 8 (4): 417–29

Hobson, R.H. (1985) *Forms of Feeling: The Heart of Psychotherapy*, London: Tavistock Publications

Holmes, J. (1994) 'Brief dynamic psychotherapy', in *Advances in Psychiatric Treatment, The Royal College of Psychiatrists, Journal of Continuing Professional Development*, 1 (1): 9–15

Holmes, J. (1997) 'Too early, too late: Endings in psychotherapy – an attachment perspective', *British Journal of Psychotherapy*, 13 (2): 159–71

Howard, K.I., Kopta, S.M., Krause, M.S. and Orlinsky, P.E. (1986) 'The dose–response relationship in psychotherapy', *American Psychologist*, 41: 159–64

Jacques, E. (1955) 'Social systems as a defence against anxiety', in *New Directions in Psycho-Analysis*, ed. M. Klein, London: Maresfield Reprints. pp. 478–98

Jacques, E. (1965) 'Death and the midlife crisis', *The International Journal of Psycho-Analysis*, 46: 502–14

Jones, D. (1986) 'General practitioner attachments and the multidisciplinary team', *British Journal of Psychotherapy*, 2 (3): 196–200

Jones, H., Murphy, A., Neaman, G., Tollemarche R. and Vasserman, D. (1994) 'Psychotherapy and counselling in a GP practice: Making use of the setting', *British Journal of Psychotherapy*, 10 (4): 543–51

Joseph, B. (1989) 'Transference: the total situation', *Psychic Equilibrium and Psychic Change. Selected Papers*, ed. M. Feldman and E. Bott Spillius, London and New York: Tavistock/Routledge

Jung, C.G. (1909) 'A contribution to the psychology of rumour', in *Collected Works 4*, *The Collected Works of C.G. Jung*, ed. by H. Read, M. Fordham and G. Adler, trans. by R. Hull, London: Routledge and Kegan Paul

Jung, C.G. (1921) 'Psychological types', in *Collected Works 6*

Klein, M. (1952) 'Notes on some schizoid mechanisms', in *Developments in Psychoanalysis*, ed. Joan Riviere, London: Hogarth Press

Kohut, H. (1977) *The Restoration of the Self*, New York: International Universities Press

Kuhn, T. (1962) *The Structure of Scientific Revolutions*, Chicago: University of Chicago Press

Kutek, A. (1999) 'The terminal as a substitute for the interminable?', *Psychodynamic Counselling*, 5 (1): 7–24

Langs, R. (1994) *Doing Supervision and Being Supervised*, London: Karnac

Laplanche, J. and Pontalis, J.B. (1985) *The Language of Psycho-Analysis*, London: Hogarth Press

Laufer, M. and Laufer, E. (1984) *Adolescence and Developmental Breakdown: A Psychoanalytic View*, New Haven and London: Yale University Press.

Launer, J. (1994) 'Psychotherapy in the general practice surgery: Working with and without a secure therapeutic frame', *British Journal of Psychotherapy*, 11 (1): 120–6

Lees, J. (1997) 'An approach to counselling in general practice', *Psychodynamic Counselling*, 3 (1): 33–48

Lees, J. (ed.) (1999a) *Clinical Counselling in Context*, London: Routledge

Lees, J. (ed.) (1999b) *Clinical Counselling in Primary Care*, London: Routledge

Leppar, G. (1996) 'Between science and hermeneutics: Towards a contemporary empirical approach to the study of interpretation in analytic psychotherapy', *British Journal of Psychotherapy*, 13 (23): 219–31

Limentani, A. (1972) 'The assessment of analysability: a major hazard in selection for psychoanalysis', *International Journal of Psychoanalysis*, 53

Macaskill, N. (1985) 'Homework assignments in brief psychotherapy', *British Journal of Psychotherapy*, 2 (2): 134–41

McDougall, J. (1986) *Theatres of the Mind: Illusion and Truth on the Psychoanalytic Stage*, London: Free Association Books

McDougall, J. (1989) *Theatres of the Body*, London: Free Association Books

MacKenzie, B. (1996) 'The enemy within: An exploration of the concept of boundaries in a GP's surgery', *Psychodynamic Counselling*, 2 (3): 390–400

MacLoughlin, B. (1995) *Developing Psychodynamic Counselling*, London: Sage

Mahler, M.S., Pine, F. and Bergman, A. (1975) *The Psychological Birth of the Human Infant*, London: Maresfield Library

Main, T. (1989) *The Ailment and Other Psychoanalytic Essays*, London: Free Association Books

Malan, D.H. (1963) *A Study of Brief Psychotherapy*, London: Tavistock Publications

Malan, D.H. (1979) *Individual Psychotherapy and the Science of Psychodynamics*, London: Butterworth

Mander, G. (1995) 'In praise of once-weekly work: Making a virtue of necessity or treatment of choice?', *British Journal of Psychotherapy*, 123 (1): 3–14

Mander, G. (1998a) 'What has happned to pastoral care and counselling in Britain?', *Contact*, 126 (1): 8–13

Mander, G. (1998b) 'Supervising short-term psychodynamic work', *Counselling*, 9 (4): 301–5

Mann, J. (1973) *Time-Limited Psychotherapy*, Cambridge, MA and London: Harvard University Press

Marteau, L. (1986) *Existential Short-Term Therapy*, London: Dympna Centre

May, R. (1997) Review of *Counselling in Further and Higher Education*, by Elsa Bell, *Psychodynamic Counselling*, 3 (3): 341

Menninger, K. (1958) 'The psychiatric diagnosis', in *Manual for Psychiatric Case Study*, eds K. Menninger et al., London: The Tavistock Institute of Human Relations

Menzies-Lyth, I.E.P. (1970) *The Functioning of Social Systems as a Defence against Anxiety*, London: The Tavistock Institute of Human Relations

Messer, S.B. and Warren, C.S. (1995) *Models of Brief Psychodynamic Therapy: A Comparative Approach*, New York and London: Guilford Press

Miller-Pietroni, M. (1999) 'The postmodern context of counselling in general practice', in *Clinical Counselling in Primary Care*, ed. J. Lees, London: Routledge

Molnos, A. (1995) *A Question of Time: Essentials of Brief Dynamic Psychotherapy*, London: Karnac

Momigliano, L.N. (1992) *Continuity and Change in Psychoanalysis*, London: Karnac

Murphy, A. (1997) 'The conjunction of the clinical and collaborative in the setting of general practice', *Journal of the Institute of Psychotherapy and Counselling*, 6: 20–4

O'Carroll, L. (1997) 'Psychodynamic counselling in an educational setting: containing, transference and clientele', *Psychodynamic Counselling*, 3 (3): 303–20

O'Connell, B. (1999) *Solution-Focused Therapy*, London: Sage

O'Hanlon, W.H. and Weiner Davis, M. (1989) *In Search of Solutions*, New York: Norton

Pingitore, D. (1996) 'The corporatization of psychotherapy: A study in professional transformation', *Free Associations*, 7, Part 1 (41): 101–27

Popper, K. (1967) *Conjectures and Refutations: The Growth of Scientific Knowledge*, London: Routledge

Porter, R. (1986) 'Psychotherapy research: Psychological measures and intrapsychic events', *Journal of the Royal Society of Medicine*, 79: 257–61

Rawson, P. (1992) 'Focal and short-term psychotherapy is a treatment of choice', *Counselling*, 3 (2): 106–7

Roberts, J. (1994) 'Time-limited counselling', *Psychodynamic Counselling*, 1 (1): 93–105

Roberts, J. (1997) 'Where ethical codes meet with managerial control: The business culture and its effect on the theory and practice of psychodynamic counselling – or some thoughts on hiring or firing', *Psychodynamic Counselling*, 3 (1): 83–8

Rosenfeld, H. (1964) 'On the psychopathology of hypochondriasis', *Psychotic States*, London: Karnac. pp. 180–99

Rustin, M. (1997) 'The generation of psychological knowledge: Sociological and clinical perspectives, Part One: "Give me a consulting room. . ."', *British Journal of Psychotherapy*, 13 (4): 527–41

Ryle, A. (1979) 'The focus in brief psychotherapy: Dilemmas, traps, and snags in target problems', *British Journal of Psychiatry*, 134: 46–64

Ryle, A. (1983) 'The value of written communications in dynamic psychotherapy', *British Journal of Psychiatry*, 138: 185

Ryle, A. (1990) *Cognitive Analytic Therapy: Active Participation in Change*, Chichester: Wiley

Ryle, A., Spencer, J. and Yawek, C. (1992) 'When less is more or at least enough', *British Journal of Psychotherapy*, 8 (4): 401–12

Ryle, A. (1993) 'Addiction to the death instinct? A critical review of Joseph's paper "Addiction to Near Death"', *British Journal of Psychotherapy*, 10 (1): 88–93

Ryle, A. (1994) 'Psychoanalysis and cognitive analytic therapy', *British Journal of Psychotherapy*, 10 (3): 402–4

Ryle, A. (1995) 'Psychoanalysis, cognitive analytic therapy, mind and self', *British Journal of Psychotherapy*, 11 (4): 568–74

Samuels, A., Shorter, B. and Plaut, F. (1986) *A Critical Dictionary of Jungian Analysis*, London and New York: Routledge

Sanders, K. (1986) *A Matter of Interest: Clinical Notes of a Psychoanalyst in General Practice*, Strath Tay, Perthshire: Clunie Press

Sandler, J., Dare, C. and Holder, A. (1973) *The Patient and the Analyst*, London: Karnac

Schafer, R. (1982) 'Discussion of transference and countertransference in brief psychotherapy', in *Between Analyst and Patient: New Dimensions in Countertransference and Transference*, ed. H.C. Meyers. New York: Analytic Press

Scott, A. (1993) 'Response to Anthony Ryle', *British Journal of Psychotherapy*, 10 (1): 93–5

Searles, H.F. (1986) *My Work with Borderline Patients*, New York and London: Jason Aronson

Seaton, S. (1996) 'Introducing counselling in secondary schools: A case study with reference to frame issues', *Psychodynamic Counselling*, 2 (4): 498–516

de Shazer, S. (1975) *Keys to Solution in Brief Therapy*, New York: W.W. Norton

de Shazer, S., Berg, I.K., Lipchike, E., Nunnally, E., Molinar, A., Gingerich, W. and Weiner-David, M. (1986) 'Brief therapy: focused solution development', *Family Process*, pp. 207–21

Sifneos, P.E. (1979) *Short-Term Dynamic Psychotherapy Evaluation and Technique*, New York: Plenum Press

Smith, M.L., Glass, G.V. and Miller, T.I. (1980) *The Benefits of Psychotherapy*. Baltimore, MA: Johns Hopkins University Press

Starling, E.H. (1912) *Royal Commission on University Education in London, 5th Report of the Commissioners* CD 6311, London: HMSO, pp. 194–6

Stern, D.N. (1985) *The Interpersonal World of the Child*, New York: Basic Books

Sudbery J. and Winstanley, I. (1998) 'Applying psychodynamic insights in brief counselling', *Psychodynamic Counselling*, 4 (3): 367–82

Talmon, M. (1990) *Single Session Therapy: Maximising the Effect of the First (and Often Only) Session*, San Francisco: Jossey-Bass

Target, M. (1998) 'Approaches to evaluation', *European Journal of Psychotherapy, Counselling and Health*, 1 (1): 79–92

Tolley, K. and Rowland, N. (1995) *Evaluating the Cost Effectiveness in Health Care*, London: Routledge

Walter, B. (1947) *Theme and Variations*, London: Hamish Hamilton

Winnicott, D.W. (1958) 'The capacity to be alone', in *The Maturational Processes and the Facilitating Environment*, Studies in Emotional Development. London: Hogarth Press

Winnicott, D.W. (1965) *The Maturational Processes and the Facilitating Environment: Studies in the Theory of Emotional Development*, London: Hogarth Press

Winnicott, D.W. (1971) The Use of an Object and Relating through Identification, *Playing and Reality*, Harmondsworth: Penguin Books

Wolberg, L.R. (1980) *Handbook of Short-Term Psychotherapy*, New York: Theme-Stratton

Wright, K. (1991) *Vision and Separation*, London: Free Association Books

Index